GOOD HORSE
BAD HABITS

Also by Heather Smith Thomas

Books about Horses:

Care and Management of Horses
The Horse Conformation Handbook
A Horse in Your Life: A Guide for the New Owner
Horses: A Golden Exploring Earth Book
Horses: Their Breeding, Care and Training
Storey's Guide to Raising Horses
Storey's Guide to Training Horses
Stable Smarts
Understanding Equine Hoof Care
The Wild Horse Controversy
Your Horse and You

Other Books:

Beyond the Flames—A Family Touched by Fire
Cattle Health Handbook.
Essential Guide to Calving
Getting Started With Beef and Dairy Cattle
Red Meat: The Original Health Food
Sammy the Salmon
Storey's Guide to Raising Beef Cattle
A Week in the Woods
Your Calf: A Kids Guide to Raising and Showing Beef and Dairy Calves

GOOD HORSE
BAD HABITS

Practical solutions to problem behavior in the barn, under saddle, and out in the world

Heather Smith Thomas

Forewords by Kimberly S. Brown and Rhonda Massingham Hart

TRAFALGAR SQUARE
North Pomfret, Vermont

This book is dedicated to my granddaughter Heather Carrie Thomas—a very talented young woman who shares my passion for horses and whose skill as a horse trainer has now surpassed my own.

First published in 2014 by
Trafalgar Square Books
North Pomfret, Vermont 05053

Disclaimer of Liability
The author and publisher shall have neither liability nor responsibility to any person or entity with respect to any loss or damage caused or alleged to be caused directly or indirectly by the information contained in this book. While the book is as accurate as the author can make it, there may be errors, omissions, and inaccuracies.

Trafalgar Square Books encourages the use of approved safety helmets in all equestrian sports and activities.

Library of Congress Cataloging-in-Publication Data
Thomas, Heather Smith, 1944-.

Good horse, bad habits : practical solutions to problem behavior in the barn, under saddle, and out in the world / Heather Smith Thomas.
     pages cm
  Includes index.

  ISBN 978-1-57076-621-3

  1. Horses--Training, 2. Horses--Behavior. I. Title.

SF287.T457 2013
636.1'0835--dc23
                              2013009935

Book design by Gryphon Design Collective
Cover design by RM Didier
Typefaces: Roboto

Printed in China

10 9 8 7 6 5 4 3 2 1

Contents

4: BAD HABITS ON THE ROAD 271

Foreword by Kimberly S. Brown

Humans are students, constantly learning from our environment and the people around us. As horse people, sometimes we teach horses, and sometimes we learn from horses. If someone tells you he or she has "mastered" anything with a horse, run quickly away from that person and don't look back. There is no "final stage" in horse training, there is only the "next stage."

Heather Smith Thomas is an award-winning equine journalist and a lifelong student of horses and the people who work with them. From the hands-on to the scientific, Heather has immersed her career in not only learning about horses and their behavior, but in helping readers understand what she and others have learned. And she is the first to admit that there is still much she can learn from others who study horses (including her adult horse-training granddaughter—and name-sake—Heather Carrie Thomas).

As a child growing up on a working ranch, horses were necessary in Heather's world, and they were also beloved. Heather has brought numerous horses into the world, raised them, trained them, worked with them on the ranch and in the competitive field, and then seen them off to their next life.

It is wonderful that Heather wants to share her decades of experience: how to understand the behaviors of horses, and how to modify those behaviors so horses can live better in the world of humans. Sometimes just recognizing the basis for an unwanted behavior is the key to unlocking the potential of a specific horse. Other times, all we need is a way to become better at communicating and training our horses so they can do what is needed or asked of them.

A "problem" is simply an opportunity waiting for the right person to come along. Let Heather's words help you look for and understand the "opportunities" in your horses.

Kimberly S. Brown is a lifelong horsewoman and award-winning journalist who spent most of her life in Kentucky and now lives in Wyoming. With two adult daughters who also are horse owners, Kimberly understands the frustrations of trying to select, train, and live with those special animals we love so much. Kimberly has spent decades working with mounted police officers and their horses to enhance that unique relationship and job, as well as having a special place in her heart for re-training/re-homing Thoroughbreds and supporting the marvelous horses used for handicapped riding programs. Kimberly created the award-winning The Horse *brand for Blood-Horse Publications, then after retiring from publishing for several years, returned to harness to work on the business side of the equine publishing industry with veterinarians and farm/stable owners and managers with the* EquiManagement *and* Stable Management *brands.*

Foreword   by Rhonda Massingham Hart

It seems as inevitable in horse ownership as it is in parenthood: You have this beautiful, intelligent, amazing creature—that you love—but when he or she does that "thing" (you know the "thing"...the "problem"...the "bad habit"), you just want to ship him or her on out and start over. It takes only one or two—or a few—bad habits to ruin a good time (and potentially a beautiful relationship).

If you're like me, what you want in a horse is cooperation. Predictability. Dare I say we want our precious horse time to be easy and fun? If only horses came with a guidebook: "When he does 'A,' you do 'B,' and he'll stop doing 'A,' and do 'C' instead."

"Pfft!" you might say. "Oversimplification!"

Not necessarily. Horses, like kids, tend to take the path of least resistance. It's up to you to know—or to set up—the path that leads to the behavior you want. After all, once you know them, horses are pretty darned predictable. And all you have to know is the physiological and psychological basis of all equine behavior, and everything about your individual horse's past, current health, and the individual aspects of his environment.

Sound overwhelming and perhaps impossible? Don't worry! All you really need to know is where to find a copy of *Good Horses, Bad Habits* by Heather Smith Thomas. Heather *does* understand the basis of equine behavior, as well as the predictable effects of past training, health, diet, development, and environment. And she shares that knowledge in this book.

I was a fan of Heather Smith Thomas's writing long before I was lucky enough to work with her. I had at least a dozen of her books, and her name was a household word in my circles. She has a profound wealth of knowledge and delivers it with clarity and purpose. You never close the page wondering, "*What* was that about?"

Heather's knowledge and wisdom is born of experience. She has been a working rancher for decades. On a daily basis, all year long, in all kinds of weather and situations, she has to depend on a cooperative, predictable horse. So when *Good Horse, Bad Habits* came along, I expected insight, deep understanding, and effective solutions. She provides all that and then some.

One thing an experienced rancher always has is a back-up plan (or two). And the rancher is always willing to look at the situation from the horse's point of view. It's the only sure way to understand a bad habit enough to change it. Hats off to Heather for yet another outstanding contribution to the equine world. Simple, sensible, and most importantly, effective ways to alter or eliminate bad horse habits and make your horse time, a good time. (And I'll bet her kids do dishes.)

Rhonda Massingham Hart is a lifelong student of the horse, former publisher and editor of The Gaited Horse Magazine, *author of* Trail Riding: Train, Prepare, Pack Up & Hit the Trail *(Awarded Best New Horse Book in 2006 by American Horse Publications) and* Among Wild Horses, *as well as a horse owner and a mom.*

Alphabetical List of Bad Habits

Introduction

The purpose of this book is to provide a
quick-and-easy reference guide to the most
common types of bad habits in horses and
how to deal with them. Some bad habits
are the result of inconsistent handling and
improper training: The horse learns the
wrong behaviors, finds ways to avoid work, or
develops defensive tactics, such as biting or
kicking. Other problems are the result of poor
management or too much confinement, such
as when a nervous or frustrated horse chan-
nels his extra energy into a habit like stall
walking or weaving.

The chapters in this book deal with specific types of bad habits, from stable "vices" to those encountered when handling a horse on the ground, and from problems under saddle to issues related to loading and trailering. In many instances, there's more than one reasonable remedy for a certain problem, so multiple solutions may be listed. Your best way forward with your horse will depend in part upon the individual animal and the reasons behind his unwanted behavior. But when one course of action does not work, you can refer again to this book and try another.

How to Choose the Best Solution for Your Horse

Often the first step in dealing with a "bad habit" is to take a hard look at the horse's situation and try to understand *why* he is acting (or reacting) the way he does. This will generally help you find the proper way to address the problem and choose the right type of solution for changing his actions. In most cases, a bad habit can be resolved if you are diligent in your efforts to understand why the horse behaves the way he does and if you are consistent in your efforts to resolve the problem or retrain the horse, replacing a bad habit with an acceptable action.

When working on correcting a certain habit, however, try to determine how much "drilling" is appropriate with the problem in mind. You often get the best results when you end each lesson as soon as the horse does the correct thing. "Over-schooling" is often stressful to the horse and counter-productive, creating new insecurities or frustrations even as you seek to resolve old ones.

> » Never hesitate to consult a professional for help—for example, a veterinarian can determine if your horse's unwanted behavior stems from a physical problem, and an experienced trainer can keep you and your horse safe when the horse's bad habit is more than you can handle on your own.

Morton Mandan Bookmobile

02/11/20 02:45PM

****

PATRON: 29007000299000

MAR 1 0

Good horse, bad habits : practical solutio
CALL NO: 636.1 THO 2014
39007002230670   03/17/20

Girls who code : learn to code and
change
CALL NO: JUNIOR 005.1 SAU 2017
39007002431567   03/17/20

TOTAL: 2

The method you choose should be one that you feel confident and comfortable with—that you think you can accomplish. Do not try a solution that pushes you beyond your range of experience and ability. Not all the methods listed in this book are "easy," and some might not be safe for you to try without the help of a more experienced horseperson.

Remember that a certain tactic might work well for one person (or one horse) but might not work at all for another. This is why I included many alternatives to choose from, and various options to try. It is my hope that these suggested solutions to common problem behaviors and bad habits will ultimately make your life with horses an easier, safer, and more pleasurable one.

-1-

Bad Habits
In The Stable

Confined horses—particularly those kept in a stall most of the day without sufficient turnout—often develop unwanted behaviors, partly due to boredom and partly due to "frustration" living in what is for horses an unnatural situation. Confinement is hard on a horse's mind, as well as his body. An otherwise happy, easygoing individual may become grumpy and irritable, and may take out his frustrations on nearby horses or the people who handle him.

Depending on the horse's personality, the bad habits that develop may stem from his efforts to simply pass the time and entertain himself; they may stem from the irritation and frustration he feels as a result of being confined; or they may be related to actual attempts to escape confinement. Whatever the origin, bad habits in the stable must be dealt with if they are unhealthy for the horse, destructive, or pose a safety risk for humans.

Most of the habits that horsemen for centuries have called "stall vices" are actually compulsive behaviors, now termed *stereotypies*. These are much more difficult to correct than a "bad habit," since the horse becomes addicted to his own *endorphins*—the release of internal chemicals that give a sense of pleasure and well-being triggered by the muscle movement of his repetitive behavior.

Horses today are often bored and frustrated, fed high energy feeds but confined with no way to express social needs or burn off energy. When a horse has a lot of unused energy, he's going to do something to get rid of it. In such cases, some studies suggest he may develop rhythmic actions as a way of coping with this stress by triggering endorphin release. Depending on the horse, he may channel his frustration/excess energy into head bobbing, weaving, stall walking, cribbing, kicking the walls, or biting at himself, and discover the related "endorphin rush" by accident (while pacing by the door after being put in a stall, or learning to crib while chewing wood out of boredom or frustration between meals since he can't graze). The endorphins make him feel good, so he repeats the action, and it becomes a habit.

> » **Horses today are often bored and frustrated, fed high energy feeds but confined with no way to express social needs or burn off energy.**

The bad habit/compulsion stems from a need-related urge developed in an unnatural environment that thwarts the opportunity for satisfying the need. It can also be triggered by unrelieved stress of any kind, such as isolation, confinement, insufficient exercise, and boredom, to name just a few. Stress can also influence the development of a compulsion. Once begun, however, the compulsive behavior becomes a need in itself, and the habit continues even when the original stress factor is alleviated. The horse gets a "fix" by going through the repetitive motions: A cribber keeps cribbing and a stall walker keeps pacing—just for the feeling of pleasure he gets.

Stereotypic behaviors are the hardest habits to change because the horse continues to crave endorphin release, even when his environment is changed and improved, and he's no longer under stress. Even if you can get the horse to halt the unwanted activity for a period of time, he may revert to it whenever he is uncomfortable, bored, or stressed.

In the pages ahead I mention both bad habits and stereotypies common to the stabled horse.

Problems With Eating

CHEWS WOOD

Horses are browsers and often nibble on trees—eating bark, leaves, or branch tips—especially if grass is sparse, dry, or snow-covered. The confined horse may also chew wood in a related scenario, such as on a cold night when he runs out of hay. Horses without enough fiber in their diet (fed grain or pellets and a minimum of hay) chew wood because they crave more "fill." A horse with a nutritional deficiency or ulcers will also chew wood.

However, a confined horse may chew wood even when he has plenty of food. He may chew up fence posts, rails, stall dividers, or feed mangers just because he's bored.

A wood chewer can kill paddock trees, destroy fences and stalls, and may swallow splinters that could injure the stomach or become the core of an *enterolith* (a "stone" in the digestive tract composed of mineral salts that build up around a foreign body).

How to Change This Habit

 First make sure the horse doesn't have a nutritional deficiency and that his needs for fiber are being met. Since horses chew wood when hungry, cold, or suffering from the discomfort of ulcers or some other digestive tract problem, you must address the underlying issue that may be the cause of his nibbling. Make an appointment with the veterinarian to determine whether your horse is deficient in a particular area of his diet or if he suffers from ulcers.

» **When a horse is given all the grass hay he can eat during a cold night, he'll usually leave the fences and stall walls alone.**

SOLUTION **2**

When lack of roughage in the diet is the problem, increase the horse's hay ration, using a low calorie grass hay. Horses need fiber for proper digestion, to give them a "feeling of fullness," and to help generate body heat during cold or wet weather. The fermentation breakdown of fiber in the hindgut (the large intestine, which consists of the cecum and large colon) creates heat, and by keeping the hindgut partly full, the horse doesn't feel hungry. When a horse is given all the grass hay he can eat during a cold night, he'll usually leave the fences and stall walls alone.

Even if he's getting all the nutrients he needs, an energy-dense diet of grain, pellets, or small amounts of quality hay fed just twice a day leaves a horse short on chew time and "fill." A concentrated diet, especially grain, is unnatural for the horse. After he eats his grain he experiences a rise in blood sugar, followed by a rise in insulin, which creates a drop in blood sugar that can last for several hours, during which he feels a need to eat. During this part of the day when his stomach is empty, he may resort to chewing wood.

SOLUTION **3**

Increase the horse's exercise. Many horses chew wood when they are fed high quality feeds and confined for long periods with nothing to do. A lot of wood chewing takes place at night and in the early morning before feeding time. If the horse is ridden or exercised a lot during the day, he won't be as restless and bored at night. He'll be content to rest and eat, unless he's shortchanged on roughage (see Solution 2). Horses at pasture graze at night, but confined horses don't have much to occupy their time, so they chew wood. This can be resolved by giving the horse more exercise during the day so he is eager for "rest time" and more grass hay in the evening so he is occupied longer.

When a horse on green pasture starts chewing wood, it may indicate the grass is too "lush" (high water content, low fiber). This kind of grass goes through the digestive tract too rapidly; the horse is shortchanged on fiber and nutrients. This problem can be solved by feeding a little hay along with the green pasture until the nutrient and fiber content of the grasses increase later in the season as the grass growth slows.

Be sure not to confine young horses. Horses that grow up in wide open spaces don't become wood chewers as readily as horses that grow up in stalls and small paddocks. Many pasture-raised horses never develop wood chewing habits. The confined, bored young horse learns it early.

What If Nothing Works?

Once a horse develops the wood-chewing habit, he may not chew when he's out at pasture, but will likely resort to gnawing on the fence or stall whenever he's confined. When you can't keep him from chewing, you can at least protect your facilities by:

- Running a strand of electric wire along the fence (to keep him away from it).
- Covering exposed wooden surfaces with chicken wire (the horse can't get to the wood and the wire is irritating to his teeth so he'll leave it alone).
- Lining stall walls and mangers with metal edges.
- Or applying one of a variety of foul-tasting "anti-chew" products over the areas he chews. Rub a bar of soap or Tabasco sauce on the edge of the feed manger and other favorite chew spots, or use a commercial product. Note that these require frequent application and may be only

partially effective. Some horses won't touch the bad-tasting stuff while others may keep chewing. Whatever you apply as a deterrent, make sure it's nontoxic. Some kinds of wood preservative, for instance, are not safe for horses to ingest.

PROBLEMS WITH EATING

When the horse is killing the trees in your pasture because he is chewing and/or eating their bark, wrap the trunks (as high as he can reach) with several layers of burlap, then tie it securely with baling twine. Smaller trees can be enclosed with a circle of net wire, secured to steel posts. As a last resort to save your trees and paddock fences, give the horse an alternative source of fiber to nibble on, such as clean straw or even a few loose branches from nontoxic trees.

DESTROYS FEEDERS/WATERERS/BUCKETS

Some horses like to play with their feeders or source of water supply just for something to do. They chew on them or paw at them, continually spilling their feed or water and ultimately destroying the mangers, tubs, or buckets.

How to Change This Habit

When the horse is fed or watered in a ground-level tub, and he likes to paw at it or put his feet in it, simply securing the tub in a higher location will help. Buckets can be hung on the wall of a stall or on the fence of the paddock with double-ended snaps and eye bolts, or set into bucket holders attached to the wall or fence. A simple bucket holder can be created by recycling an old, larger bucket: Securely attach the bigger bucket on the wall or fence in a corner of the stall or paddock, and the horse's feed or water bucket can be set into the now "stationary" one. This offers tub/bucket protection while enabling easy removal for cleaning/refilling.

When this bad habit is exhibited in the horse's paddock, a ground-level water or feed tub can be set inside a tire to keep the horse from grabbing the tub with his teeth, playing with it, pawing at it, or tipping it over.

If you try Solution 2, but the horse still finds a way to pull the tub out of the tire with his teeth, or if he continues to put his feet in it, set one tire on top of another so you can set the feed tub into the top tire. Thread two or three pieces of smooth wire through the center hole of the top tire and fasten them in tight loops around the tire. Use a rubber water/feed tub with eye bolts (or add eye bolts in the rim of one you have), and use two or three double-ended snaps to clip the tub to the smooth wire loops.This will hold the tub secure so the horse can't pull it out of the tire, but it will be easy to unsnap and pull the tub out to wash or dump.

In most instances, the horse plays with his feeder, tub, or bucket because he's confined and bored. In addition to making it harder for the horse to grab or paw at his tub or bucket (as suggested in the previous Solutions), address the issue of boredom and give him more to do. Free-choice pasture with access to a run-in shelter, or at the very least having more turnout time, especially with other horses, is often the best solution. Spending more time with the horse (grooming, riding, training) will also help keep his mind occupied and provide a variety of outlets for excess energy.

When such changes in management are impossible, give the horse toys to play with in his stall or paddock so he can expend his energy pawing at or chewing on *them* instead of the feed and water tubs. Change the toys regularly so he'll remain interested in them.

What If Nothing Works?

If you can't keep your horse from demolishing his feed tub or manger, put his hay on the stall floor and his grain on top of the hay. If he destroys every watering system you can create, keep a full bucket outside his stall or paddock during the day and set a timer to offer him as much as he'll drink on the spot, at least four times a day. If you resort to this method of hand-watering, however, you must be absolutely sure to consistently provide hydration, especially in hot weather. If you or a barn manager is not on hand to ensure regular watering can occur, then it is not an option.

PROBLEMS WITH EATING

EATS BEDDING

Some horses eat their bedding when they are confined in a stall. This problem is most common when straw is used for bedding. Consuming straw can be harmless or harmful, depending on the quality of the straw and how much the horse eats. Since it is much coarser than hay, eating a lot of straw may cause indigestion or impaction. If it is moldy, it may cause a horse to colic (experience mild to severe abdominal pain due to gastrointestinal disturbance) or a pregnant mare to abort.

Shavings and wood chips are other popular beddings that a horse may nibble. Shavings are often better than wood chips because wood chips may cause choke, splinters, digestive tract obstructions, among other problems, when a horse eats them. Not only are horses less apt to eat shavings, but this kind of bedding is not as likely to cause a digestive issue.

How to Change This Habit

 The best solution in this case is to keep the horse at pasture with a run-in shelter or in a covered pen—rather than a standard box stall— where he won't need bedding.

 If the horse must be in a stall and your preference is straw bedding, select a type of straw that he won't eat. Every horse is different. Some may readily eat oat straw but won't touch wheat or barley. Wheat straw is less palatable than oat, rye, or barley straw (not as readily eaten), while less abrasive than barley. The sharp awns of the barley seed heads (if there is any grain left in the straw) can become embedded in a horse's mouth when he eats the bedding.

» **Shredded paper, paper pulp, recycled newspaper, peat moss, rice hulls, peanut shells, and volcanic aggregate are all possible bedding alternatives for the horse that eats straw or shavings.**

Alternative materials for bedding may work better than straw when a horse tends to eat his bedding. As mentioned earlier (see p. 13), you might try using shavings, wood chips, or sawdust (make sure it's not too fine and dusty). Shavings from softer woods, like pine and fir, make good bedding and are more absorbent than shavings from hardwood trees. In addition, some types of hardwood are not safe—for example, black walnut is toxic to horses, and oak is too acidic for good hoof health.

Other materials that can be used for bedding (and which the horse is not as likely to try to eat) include shredded paper, paper pulp (resembling the soft cardboard used in egg cartons), recycled newspaper, peat moss, rice hulls, and peanut shells. Volcanic aggregate (a sandy material) is porous and lightweight and can be used by itself or as a layer under other types of bedding to improve drainage. If the horse is fed on the floor of the stall, however, some of this material might be ingested and could cause sand colic.

Another way to halt or reduce bedding consumption is to keep hay in front of the horse at all times. With roughage to satisfy his need to chew, he will leave the bedding alone. Feeding hay on the floor (or in a safe ground-level feeder in the corner of the stall) is more natural for the horse than in a hay net or wall feeder where he has to reach up for it.

If there's always hay in your horse's stall but he still insists on eating the bedding, check the quality of the hay you are feeding.

You may need to switch to a more palatable type or a better quality hay so the horse finds it appetizing.

 Some horse owners with this issue successfully change the habit when they apply a strong-smelling spray (such as an aromatic herbal household room spray) over their horse's bedding. While this may indeed deter the bedding eater, always make sure that any spray products are nontoxic, in case they are ingested.

What If Nothing Works?

If the horse is a compulsive bedding eater, the only solution may be to use no bedding at all, or to use plain sand or volcanic aggregate (see Solution 3). If you use sand or a sand-like bedding, however, make sure the horse's hay and grain are fed in an area of the stall or in a type of feeder where he isn't likely to spill onto the bedding. The horse may develop *sand colic* (abdominal pain caused by the collection of sand in the gastrointestinal tract) if he consumes sand bedding while "cleaning up" wisps of hay or dropped grain.

EATS GRAIN TOO FAST

Devouring grain too quickly is a habit that some horses develop when confined because—as with other bad habits we've mentioned already—they have nothing else to occupy their time. A grazing horse on free-choice pasture can eat whenever he feels like it, leisurely and periodically through the day. By contrast, the confined horse gets his meals only once or twice a day; he therefore looks forward to feeding time, and may bolt his grain in a hurry when he gets it.

This tendency is exacerbated if the horse is fed while turned out with others in a pen or paddock, especially when he's not the dominant animal. The subordinate horse may fear another horse will eat his grain if he doesn't consume it quickly.

Regardless of the reason for his haste, eating too fast can be unhealthy for the horse, since it poses more risk for *choke* (blockage of the esophagus), *colic*, and other digestive ailments. Grain that is hastily eaten and not well chewed is not broken down as readily in the horse's stomach, and some of it may go on through the digestive tract without being utilized (thus not doing the horse much good). Even more harmful is the fact that any grain passing through the stomach and small intestine undigested goes into the *hindgut,* where forage is fermented and broken down into useable nutrients, and where undigested grain can cause serious problems. The fermentation of grain creates a different environment in the hindgut, altering the population of microbes. This can lead to production of bacterial toxins, which in turn can lead to *colic* or *laminitis* (inflammation of the soft tissue structures that connect the bones of the foot to the hoof wall).

How to Change This Habit

If the horse is being fed while loose in a herd, remove him from the group at feeding time, giving him time to eat his meal by himself in a stall or a separate paddock. This may be all that's needed to slow down an insecure individual, once he realizes that other horses cannot threaten him or steal his food.

» **Place a few large (fist-size) rocks or thick rubber dog toys in the horse's feed tub to force the horse to eat his grain more slowly and carefully.**

If the horse continues to bolt his grain despite isolation at mealtime (or if the horse was fed alone in the first place), place a few large (fist-size) round rocks in the horse's feed tub or feed box. Working around these obstacles forces the horse to eat more slowly and carefully. If you don't like the sound of the rocks banging around in the feeder, use some thick rubber dog toys instead. These may be easier on your horse's muzzle than the rocks, as well as easier on your ears. When the horse flips his grain out of the feed tub in an effort to get rid of the rocks/dog toys, use a deeper tub.

When your horse is fed hay on a clean dry surface, such as a hay feeder with a solid bottom, or on a solid stall floor or a rubber mat, an alternative method is to place his grain on top of or between the flakes of hay. This way he eats the grain along with the hay, which slows him down.

If you have a clean, dry feeding surface, another alternative is to use a horse toy: There are some that can be filled with grain and will then dispense the feed slowly as the horse rolls the toy around and plays with it.

One solution when feeding a fairly large ration of grain (to a horse that needs the extra calories and nutrition—such as a lactating mare or a hard-working competitor) is to split the daily ration into five or six small meals and feed many small portions throughout the day instead of just two at the standard morning and evening times. Multiple small meals are more natural for the horse (more like grazing), and he may not be so "greedy" if fed more often. Smaller portions are also much safer, minimizing the risk of colic or laminitis.

What If Nothing Works?

You may never be able to change your horse's habit of gobbling his grain; some horses continue to feel the need for haste, regardless of what you may do to try to change their behavior. At the very least, the Solutions listed here will slow down the too hasty consumption enough that the horse won't put his health at risk.

PICA/UNUSUAL APPETITE

When a horse insists on eating bedding (see p. 13) or other "unnatural" things (manure, dirt, sand, bark), it can be a sign of dietary deficiency, but it can also simply be a habit that developed due to boredom. *Pica* (a pattern of eating non-food materials) can have serious consequences if allowed to continue. The horse may ingest toxic amounts of poisonous substances if he regularly chews on treated fence posts or surfaces covered with lead paint, for instance. He may choke if foreign material lodges in the esophagus; suffer perforation of the esophagus or stomach after ingesting sharp objects or wood splinters; and/or develop intestinal obstruction from eating dirt or sand.

How to Change This Habit

The first thing to do when a horse is eating, licking, or chewing on "strange" things is to determine whether he's suffering from a nutritional deficiency, or if he is merely bored or curious. When the horse's diet is lacking in certain vitamins or minerals (such as phosphorus or salt) or short on roughage (the cause of most wood chewing—see p. 8), the deficiency must be corrected.

Lack of salt may cause a horse to chew leather, lick himself excessively, chew or lick rocks and treated fence posts, or eat dirt or sand. This habit can be alleviated by giving him free access to salt.

Increasing the hay ration will often halt unusual wood chewing or bark eating. As discussed on p. 10, even when a horse is on lush green pasture, he may be lacking fiber, in which case he can be given hay to prevent development of this habit.

When a horse persists in eating things he shouldn't, a checkup by your vet is in order since chronic abdominal pain or other disorders may be a cause of pica, and/or a thorough analysis of his diet may be necessary.

When you suspect the horse may be eating or chewing on unusual objects because of boredom, turn the horse out more, if at all possible, in a large pasture or at least a generous-sized paddock. When there isn't pasture available, give him constant access to hay, which will often halt the problem.

What If Nothing Works?

Pica rarely continues when a horse's environment is changed (giving him more room to move so he's not confined and bored, or more pasture to graze or hay to eat so he has more "fill" and "chew time") or a dietary deficiency is corrected. Foals are an exception—they lick or chew on just about anything due to curiosity. They also eat fresh manure expelled by adult horses, often following their dam and nibbling on any manure she drops. Manure eating (*coprophagia*) is normal behavior in foals, as it enables them to obtain the necessary microflora needed to start a microbe population in their own hindgut for fermenting and digesting forage.

"WASTES" (TRAMPLES/URINATES ON) HAY

Some horses continually walk through their hay or defecate and urinate on it. Hay that is trampled or fouled with feces or urine is rarely eaten; the horse wastes it. Male horses are especially prone to this habit, and once it starts, it's hard to stop.

Confined horses tend to defecate and urinate in certain areas of their stall or paddock, always going to the same spots to relieve themselves. If they choose the area where hay is fed, you've got a problem. When there are several horses in a paddock and one starts urinating on the hay, more of them may pick up the habit because members of a herd tend to urinate and defecate in communal areas.

>> When one horse urinates on the hay in a group turnout, others may pick up the habit because members of a herd tend to urinate and defecate in communal areas.

How to Change This Habit

The easiest way to solve this is problem to turn the horse out on plentiful, free-choice pasture and discontinue feeding hay.

When the horse can't have access to free-choice pasture and must be fed hay, don't feed the hay on the ground or stall floor. Some horses will avoid soiling their hay or pawing it around with their feet when you put the hay in a corner, but others will just paw it out of the corner and waste it. For these horses, you need a hay feeder in the corner of the stall or paddock.

A simple manger, with the hay still fed at ground level (as is preferable for horses), will usually work to protect the hay from being trampled or soiled. When there's more than one horse in a paddock and a corner feeder is not ideal (since a dominant horse may hog it and keep others away), create a fence-line "feed bunk" or hay rack, or use several feeders in different spots so there's room for everyone to eat.

If your horse habitually backs up to the hay feeder to urinate or defecate onto the hay within it, use a feeder that is high enough on the wall or fence to prevent this, or hang the hay in a hay net.

What If Nothing Works?

Unfortunately, you may not be able to change this habit, and the horse may always stir up his hay or soil it when it is fed on the ground or stall floor. In such cases, you may have to continue to protect the edibility of the hay by using an alternative feeding arrangement.

Stall Vices

AGGRESSIVE TOWARD PASSERSBY (HORSES/PEOPLE)

Some horses defend their "personal" space (their own stall) to the point of "protecting" it against all comers. These horses may charge at any horse or person that approaches or passes by their stall, lunging at them over the door or coming right up against the bars of the door with ears back and teeth bared.

How to Change This Habit

SOLUTION
1

Keep in mind that there might be several reasons a horse is defending his/her space. A mare with a foal may be an over-protective mother, attempting to defend her foal from perceived threats. An insecure horse may be exhibiting fight-or-flight instincts: Since he can't run away (because he is confined in the stall) he is taking the next logical course of action in his mind—attacking those who approach *before* they can attack him. Most "bad-mannered," aggressive horses are exhibiting this behavior because of an underlying fear or insecurity.

Try to evaluate your horse's behavior appropriately so you can deal with it properly. In most instances, punishment is counterproductive because it simply reinforces the horse's conviction that people/horses who are going by the stall or approaching it are to be feared and require self-preservative aggression.

A change in living arrangements is usually the best solution, letting this kind of horse live outside in a pasture or a paddock with a run-in shelter. A mare with a foal, for instance, should not be kept locked up in a stall. Confinement is not healthy (mentally or physically) for either one of them. Any horse that becomes aggressive in a stall will do better if turned out.

When Solution 2 isn't feasible, try to find an equine buddy that the horse gets along with, and put that horse in the neighboring stall. Ensure there are openings between the two stalls so the horses can see, smell, and touch one another. Healthy social interaction will often resolve this problem.

If the horse still rushes at anyone who passes his stall, aim to convince him that an approaching person/horse is *not* a threat. Spend time working on getting the horse to accept you into what he considers his space. Move slowly toward his stall in a neutral, non-threatening manner. If he seems uncomfortable with your movements and proximity, retreat a step or two, then step forward again. You may have to advance and retreat several times before he no longer considers you a threat that he must attack first.

When you get within reach, reward him with praise and a treat, then leave him alone for a while before trying it again. It may take many days of quiet, patient approach-and-retreat to change his attitude, but this method generally works better than punishment, especially when the horse is reacting out of insecurity. When you counter his lunges over or at the door with yelling or a physical reprimand, you only reinforce his feeling that you are a threat and he must defend his space.

What If Nothing Works?

When the horse's stall is in an area where there's a lot of traffic back and forth or people/horses often walking directly toward his stall, he may find the constant "threat" to his space overwhelming. If you can't resolve the problem of his "bad attitude" and aggression, move him to a different stall where there is less traffic so he feels less threatened. If the barn stalls have Dutch or half doors, use a stall guard across the top or add wire or grillwork at the top so he can still see out but can't lunge over or reach through to bite.

AGGRESSIVE TOWARD PEOPLE ENTERING THE STALL

Aggression in the confined horse may take several forms. Some horses become cranky about people entering their personal space—that is, their stall. They make a point that they want to be left alone and don't want to be touched, caught, or handled. They might rush toward you with ears back and teeth bared (charging), even when you are bringing food or water.

Others tend to be the impatient type and have learned they can bully people with their size and strength. They are "unintentionally aggressive"—they are so eager to get out of their stall, every time the door is opened, they run you over or push you out of the way. Others are overly impatient come feeding time and practically knock you down as you enter the stall with hay or grain.

How to Change This Habit

As with many of the bad habits we have already mentioned, as well as those still to come, the best solution is to let this kind of aggressive horse live outside in a pasture or paddock so he doesn't feel so "caged in." The next best thing is to change his stabling arrangement, so that at the very least he has an outdoor "run" attached to his stall and can go in and out as he pleases. This often defuses the situation, lessening frustration and anxiety in the stall-bound horse so he becomes less aggressive.

If the horse can't have more living space, ensuring more turnout time between stalled hours will help.

» **Some horses tend to be impatient and have learned they can bully people with their size and strength. They are "unintentionally aggressive."**

Work on teaching the overeager horse to be patient. Don't feed him or let him come out into the aisle until he can stand quietly for a moment first. Make a practice of asking him to stand still each time you enter the stall. Drill him on "whoa" at times other than when you are feeding or haltering him, both in the stall and out of it, using the butt end of a riding crop to tap his chest to get his attention when he won't stop. Practice sessions on the lead so he begins to know "whoa" means to immediately stop and stand still. If you are consistent and *always* ask him to stop and stand *before* you feed him and *before* you take him out of the stall (and then insist in the latter that he take one step at a time rather than rush), he will soon get the picture. He'll realize that waiting at "whoa" actually gets him his feed or his "outside time" quicker, since you won't give it to him until he *does* stand still.

To prevent a horse's aggression or charging habit from becoming dangerous, be prepared to thwart it each time you come to his stall. Often the best tactic is surprise rather than physical punishment. Using force often begets more force, and you don't want to pick a fight with an aggressive horse. Startling the horse with a spray of water from a squirt gun, aimed at his face, will often halt him midcharge, and he'll stop and reconsider. As mentioned, many horses charge because they feel they can get away with it; they've dominated humans in the past and are taking advantage of someone's timidity. If every time a horse charges at you he is thwarted, he will start to see you in a different light and will realize he can't get away with bullying you. You need to shift who is dominant and who is submissive in your relationship. The horse must respect you as the leader instead of thinking he is the boss.

What If Nothing Works?

If you can't change the horse that is aggressive at feeding time, devise a way to feed him without going into his stall. His grain can be delivered through a hole or a sliding "door" cut into the stall wall; erect a hay feeder you can reach from outside the stall.

However, if you can't defuse aggressive charging that is becoming danger-ous, seek professional help from an experienced and respected trainer.

BECOMES CAST (HABITUALLY)

When a horse lies or rolls too close to the stall wall or paddock fence he may get stuck on his back; he can't get his legs underneath himself to get up. This is called "becoming cast." Some horses repeatedly find themselves cast if their favorite resting spot is very close to a wall or fence—especially if they like to roll before getting up.

How to Change This Habit

SOLUTION 1

First, if the horse is rolling far more often than is "natural," make sure there's not an underlying reason for the behavior. Sporadic bouts of mild colic may cause him to roll, as well as distract him to such a degree that he fails to pay attention to *where* he's rolling. A skin disease or external parasites may make him itchy and prone to rolling in an attempt to scratch hard to reach places. In some cases, resolving the reason the horse is rolling will put a stop to the habitual entrapment problem.

When dealing with a horse that becomes cast in the stall, give him a bigger stall or extra bedding around the edges of the stall to discourage him from lying too close to the walls. If that doesn't work, install a slanting board shelf or *anti-cast strip* around the bottom of the stall (the stall should be a large one) so there aren't any abrupt corners for the horse to get stuck in when on his back. When he rolls up against the slanted surface of the "shelf," the horse can usually roll back over or slide away from it because his withers aren't wedged in the corner between the wall and floor.

If your horse generally becomes cast in the paddock, line the fence where he usually rolls and gets stuck with tires, so he can't get too close to the fence.

What If Nothing Works?

If the horse insists on rolling too close to the wall or fence in spite of your barricades, you can try an "anti-cast roller," which consists of a surcingle with a smooth, round protrusion ("handle") at the top that keeps him from rolling clear over. When adjusted properly, it may help minimize his chances of getting cast.

CHEWS LEG WRAPS/BANDAGES/BOOTS

Bored horses may chew on leg wraps, bandages, or boots. This is similar to blanket chewing (see p. 46); the horse enjoys fiddling with the leg wraps because it gives him something to do.

How to Change This Habit

First make sure the wraps, bandages, or boots are not too tight or causing pain or discomfort. If soap residue remains in the wraps from previous washing, this could cause itching and sensitive skin and the horse will bite at them.

When the only reason the horse is chewing his leg wraps is to entertain himself, apply a foul-smelling or bad-tasting product to the wraps so he'll leave them alone.

- One solution is to mix powdered laundry soap with a little water to create a paste to coat the exterior of the wraps/bandages/boots. Make sure it has a thick consistency so it won't soak through cloth and irritate his skin.

- Apply the paste to the outer surface of the leg wraps after they are on the horse. The horse definitely will *not* like the taste.

- When you wash the wraps later, make sure they are thoroughly rinsed so there isn't any soap residue before the next use.

- Another way to deter chewing is to do a final rinse with vinegar added to the water whenever you wash the leg wraps. The smell and taste of vinegar will keep most horses from chewing them.

STALL VICES

What If Nothing Works?

When you can't stop the horse from chewing his leg wraps, bandages, or boots, ask yourself if they are absolutely necessary to his health. If the answer is "no," leave them off.

If they must be used in the stall and during turnout for medical reasons, you may have to resort to a *neck cradle* (often made of wooden dowels and wooden spacers that go under the neck with adjustable straps that go over the crest). Adjust the cradle so the horse can still lower his head far enough to eat and drink comfortably (it helps if he is offered feed and water in tubs, buckets, or racks that are up off the ground) but so that he can't bend his neck quite far enough to reach his front legs or reach around behind to nip at a hind leg.

CRIBS/WINDSUCKS

The term "cribbing" is often used for wood chewing (see p. 8), but these are very different problems. Many horses chew wood but never learn how to crib. Cribbing is an activity in which the horse grabs a horizontal surface such as a fence rail or manger (called a "crib" in earlier days). He anchors his top incisors over the object or presses them into the wood and lets his lower jaw hang slack, then flexes his neck and pulls back, giving a backward jerk of his chin with his mouth open, and swallowing air with a grunting sound. This is also called "windsucking" by some, but this latter term can be confusing because it is also used to describe mares that suck air into the vagina when trotting or galloping.

Cribbing is one of the most annoying and common stall vices. The grunting sound of a cribber is offensive, and the activity is destructive to facilities and unhealthy for the horse. Cribbers destroy stalls, mangers, feeders, and any other wooden structures they can grab, and create excessive wear on their top incisors—eventually wearing them down to nothing. When the teeth become so worn that they no longer meet, the horse has difficulty grazing. Sometimes the teeth begin to slant forward due to the repeated pulling against solid objects. Impaired chewing due to damaged teeth may lead to weight loss or colic. An additional worry is the danger of wood slivers damaging the horse's throat or stomach. To make matters worse, serious cribbers lose weight because the habit is so addictive, they'd rather crib than eat.

> » **The term "cribbing" is often used for wood chewing, but these are very different problems.**

Cribbers have a higher incidence of gastrointestinal problems (colic, gastritis, and ulcers), but at the time of writing, researchers aren't sure whether this is due to cribbing or if discomfort from the digestive problem is part of the stress that leads to formation of a cribbing habit. (Colic, ulcers, and cribbing can all be caused by underlying stress factors.) Some researchers also feel there is a genetic aspect to cribbing, since some breeds and some family lines are much more prone to cribbing than others. A horse with a nervous personality may be more likely to start a cribbing habit than a calm, mellow individual.

Cribbers develop unsightly large muscles under the neck, due to this continual activity. The thickened muscles interfere with flexibility of the neck, making it harder to collect a horse for athletic maneuvers when he is ridden.

STALL VICES

How to Change This Habit

Always keep in mind that cribbing is a sign of something wrong with the horse's mental/physical environment; it is a compulsion the horse developed as a way to cope with stress. The stress may be due to the way he lives (confined in a stall rather than out at pasture with other horses) or the way he is handled. The stress of certain training methods may also cause some horses to start cribbing.

Since a high percentage of confined horses suffer from gastric ulcers (and some studies suggest that the act of cribbing may help ease their pain because of *endorphin release*—see p. 6) the first step should be to check and/or treat the horse for ulcers, and rule out any other physical problems that might be contributing to his need for endorphins.

The horse's total environment should be evaluated. If the horse is confined in a stall, deprived of social contact with other horses, and unable to move about and graze, this may be the reason he's cribbing. Some horses can adjust to life in a stall, but others can't handle it. If conditions that are not natural to the horse (social deprivation, diet lacking in roughage) are driving your horse to compulsive behavior, adjust his care and management to better accommodate his needs.

The best "cure" is full-time turnout on pasture, but when this is not feasible, give him as much out-of-doors time as possible (at least half of each 24-hour period), and feed him in ways to better occupy him (smaller meals more often). Allow him as much room to move and activity as possible so he has things to see and do. Here are some ways you can do this:

- If the horse must spend most of his time in a box stall, make sure it has windows, a Dutch (half) door or stall guard that enables him to look out, and/or walls that allow him to see, hear, and smell his neighbors. Isolation from other horses is even more frustrating to a horse than confinement—for example, it has been found that horses in rows of tie ("standing") stalls that are more limiting in terms of movement but in close proximity to other horses don't crib as much as horses loose in box stalls. And, horses in box stalls are less apt to crib when the stalls are not separated by solid walls, but by partitions with bars or wire so they can see through and touch noses with their neighbors.

- Provide companionship, such as another horse in the next stall, as bonding with a neighboring horse can satisfy a horse's social needs. If he can't have a next-door buddy, provide a companion animal that can live in his stall with him, such as a goat, sheep, duck, chicken, dog, or small donkey.

- If it's impossible to give the horse a companion, add "glassless" or unbreakable mirrors in the stall (you can protect them with wire mesh for further safety) so he can see his reflection. Research has shown that a solitary horse in a box stall is less apt to crib when the stall has mirrors.

- Give him something to do in the stall, such as providing "toys" to play with. This won't meet his needs for space or socialization but can help refocus his attention on something besides his obsessive habit. An old rubber tub, tire, big rubber ball, traffic cone, squeaky dog toy, partially deflated basketball, or a plastic jug hung from the ceiling (any indestructible, smooth, safe object) may help keep him occupied. You can add a noise component:

Fill the jug with rocks so he can rattle it, or hang it by a string of bells that ring when it swings. Change the toys periodically to keep him entertained.

» **Add "glassless" or unbreakable mirrors in the horse's stall so he can see his reflection. Research has shown that a solitary horse in a box stall is less apt to crib when the stall has mirrors.**

- A radio playing softly in the barn can help divert the horse's attention and keep him mentally occupied.

- Increase the hay ration (using a low-calorie mature grass hay, not rich alfalfa) and find ways to increase his eating time in the stall or paddock. Control the amount of hay he can grab at once: One method is to double- or triple-layer your hay net to make him work harder to get the hay out so he spends more time eating. Hang hay in every corner of the stall so he moves around more while he eats. When using a hay feeder, put 2-inch wire mesh along the front of it (with openings too small to put a foot through the mesh if he paws) so he can only pull out small amounts at a time, or use a hay rack with narrow openings.(There are also some commercial slow-feeder hay racks and hay bags available.) When he's in the paddock, spread the hay around in many small piles so he must go from one to another. This way he spends more of the day "grazing," pulling out a few wisps at a time, rather than eating all his roughage quickly, leaving him with nothing to do for hours.

- Feed less grain. Horses fed a large amount of grain are generally more "hyper" and frustrated when confined, having no way to burn off the extra energy—so they are more apt to develop unwanted behavior as a coping mechanism. If the horse must have the extra calories (for high level athletic performance or for lactation), feed smaller amounts of grain more often so the horse spends more time at the feed tub and less time being bored, or feed the extra calories in the form of a fat supplement.

- Do more with the horse. Take him out for more frequent exercise, in hand or under saddle. If he's young, train him to pony so he can accompany you with other horses. One deterrent to cribbing is more work; hard-working horses have less excess energy to burn. A good grooming session once or twice a day can also help the attitude of an isolated, solitary horse, partially replacing the physical contact the horse would get from herdmates.

- As mentioned already in this book, don't confine a young horse. Young horses (under the age of four) are more apt to develop *stereotypies* (see p. 6) when stalled than older horses because youngsters have high energy levels and are more readily frustrated by confinement. In addition, a foal or yearling that starts a compulsive behavior tends to continue it through life, even when his environment and/or management is later improved, while older horses are less apt to develop problems when stalled much of their day—that is, if they had the benefit of pasture and socialization during their "growing up years."

Horse experts continue to debate whether horses mimic their elders, whether a cribber in the barn may start others cribbing, and if a foal may learn the habit from his mother (some research suggests a foal may also be genetically "wired" to crib). Young horses may start cribbing when teething, or during weaning, due to stress.

Even if you eliminate physical and mental stresses, and provide the horse a more natural lifestyle (ample turnout and companionship), some horses will continue to crib because they've become dependent upon their addiction. You can't "break" the habit, but you can halt, or at least limit, the destructive behavior by using a *cribbing strap*. This leather (or leather and metal) "collar" is fastened snugly around the horse's throatlatch and makes it uncomfortable for him to tense the muscles that retract the larynx while cribbing. It must be tight enough when the horse's head is up that it will create some pressure, but not be so tight it's hard to unbuckle. It should loosen when the horse lowers his head, and should not interfere with eating and drinking.

Many cribbing straps have a heart-shaped piece of metal or stiff leather at the throat. Some include a strap that goes over the forehead in front of the ears. Whatever kind you choose, a properly fitted collar will prevent cribbing when the horse is wearing it, but most horses resume cribbing when it is removed.

A disadvantage to cribbing straps is that they can rub out the horse's mane and the hair at his throatlatch, or create sores. There's also risk of the strap catching on something and trapping or strangling the horse.

Some horse owners prefer to use a muzzle attached to a breakable halter to prevent cribbing. Muzzles come in different styles: A *grazing muzzle* allows the horse to breathe and drink freely but limits the amount he can reach to eat (it only allows longer blades of grass or hay to stick through), and so must be removed when he's fed meals. A *cribbing muzzle* will keep the horse from grabbing wood but still allows him to easily nibble hay. Since it takes longer for a horse using the latter type of muzzle to eat, food can keep him busy more of the day.

Some horse owners use homeopathic remedies for cribbers, including herbal remedies, aromatherapy, or even acupuncture. In some cases, these may help in the early stages of cribbing, especially if you also make changes in the horse's care and management, removing possible sources of the stress that is causing the behavior.

As a last resort, surgery is an option. In the technique most commonly used today, this involves cutting nerves to the muscles under the neck that are used by the horse in the act of cribbing (muscles that retract the larynx to suck in air) and/or removing portions of those neck muscles. Earlier surgical methods were successful in only about 60 percent of cases (some horses eventually began cribbing again) and left some horses disfigured.

Merely cutting the nerves to the muscles works best if done early, when the habit is just starting; if a horse had been cribbing for a long time, there is a chance he is still be able to crib after surgery because the more a horse cribs, the more he recruits other muscles to participate in this action. Note that the newer techniques have improved the surgical results by cutting the muscles in a more forward location (under the jaws) and taking out more muscle, thus reducing possibility of the transected muscle ends growing back together. A laser is used to cut the muscles and nerves, reducing bleeding (which can lead to a clot and fibrous tissue formation).

What If Nothing Works?

Remember, cribbing is a perfect example of truth in the old adage that says *an ounce of prevention is worth a pound of cure*. If, however, a horse starts cribbing in spite of what you think is a "good" or "natural" environment, it is crucial to try to halt the behavior as quickly as possible, before the horse becomes an "endorphin junkie." Once the habit is well established, it can be impossible to cure entirely.

When dealing with a cribber, remember that punishment is not effective, and devices used to thwart cribbing behavior do nothing to relieve the cause of the habit. Cribbing straps or muzzles, putting round metal edges on wooden surfaces in stalls so the horse can't grab them, surgery, and so on, are all merely addressing the symptom and not the cause. A change in environment or training program (reducing or eliminating the stress that's causing the horse to crib) is the best "solution," although it will not actually *end* the problem if the horse is already addicted to his habit.

>> **Cribbing is a perfect example of truth in the old adage that says *an ounce of prevention is worth a pound of cure.***

When faced with a horse that is clearly addicted and all attempts to change his behavior have failed, determine whether or not the habit is damaging to his health. If it isn't, it may be best to just let him continue his coping mechanism, finding a way to live with his habit, such as installing a sturdy, rubber-covered bar in his stall that he can crib on safely, without damaging his teeth or the stall.

Since you usually can't stop cribbing once it starts, you must try to prevent it in the first place, by keeping the horse in a more natural and less stressful environment. You can't just stick the horse in a stall when you're not using him, and forget about him.

STALL VICES

CROWDS

Some horses don't respect your personal space and crowd you when you are in the stall, stepping on your toes or pushing you into the wall. An aggressive horse that crowds (see p. 23) can actually be quite dangerous, so it is important to change this bad habit.

How to Change This Habit

First determine whether the horse is crowding and bumping into you because he's afraid or uncomfortable or if he is just intentionally pushy. If he is a nervous, timid individual, he may be worried about something that's happening or that he thinks is about to happen. If he's so focused on his fear that he isn't paying attention to you and your personal space, he needs patience rather than punishment; the latter will just make him more stressed, upset, and uncontrollable.

When the horse is aggressive and bumping into you or trying to smash you into the wall on purpose, he needs to learn to respect your personal space. This may take additional training in "neutral territory" (out in a paddock or arena) and not just in the stall. The horse must learn to respect you at all times. Create an imaginary box around yourself in your mind—a space into which the horse is not allowed. Every time he pushes into your space, he should be made uncomfortable—by running into your hand, elbow, a stick, or the butt end of a whip. Raising your hands toward his face and making "pushing" gestures with them can tell him to "Back up!" since horses instinctively move away from anything "threatening" their head. He must learn to stay back, and also to move back out of your space instantly on command. Every time he steps into your space, immediately insist that he back up or move over to where he belongs.

» **If a horse is afraid or anxious and so focused on his fear that he isn't paying attention to you and your personal space, he needs patience rather than punishment.**

A good way to start this type of retraining is by teaching him to move away from pressure. (As mentioned, practice in a safe space other than his stall, at first.)

- Start by applying light pressure with your hand on various parts of his body: head, chest, and sides.

- When he responds and steps back or moves over, reward him with praise and gentle rubbing.

- When he doesn't respond, press a little harder, and if that doesn't work, try "tapping"—a repetitive "press and release" with your hand or tap with the butt of your whip. Once he learns to respond correctly and quickly, you can refine the cue, bringing it back to the gentle pressure you tried at first.

- When the horse will move back or move over for you out in the open, repeat the same lesson in the stall.

What If Nothing Works?

If despite time spent retraining the horse to respect personal space the horse still insists on shoving you into the wall, carry a short, stout blunt stick with you every time you go into his stall. Hold the stick horizontally in front of you so that when he crowds, he runs into the stick instead of you. A sawed-off piece of shovel or broom handle works well for this: Cut it so it is a little longer than you are wide. This is intended to protect you from injury or uncomfortable squashing. In many instances this strategy may also teach the horse that it's uncomfortable for him to move into your space, since when he gets too close, the stick presses into his body. He may press on it for a moment at first but will soon move away.

STALL VICES

PAWS

This is another habit often seen in confined horses. Some horses paw every time they are frustrated, nervous, or impatient, as at feeding time, or when the feed tub or water bucket is empty. Horses often continue their feeding time pawing habit because they "learn" that the behavior is ultimately always rewarded with food.

How to Change This Habit

SOLUTION 1

A reward system is often more successful than punishment. For those of you with the time and patience, giving the horse a bite of feed whenever he *stops* pawing for a moment (and *never* feeding him when or right *after* he paws) can modify the horse's behavior— he eventually realizes he never gets fed when he paws, only when he doesn't.

SOLUTION

2

"Self-punishment" techniques also work on many horses that paw. You can have success if you stand out of sight, outside the stall, with a squirt gun in hand, and give the horse a surprising spritz on the neck or shoulder whenever he starts to paw. Another method that can be effective is to suspend a short length of chain from a leather strap attached above the fetlock joint (or just above the knee, if you prefer). The whack and irritation from the chain bumping against his leg and/or foot when he paws can deter him from repeating the motion, and it is less likely to damage the leg than the continual concussion of pawing the ground or striking against the stall wall.

> » **In a natural environment with plenty of room to roam and free-choice pasture, the horse isn't frustrated and always waiting for feeding time, so has no reason to paw.**

What If Nothing Works?

When the horse continues to paw in spite of your efforts, the best solution is turnout on pasture. In a natural environment with plenty of room to roam and free-choice pasture, the horse isn't frustrated and always waiting for feeding time, so has no reason to paw. At the very least, give the horse more turnout time or feed the horse in an outside run instead of in the stall. To a great degree, you may just have to live with the pawing habit and adjust the facility so he's not destroying the barn nor hitting anything that would injure his feet.

RUBS MANE/TAIL

Itchiness may cause a horse to rub his mane or tail on any available surface, such as stall walls, doors, fences, or trees. The itchiness may be caused by *internal parasites* (such as pinworms that lay eggs on and around the anus), or *external parasites* like mites, ticks, or lice (the latter are often located at the base of the mane). Tail rubbing can also be due to itchiness in the udder or sheath area; the horse can't quite reach the itch and is rubbing as close as he/she can get to it. Once an area is irritated and sensitive (or raw from all the rubbing), the horse seems even more inclined to rub it.

STALL VICES

How to Change This Habit

SOLUTION 1   First address the underlying reason for rubbing. Make sure the horse is regularly dewormed, and check for external parasites. If the horse has lice, ticks, or mites, consult your veterinarian and use an appropriate insecticide.

SOLUTION 2   Relieve the itch. If the area is raw, use a soothing ointment recommended by your vet. When the cause of the horse's itch is a dirty sheath or udder, clean it. Bathing the horse with a mild shampoo may get rid of some of the irritating factors, but be sure to rinse thoroughly to get rid of all soap. And note: You should not wash a horse too often or you'll remove the natural oils in his skin/hair coat that keep it healthy. Too-dry skin may also cause itchiness. Once the reason for itching is removed and the itchiness is relieved, most horses will stop rubbing, but others continue—especially when confined—just for something to do.

» **Do not wash a horse too often or you'll remove the natural oils in his skin/hair coat that keep it healthy.**

What If Nothing Works?

When the horse continues to rub his tail even after the original cause has been dealt with, you can protect the horse and the stall walls by installing a *tail board/rail*. Like a *kick board* (see p. 44), the tail board keeps the horse from getting close to the wall. It is a "shelf" that goes all the way around the inside of the stall, put at a height (for that individual horse) a little below the point of his buttocks. Paddock fences can be lined with a strand of electric fencing to keep him away from them.

To help protect his tail so he can't break off the hairs with constant rubbing or attempts at rubbing, braid the tail and put it in a tail bag.

SELF-MUTILATION

This is one of the most destructive and frustrating stereotypies in horses, and in most cases, seems to be a response to stress. The horse bites at himself, often spinning around to nip at his flanks or legs, or curling his neck to bite his own chest. Some horses grunt, "bark," or squeal during or right after nipping themselves; kick out with one hind leg or make repeated kicking motions; or shake their head and turn in circles.

This destructive activity occurs most frequently in stallions (partly because they are often kept isolated and confined—it is not seen in stallions who are allowed to live with other horses), less frequently in geldings, and even less often in mares. At first the problem may be mistaken as a symptom of colic, fly infestation, parasites, skin diseases, or ulcers. Susceptibility to this problem may be inherited; it may be a neurological condition brought on in certain horses by stress (somewhat similar to Tourette's syndrome in humans). Once begun, some studies suggest the habitual behavior becomes addictive due to the release of endorphins (see p. 6), which not only activate reward centers in the brain, but also increase the horse's pain threshold, so he feels very little discomfort following his self-inflicted abuse.

How to Change This Habit

Self-mutilation can often be halted if the horse's routine and/or living situation are changed immediately, at the first sign of the habit's onset. If the horse is confined, give him more turnout and a companion. The best solution for a stallion is free-choice pasture with one or more pregnant mares. Horses living in groups rarely develop the self-mutilation habit because they can release any extra energy, aggression, displeasure, or frustration in natural social interactions— playing and chasing.

 Drug treatment can help some horses but not others. Those that have had limited success include steroids, medications that act as opiate-receptor blockers, and dopamine antagonists. When medication does work, the effects are usually only temporary—unless the horse's care and management are also changed at the same time.

 Castration resolves this problem for some stallions, especially if they are then allowed to live a more natural life, with more turnout in the company of other horses.

What If Nothing Works?

In extreme cases in which the habit continues despite turnout, socialization, castration, and/or medication, euthanasia may have to be considered if the horse has no quality of life and becomes a serious danger to himself and his handlers.

STALL BANGS/KICKS THE WALL

Some horses kick at their stall or paddock fence because they don't like the horse next door; some kick because they are impatient to be fed (and only do it at feeding time); and with others it becomes a stereotypical compulsion—when they are bored or frustrated, they pass time by rhythmically kicking the wall.

At its least, this habit can lead to loosened shoes. Horses may also develop hock or tendon injuries from hitting their hind legs against the stall walls or from hyperextension of the joints. They may fracture a pastern bone or coffin bone if they kick forcefully. When stall walls are cinderblock, horses may break or crush part of a block (since the blocks are hollow) and injure

STALL VICES

their feet. When walls consist of horizontal wooden boards, dangers exist as well, because horses may kick through them, possibly wedging a foot or leg.

> » **Horses may develop hock or tendon injuries from hitting their hind legs against the stall walls or from hyperextension of the joints when they kick.**

How to Change This Habit

If the horse only kicks at feeding time or when someone is in the barn—as a way to demand attention or impatiently beg to be fed first—this habit is a *ritualized pattern* rather than a true *sterotypy*: The behavior is only associated with feeding or other specific stimuli and not a compulsive/obsessive addiction.

To break the feeding-time wall banging, do not "reward" the horse with his feed until he has stopped kicking and stands quietly. If you feed him his dinner every time he kicks to demand it, he's reward-ed for his impatient, destructive behavior and will continue it. This solution requires you spend a little extra time with your horse during feeding for a few days, since you must wait until he stops kicking before you feed him. The problem with ending this habit in most cases is the owner or barn manager is in a hurry and must complete chores in a certain time frame, so the kicking horse is fed even though he's behaving badly. When he's fed every time he kicks, it only makes sense that he continues the habit.

If you can reinforce a "reward/punishment system" by feeding when the horse is quiet (as described in Solution 1) and reprimanding him when he kicks, this speeds the process of changing the bad habit. However, use caution in how you convey to him that kicking is undesirable. Do *not* reprimand him by yelling or by going into the stall to punish him. Yelling is rarely effective and may only make him upset or more agitated. Entering the stall is counterproductive: When he sees you coming, the horse likely stops kicking, and thus you are most likely punishing him for *stopping* (the opposite of what you want).

A better way is to punish the horse for the act of kicking is to do so from a distance and in a way that you can do it *as the horse is kicking*. You want to use "self-punishment" (see p. 38), so the horse does not associate *you* with the discomfort of the punishment, but instead thinks he caused it himself. This can be done with a spritz of a squirt gun, the goal being to startle the horse enough that he halts the undesirable activity. If every time the horse kicks he receives the unexpected and unpleasant sensation of a spray of cold water, he is far more likely to halt the habit.

» **In most cases of stall kicking, the owner or barn manager is in a hurry and must complete chores in a certain time frame, so the kicking horse is fed ("rewarded") even when he behaves badly.**

SOLUTION 3

If the horse kicks when you are not around to stop the unwanted behavior, suspend a short chain from a soft, padded leather strap attached around his hind pastern or around the leg above the hock. The startling sensation the chain creates when the horse kicks the wall is usually unpleasant enough to halt chronic kicking—each time he kicks, the chain slaps back and bangs his leg, acting as self-punishment.

SOLUTION 4

When the horse kicks because he doesn't get along with the horse in the next stall, move the horse or change his neighbors.

SOLUTION 5

The horse that kicks compulsively (as a way to trigger *endorphin release* and experience pleasure—see p. 6) may stand with his hindquarters next to the stall wall, rhythmically kicking with one hind foot and bobbing his head at the same time. Or, he may rock backward and forward, then kick out with both hind feet at once, giving several hard kicks in a row.

The best way to correct the compulsive kicker is to leave him out-doors—with free-choice pasture and a run-in shelter—instead of in a stall. If pasture living isn't possible, you might try a tie (standing) stall instead of a box stall, so he doesn't have a wall behind him to strike (though some compulsive kickers in tie stalls may turn side-ways and kick at the side wall with one hind foot).

If the horse must be in a box stall, give him more to do to reduce his boredom and frustration level, such as: horse toys, more hay to eat (fed in a manner that forces him to eat slowly to occupy more of his time), or a companion animal. The management tactics that help alleviate other stereotypical behaviors, including cribbing (p. 31), weaving (p. 48), and stall walking (p. 45) may also be helpful when dealing with stall kicking.

» **When dealing with a compulsive stall kicker, take precautions to make sure he doesn't injure himself or damage the barn.**

What If Nothing Works?

If you can't keep the horse from kicking the walls of his stall, take some precautions to make sure he doesn't injure himself or damage the barn. If an outside wall is cinderblock or metal, line it with boards to keep him from possibly kicking through the outer material. Place the kick boards vertically instead of horizontally, with shorter span and less "give" in the center, so he's less apt to crack them and put a foot between two boards if he kicks hard.

An alternative is to pad the stall walls with rubber mats to protect both the horse and the walls, and also muffle the sound of the kicking. Some horses actually lose interest in kicking when their actions aren't creating a lot of noise.

STALL/FENCE WALKS

Some horses pace back and forth in their stall or paddock in a certain pattern, or circle their stall continually. *Frantic* stall walking or fence running occurs when a horse is very upset at being separated from other horses (or a mare is separated from her foal at weaning time). The horse may whinny and "scream" with displeasure. This type of behavior generally ceases as soon as the horse is reunited with his friends or put near other horses.

STALL VICES

Methodical stall/fence walking, by contrast, is a compulsive stereotypic behavior: The horse does it repeatedly and in response to an unnatural environment or perceived stress. He always walks in the same direction, often turns the same way, and leaves a well-worn trail.

When the horse consistently walks or runs along the stall wall or paddock fence a short ways, then stops and pivots in the same direction every time, he may develop joint problems or abnormal wear on his feet from the constant activity that stresses one side of the body more than the other.

> » *Frantic* stall/fence walking behavior is related to separation from friends and generally ceases as soon as the horse is reunited with other horses.

How to Change This Habit

Stall/fence walking are caused by the same conditions that spawn weaving—some horses just channel their frustrations into repetitive walking patterns. Thus the same suggested remedies for weaving will also work for the horse that paces his stall or walks the fence—see p. 48 for solutions.

What If Nothing Works?

If you can't change the horse's management and environment enough to halt this activity by removing stress and alleviating boredom, and if he only exhibits the behavior on occasion or when he is nervous (and does no harm to himself), it may be best to not worry about it.

If his constant walking displaces all the bedding from one side of his stall (or its outer edges) or grinds it to dust, just use straw instead of shavings.

TEARS BLANKETS

Some horses, due to nervousness or frustration at being confined, amuse themselves by nipping and tearing at their blankets. Others may bite at the blanket if it fits poorly and causes discomfort.

How to Change This Habit

 First make sure there isn't a physical reason the horse is chewing or tearing the blanket. If the horse is dirty or sweaty, he may be itchy. If the blanket is dirty, it may be irritating his skin. It is also possible that a new blanket has starch, glazing, or other additives that cause the horse discomfort (and therefore, blankets should be washed before use). A freshly laundered blanket may cause irritation when soap was used in the wash and wasn't completely rinsed out. (A horse with sensitive skin may develop a serious skin reaction to laundry detergent.) A poorly fitting blanket may rub the horse in various places, making it uncomfortable or annoying. When there is a physical problem related to care of, style, or fit of the blanket, address this issue before blanketing the horse again.

» **A freshly laundered blanket may cause irritation when soap was used in the wash and wasn't completely rinsed out.**

When there's nothing wrong with the blanket and the horse is tearing it just to amuse himself, there are ways to stop him. Rubbing a strong-smelling soap or dabbing a mentholated medication on the areas he tends to bite at or tear discourages most horses. Another option is to apply Bitter Apple Spray, a topical taste deterrent available through many pet shops and online animal care websites, on the blanket. It has a foul taste but doesn't leave a messy residue or stain.

STALL VICES

Another way to halt the blanket-tearing habit is to physically prevent the horse from biting at the blanket. A leather "blanket bib" that fits under his chin and clips to the noseband of his halter allows him to eat or drink, but prevents him from taking hold of his blanket with his teeth. A cheaper alternative that is often even more effective is to tie many short pieces of baling twine (about the length from where his jaw meets his neck to the tip of his nose) to the throatlatch of his halter, making a thick "beard" of twine that he can't bite through when he flexes his neck.

What If Nothing Works?

If the horse insists on trying to rip and tear his blankets in spite of your efforts, consider adjusting his lifestyle so you can leave the blankets off. Unless he needs a blanket for health reasons, he may very likely be better off without it.

WEAVES

This is form of *stereotypical behavior*—a compulsive habit developed in response to stress of confinement (see p. 6). A weaving horse sways back and forth, shifting weight from one front leg to the other. He generally does it in the same place in his stall or paddock, such as by the door or gate. He may rock from side to side or lift his whole front end off the ground and pivot back and forth on his hind legs. Other weavers just bob their head up and down continually.

This habit may start "by accident" as the confined horse tries to get out of his pen or stall. He takes a step in one direction, but can't go anywhere, so repeats the movement the other way, and then back again, over and over as a constant shifting of his weight. Some studies suggest the *endorphin levels* in his blood rise when he exerts himself in such repetitive action, and when he discovers that the motion relieves his stress and makes him feel good, he begins to engage in the action every time he is anxious, frustrated, or bored. When his endorphin levels rise to a certain point, the horse feels "satisfied" and stops weaving. When they drop, he craves that good feeling and starts weaving again.

> » **The horse that weaves generally always does it in the same place in his stall or paddock, such as by the door or gate.**

How to Change This Habit

 The most effective remedy for this bad habit is pasture turnout.

 When the horse can't be at pasture, living with a buddy in a paddock is the next best thing. Socializing with another horse fulfills his needs, and he won't be as frustrated by his confinement.

 If full-time turnout in a pasture or paddock is not feasible, give the horse more room to move (a bigger stall or stall-run combination) or more turnout time, and keep him near enough to other horses that he can touch them (over-the-fence contact or through-the-stall-wall contact).

 When you can't give the horse more room to move, and he must stay in a stall the majority of the time, change his management so he has company (a horse he likes that lives next door or a companion animal in his stall). Find ways to occupy more of his time—grooming, working in hand, riding. Install "unbreakable" mirrors in his stall if he can't have companionship, and provide him with horse toys to help occupy his time (see p. 32).

(see p. 32)

SOLUTION 5 Feed more roughage and less concentrated feed. Eliminating or greatly reducing the amount of grain being fed can decrease the horse's desire to weave. Studies have shown that horses being fed highly palatable feeds (especially sweet feed) are more prone to this type of behavior. In addition, as already mentioned in this book, when you feed more roughage, the horse spends more time eating and less time being bored and frustrated. Use a lower quality grass hay he can pick at throughout the day. Place the hay in a feed rack with small openings or a triple hay bag (see p. 33) so he'll have to work harder at pulling out small bites and it will take him longer to eat.

(see p. 33)

STALL VICES

>> **Eliminating or greatly reducing the amount of grain being fed can decrease the horse's desire to weave.**

SOLUTION 6 If the horse always weaves by the stall door or window, suspend two small blocks of wood with string tied to the top of the door or window frame so they hang in the "opening." Then every time the horse starts to weave, he will bump the wood blocks or their strings and start them swinging. This may distract him enough that he stops the weaving behavior.

What If Nothing Works?

If you can't change the horse's management and environment enough to stop his weaving, stay attuned to his soundness and make sure he does not develop physical problems from this constant activity. As mentioned, the horse puts stress on his leg joints as he widens his stance to shift his weight from one side to the other. The extra stress on the inside of the leg can lead to excessive wear on the inside of his feet or shoes, as well as more serious issues, such as ringbone and knee problems. You may need to enlist your farrier's help in order to try to minimize the damage to the chronic weaver's feet and legs.

>> **Extra stress on the inside of the weaving horse's legs can lead to excessive wear on the inside of his feet or shoes.**

-2-

Bad Habits
On The Ground

Most of the problems encountered when handling horses are the result of poor (or a lack of) training. Everything a person does with a horse is *training*—you are either making the horse better or making him worse whenever you work with him. A horse remembers the inadvertent "lessons" as well as the intentional ones. He learns through repetition and develops bad habits or good ones. A horse with a bad habit on the ground was generally "made that way" by improper handling.

Problems with Catching

DIFFICULT TO CATCH IN PASTURE

Before a horse can be easy to catch, he must trust you. The inexperienced or young horse must learn about people; he must come to know and understand them before he'll be willingly caught. The experienced or older horse that habitually avoids being caught has learned to distrust people. He doesn't like what happens to him after he's caught or has never been given enough incentive (reward) to want to be caught—and it is likely he also knows he can get away with being hard to catch.

Some horses are easy to catch in a stall, but out in a pasture they enjoy their freedom and would rather run than be caught. Others develop a hard-to-catch habit because they've always been chased into a corner. There are those that are not afraid of people but remain elusive because they've never learned to expect enjoyable things to happen once they are caught. Your challenge is to change the horse's mind so he'll come to you rather than run away.

>> **Before a horse can be easy to catch, he must trust you.**

How to Change This Habit

SOLUTION 1 — Use a reward. If you always give the horse a treat (a few bites of grain, a horse cookie, a carrot, or another snack he likes) once he's been caught, he'll learn to come to you.

Caution: *Do not* take a bucket of grain out to the pasture: The horse may try to grab a bite while avoiding the halter, and if there's more than one horse in the pasture, a fight may erupt, making it hard and/ or dangerous to catch one of them.

Always halter the horse first, *then* give him the treat (the horse cookie, or some grain that he can have *after* you catch him and lead him out of the pasture). If you consistently reward him, he'll learn to willingly play by the rules.

Use positive reinforcement by changing your routine. When a horse is difficult to catch or becomes more so over time, try to determine *why*. If you always work him hard after he's caught or make him do things he doesn't want to do, he might learn to avoid you.

To correct this problem, catch him every now and then just to give him a treat and turn him loose again. Or, catch him and do some-thing short and easy—for example, groom him and turn him loose again—so he isn't always anticipating hard work whenever he sees you coming. Rubbing and scratching the places he likes to be rubbed and scratched can be as just as rewarding to him as food, so use your imagination.

» **Every now and then, catch your horse and do something short and easy—for example, groom him and turn him loose again—so he isn't always anticipating hard work whenever he sees you coming.**

"Walk him down." When the horse insists on moving away when you approach him in the pasture and he's not interested in a treat, follow him slowly and patiently until, sooner or later, he lets you walk up to him. Attempt this solution on a day when you have plenty of time so you won't get frustrated and impatient.

Casually walk toward the horse without looking directly at him. Use a zigzag approach rather than moving straight toward him. If he moves away, follow slowly, even if he runs to the far corner of the pasture. When he stops moving, stop following—or even step back a little—to show you are not pressuring him. His attitude will tell you if you should wait quietly or go toward him. If he moves away from you, follow him again.

For a while the horse may keep avoiding you, but this takes effort; eventually he'll grow tired of it and let you walk up to him. Praise him when this happens, and don't be in a hurry to put the halter on. When you do, give him lots of praise and/or a treat, then just turn him loose again after a moment and leave. The first few times you walk him down like this, don't do anything else with him—just catch and pet him and turn him loose. It won't be long until he realizes that being caught by you is not a bad thing. Eventually he will stand still or just move a short distance away before stopping and letting you approach. Even when he gets to this point, you should continue to catch him every now and then to just give him a treat and turn him loose again, so he won't expect a serious workout every time he sees you coming.

It often works to use a small pen to retrain the horse that is hard to catch. This process may take several days or several weeks, depending on how ingrained his habit of distrust may be. In a small pen he can't run far away from you, and so he's more apt to resign himself to being caught. This solution is particularly effective when you catch him before every mealtime (for example, morning and evening), feeding him *only* after he's been haltered, and if you make a point of catching him at other times throughout the day (even when you are not going to ride him) just to give him a treat.

>>   **Horses in a group can become hard to catch if one or two are habitual runners.**

If the horse is with a group of horses that are hard to catch, he may evade you just because the others do. Horses in a group can become hard to catch if one or two are habitual runners. Put him in a small pen by himself and catch him several times a day to give him a treat (see Solution 4).

Pair your horse with a buddy that is always easy to catch. This often works in a pasture as well as a small pen. The horse that *wants* to be caught is a good influence on the one that avoids you. When the elusive one sees you feeding and petting his buddy, he won't want to be left out.

PROBLEMS WITH CATCHING

Build a "catch pen" in the corner of the pasture (even if it's a temporary pen created with portable round-pen panels) and feed him a small meal of grain as a special treat in the pen every day for several days (*without* catching him). If he won't come in for the grain, have several people help you gently herd him into the pen the first day or two—slowly and without running, even if it takes a while. Lock him in until he has eaten the grain, then let him out again when he's done. Once he realizes he's not going to be caught and put to work, you won't have to herd him into the pen; he'll come in on his own. Once he comes into the catch pen willingly for the grain you can start working with him in a small pen as described in Solution 4, making him realize catching is pleasant.

What If Nothing Works?

Most horses can be retrained to be easy to catch. On rare occasions, however, you may encounter an especially difficult individual with such an ingrained habit that he can't bring himself to trust you and can't be bribed with any kind of reward. When a horse still refuses to be caught but lets you get close (although not close enough to touch him), leave a halter on him with short (1- to 2-foot long) piece of rope or twine attached.

This should not be a long-term solution because it is not a good idea to leave halters on horses, especially out in a pasture. The horse may catch the halter on something and be injured (sometimes fatally). In this situation, always use a breakaway halter that comes apart if it catches on something, and make sure it fits: not too tight that it is uncomfortable or inhibits his chewing, but not so loose that it might catch on something or so that he can snag a hind foot if he reaches forward to scratch his face with one hoof.

DIFFICULT TO CATCH IN STALL/PEN

Some horses develop evasive or dangerous habits related to being caught in a small area. They may keep turning away from you (even when cornered) so you can't reach their head, or threaten to kick.

How to Change This Habit

When you enter the stall or pen, don't immediately rush to catch him if he's elusive or suspicious. Let him come to you. If it's his idea to be caught, he will be more willing in the future, and if you consistently give him a treat after haltering (see my discussion of catching the horse in the pasture on p. 52), he'll most likely decide it's not so bad to be caught.

》 **When you enter the stall or pen, don't immediately rush to catch the horse. Let him come to you.**

Work with the horse in a round pen. In a small stall you can usually walk up to even a timid or stubborn horse—if you take your time and gently corner him—but this may not be possible if you turn him out or work with him in a corral or paddock. You may have an easier time changing the mind of the suspicious, timid, or independent horse if you teach him to want to come to you in a round pen. Take advantage of his desire to run away from you, letting him travel in circles around you until he gets tired of it and realizes you are not so threatening after all.

Here's how to do it: Turn him loose in the round pen, moving away from him and toward his rear. Swing your halter rope to encourage him to take off at a trot or canter. Walk in a smaller circle within his circle, a little behind him to keep him traveling away from you. Have him go several times around the pen, then ask him to change direction by stepping across his line of travel in front of him so he'll turn and go the other way. Back away to give him the space he needs to turn toward the center of the round pen.

After he's gone around the pen several times both ways, the horse should *want* to slow down. Stop driving him forward, and let him drop to a walk or stop. If he stands and faces you, approach him in zigzags, rather than walking straight toward him. If he lets you, rub his forehead, then walk away. If he leaves before you reach him, make him do a few more laps around the pen, then let him stop again. After a few round pen lessons like this, you'll find he is willing to remain still as you walk up and catch him.

For the horse that turns his tail toward you every time you enter his stall or get close to him in his paddock, or for the horse that kicks out or threatens to kick, "whip breaking" is a way to encourage him to face you instead. The whip (or any long, blunt-ended stick will work) is not to punish: It is merely used as an extension of your arm so you can touch the horse (and his rump) while remaining at a safe distance so you won't get kicked. The whip helps in particular when you need to retrain a horse that puts his head in a corner where you can't reach it without coming up behind him (at the risk of being kicked).

» **A whip can be used as an extension of your arm so you can reach out and touch the horse (and his rump) while remaining at a safe distance so you won't get kicked.**

From a safe distance, cluck softly to the horse, asking him to move out of the corner. If he takes a step, praise him, then cluck again.

If he takes another step (bringing his head closer to you), praise him again and back away a little farther, so he realizes you're not pressuring him. If he doesn't move when you cluck, or if he turns away from you again, *tap* his rump gently with the whip or stick. *Do not* "hit" him hard or tap his legs, as that may only cause him to kick at you. Tap on his rump for as long as needed to encourage him to move over and turn his head toward you. As soon as he does, *stop* tapping, and praise him. Then cluck again, giving him a chance to take another step toward you before you start tapping on his rump again. Before long he'll discover that after you cluck he'll get tapped on the rump—*unless* he turns his head toward you. Before long, he'll learn to turn toward you when you cluck. This eliminates the frustration of not being able to get to his head and reduces your risk of being kicked.

For the very elusive or timid horse that won't let you get close enough to his head to put a lead rope around his neck or his halter on, leave a close-fitting, breakaway halter on—one that you can quietly take hold of—until you have time to retrain him and gain his trust. As an additional aid in the stall, you can leave a short piece of rope attached to the halter, and when he's turned out in a corral or pen, you may have to leave a longer lead rope trailing from the halter for a few days. *Do not* use a long rope when he's turned out in a pasture (see p. 52).

When the horse moves away from you in the stall or pen, you can quietly follow until you are close enough to put a hand on the rope. Once he realizes that he can't get away and that you can "catch" him, even from a distance, he'll give up being evasive, and you can progressively get closer and closer to him. Reward his good behavior as previously discussed (see p. 53), and soon you won't need the trailing rope or even the halter anymore.

What If Nothing Works?

Any reasonable horse can be caught (and will steadily become easier to catch) using one or more of the solutions I've outlined. When a horse is so set in his ways that he's dangerous (runs over you if cornered, aggressively kicks, or charges at you when you enter the pen or stall), you need a professional trainer's help...or a different horse.

DIFFICULT TO HALTER

Some horses will let you approach them, but then they try to avoid having the halter put on. They raise their head high or turn it to one side so you can't reach it.

How to Change This Habit

Never try to put the halter on without "catching" the horse first: As you stand next to him, quietly put the lead rope around his neck. Now you can take all the time you need to put on the halter. Don't be in a hurry—the less threatening you are about it, the more cooperative the horse will be.

Teach the horse to lower his head on cue so it will be easier to put the halter on. Introduce this lesson when the horse is already caught and haltered, so he can concentrate on one thing at a time.

- Put one hand at the top of his neck and the other hand over the bridge of his nose, applying slight downward pressure to his nose and the crest of his neck.

- When he responds by lowering his head, immediately release the pressure and give him a rub to praise him.

- Repeat the procedure. If he backs up or tries to raise his head, move with him, letting him know he's not trapped. Don't try to force him to lower his head, and always release the pressure *as soon as he responds*. He'll soon learn to lower his head each time you put your hand on the top of his neck because he realizes the pressure is always released when he responds properly.

If the horse is headshy, make sure there isn't an underlying reason (such as ear ticks, warts, or an old injury) that causes him to avoid having his ears or head touched when you try to halter him. You may need your vet to examine him, and if there is a medical problem, treat it before you work with him further.

If he's headshy from habit (due to mishandling of his ears in the past), work on getting him over his fears by gradually moving closer to his touchy areas with gentle rubs during each grooming session. Put the halter on in a manner that does not threaten him—without coming close to his ears, for instance.

Give the horse his treat (his reward for being caught) in the palm of one hand, with the treat hand positioned so he has to lower his head and put his nose into the halter to reach it.

Leave a close-fitting, breakaway halter on the horse and use it to control him while you practice putting on a second halter over it. Snap a lead rope to the breakaway halter so he can't avoid you during these practice sessions. Spend time every day (several times a day) putting a halter on and off over the one he's wearing, until he realizes that haltering is neither scary nor painful, and he no longer tries to avoid it.

What If Nothing Works?

If your horse has an unreasonable phobia about haltering, leave a breakaway safety halter on him as suggested in Solution 5. Pay close attention to fit, especially if using it when turning him out to pasture (see p. 56).

Problems with Leading

AGGRESSIVE TOWARD HANDLER

Some horses learn they can intimidate the handler in order to get their own way. Others don't want to be handled and led and use aggressive tactics like biting or striking to keep humans out of their personal space. Biting is a horse's natural defense mechanism, and he also nips and bites in play; however, for reasons of safety, biting at you as you handle or lead him should not be tolerated.

PROBLEMS WITH LEADING

How to Change This Habit

First determine the cause of the aggression. If a normally well-mannered horse suddenly becomes aggressive, it may be a sign of discomfort. Make sure there isn't a physical reason for his crankiness. Aggression can also be a sign of a neurological problem or disease that affects the brain, such as rabies.

If the horse is naturally aggressive or overly playful (such as a youngster that has not yet learned to respect humans and considers them equals, or a stallion that hasn't learned proper manners), he needs firm, consistent handling to teach him the behavior is not acceptable. Don't fight with him; this usually makes an aggressive horse more aggressive.

The best punishment is self-punishment, making sure the horse always comes into contact with something besides you when he brandishes his teeth. One suggestion is to fasten a lightweight, sharp object—such as a dog grooming comb—to your coat sleeve on the side next to the horse when you're leading him. When he tries to bite, ensure he always makes contact with the comb instead of you, and soon giving you a nip won't be so tempting to him.

> » **Don't fight with your horse; this usually makes an aggressive horse more aggressive.**

What If Nothing Works?

See Bites/Nips in the Ground Vices section (p. 149) for other solutions.

BALKS WHEN LED/RELUCTANT TO MOVE FORWARD

Some horses are "lazy" or "stubborn," refusing to move forward when asked or hanging back on the lead rope when you try to lead them.

How to Change This Habit

First of all, don't walk in front of your horse. The proper way to lead a horse is to walk beside or slightly ahead of his left shoulder, with him walking actively beside you. This is the safest way to lead and gives you the most control over the horse's actions. This way, he won't bump into you or knock you down if he gets startled and lunges forward, and you are also in the best position to slow him down when he rushes and encourage him to go faster if he's lazy or stubborn.

Hold the lead rope about 8 to 12 inches from the halter, giving him a little slack so your hand is passive. As long as the horse walks at the proper rate of speed beside you, there should not be tension on the rope. In this position you are able to control his speed: If he goes too fast, he bumps into pressure from the halter, which you should immediately release when he slows. If he goes too slowly he meets resistance and must come forward to relieve it. Your hand should be a *fixed point*—it should not pull forward or backward.

» **Hold the lead rope about 8 to 12 inches from the halter, giving him a little slack so your hand is passive.**

PROBLEMS WITH LEADING

As mentioned, do not pull on the horse's head to make him come forward. It is the horse's instinct to pull back. It takes two to create a tug of war, and he's larger and stronger. If necessary, instead of pulling on him, encourage him from behind. Use a long stick or whip as an extension of your arm. When he refuses to move forward or hangs back on the rope, reach back with the hand furthest from the horse (holding the extra length of lead rope), and touch his hindquarters with the whip.

Another method to encourage the horse forward is to loop a long lead rope around his hind end: Clip one end to the halter, then loop the rope around his rump, with the free end of the lead coming back through the halter ring. The loop should hang loosely around the rump, remaining slack when the horse is moving forward willingly (but not so slack it hangs down to his hocks or it will bump his legs and annoy him). If he hangs back, give a quick tug or two on the "rump rope" instead of pulling on his head. When he feels the pressure on his hindquarters, the horse's natural tendency is to move forward, away from pressure.

Teach the horse to move forward with a voice cue: Give a clucking or kissing sound, followed by a gentle tap on the rump with the whip if he doesn't move forward. Repeat until he learns to respond to the sound of your cue.

What If Nothing Works?

If the horse still won't move forward or hangs back when you try to lead him forward, have a helper stand to one side and behind him to encourage him with a tap on the rump with a long whip whenever you give the cue to move forward.

BOLTS/PULLS AWAY FROM HANDLER

Some horses do not respect the restraint of a halter and develop the bad habit of pulling away or bolting. This habit usually forms because the horse succeeds in getting away from the handler once or twice when frightened or upset. (Note: Wear gloves when working with the horse that doesn't lead well to avoid rope-burned hands if he tries to pull away.)

How to Change This Habit

The horse is stronger than you are, so you need everything in your favor. The mistake most people make is to maintain constant pressure on the halter when the horse is pulling (or when it seems like he might bolt), but you can't outpull a horse. Instead, leave a little slack in the rope rather than steady tension, and keep your hand passive. Then the rope will only tighten if he tries to go faster than you want him to or he tries to pull away, when he will meet the resistance of your fixed hand. If the horse shies or tries to pull away, keep your hand fixed and play out a few feet of rope if necessary as you travel with him. When he's the only one pulling, the tension on the halter ceases when *he* stops pulling. He will realize he is rewarded by a release of pressure when he slows down or stops pulling away.

» **The mistake most people make is to maintain constant pressure on the halter when the horse is pulling.**

Use a chain lead, with the chain run through the halter rings and over the horse's nose. Put a knot in the lead just behind where the chain begins, and a knot at the end of the lead, with additional knots spaced a foot apart all along it, to keep the lead from slipping through your hands if he tries to bolt or pull away. The chain is most effective, however, if you can give one quick downward pull just as he starts to bolt. The sharp pressure of the chain given once, quickly, is much more effective than a steady pull, and it is also more apt to pull his head back around toward you.

PROBLEMS WITH LEADING

Use body leverage to your advantage. When the horse starts to bolt, brace your elbow into his shoulder to give you more leverage, then give a quick jerk on his head to turn back in your direction and spin the horse around you. When he is moving in a circle, he can't bolt away.

» **When the horse starts to bolt, brace your elbow into his shoulder to give you more leverage.**

What If Nothing Works?

When you can't change the horse's behavior and he continues to pull away or bolt in hand, seek help from a professional trainer.

PRANCES/JIGS IN HAND

This is similar to Rushes When Led/Pulls Ahead of Handler (p. 72). The horse always goes too fast when led—he won't settle down and walk. Even if he respects you enough to not pull away or bolt, he still always jigs and jogs as you lead him, instead of walking calmly.

How to Change This Habit

 The horse is either nervous or has too much energy he can't contain. In either instance, more handling is key to correcting this behavior (along with a reduction in grain/calories if he is hyper because of his diet). Practice leading him often, using repeated tugs and releases on his halter (or a chain if that isn't adequate—see p. 65) to keep his attention and reward him for even a single walk step.

 Lead him in a quiet, confined area where there's nothing going on to excite or interest him so he'll be more apt to remain calm. Try working on this by simply going around and around in a pen or small paddock. The limited space, repetition of movement, and diminished distractions (less interaction with the kinds of surroundings that normally make him nervous) may defuse his over-eager attitude, and he'll be more likely to listen to you and relax.

>> **Practice leading the horse in a quiet, confined area where there's nothing going on to excite or interest him so he'll be more apt to remain calm.**

 Start your training session with round pen work on a longe line, making the horse work hard—trotting and cantering—with many changes of direction until he is very responsive to your cues and paying attention to you. Then move on to a leading lesson. The horse usually will be more responsive, relaxed, and cooperative, knowing that you are the one controlling his movements.

What If Nothing Works?

If a horse is so charged up and nervous he can't relax and walk, seek help from an experienced trainer.

PUSHY/WALKS ALL OVER HANDLER

Some horses don't respect you and don't pay attention to where you are, or they don't care. They continually bump into you, crowd you, push you, or step on your toes when you are leading or handling them.

How to Change This Habit

Create some consistent ground rules for the horse, clarifying allowable limits of behavior that he can easily understand. He must learn that humans are not to be bumped or pushed. Even if he is nervous or distracted, he must remember to respect your personal space. Often we subconsciously back up when a horse crowds into us, and some horses soon take advantage of this because this is what a submissive herdmate would do—the horse realizes he can dominate the person who steps back, just like he could dominate another horse.

Make sure the horse knows where his space is, and yours. Allow him to be *comfortable* in *his* space, but always make him *uncomfortable* if he pushes into *yours*. Create an imaginary space around you that he is not allowed to barge into: Position yourself so he bumps into your hand, elbow, or the butt end of a whip if he comes too close, or raise your hands and wave them in his face, and be consistent in enforcing this boundary.

>> **Clarify allowable limits of behavior that the horse can easily understand.**

When the horse crowds you repeatedly and you know it's not an accident (his foot *always* lands on yours or he nearly knocks you down on a regular basis), be more forceful in insisting he keep his distance. Carry a short stick with a sharp end and hold it so he'll run into *it* before he bumps into you. The important thing here is that this works as *self-punishment,* which makes the reprimand more effective. *Do not* hit the horse, yell at him, or actively move the stick toward him. This solution only works if he causes his own discomfort by running into the stick: A sharp prick teaches him it's unpleasant to invade your space.

What If Nothing Works?

If the horse crowds you at feeding time or comes aggressively toward you with ears back, impatient for food, carry a broom handle or stick and wave it back and forth in front of you as you approach. Most horses will back off and respect your space in this scenario. However, when a horse is so pushy and insensitive that he won't stop walking all over you, you need professional help or a new horse.

REARS IN HAND

Rearing is a dangerous habit some horses develop because they are impatient (they want to travel at a faster pace), they are trying to avoid the restraint from the halter or handler, or because they are being asked to do something they don't want to do.

How to Change This Habit

Do a lot more groundwork and leading practice, teaching the horse to always move forward on command. When "Go forward" is solid in his mind, he's less apt to rear up when he's upset or insecure because you can make him move on command. Repeated lessons on giving to pressure, and responding to your cues to move forward, to slow, and to halt, are the best solution to this problem.

» **When the "Go forward" cue is solid, the horse is less apt to rear up when he's upset or insecure because you can make him move on command.**

If the bad habit continues, use a chain lead over his nose (see p. 66) and be ready to use it at the first indication he's going to rear. Give a sharp downward jerk on the chain before he actually gets off the ground. Timing is important here: If the rear starts before you have a chance to intervene, *do not* punish him while he's going up. Wait until his front feet are on the way back down before you reprimand him. If you jerk on the chain lead while he's going up or at the full height of the rear, you might cause him to throw himself sideways or over backward in reaction to the pressure of the chain, or it may incite him to strike at you. It's safer (and more effective) to give a jerk on the chain just before he leaves the ground, or if necessary, after he's starting back down. Proper timing of the application of the pressure will convince him that rearing is unpleasant.

Work on becoming better in tune with the horse so you can anticipate when he might try to rear. If he starts to go up before you can correct him with a jerk on the nose chain, move back toward his rump and give him more slack on the lead rope so you have more leverage to pull his head around to the side. This makes him change position and move his hindquarters, making it harder for him to rise up on his hind legs.

Always keep safety in mind and stay to the side of the horse where you have the best leverage to pull his head around toward you. Don't position yourself in front of him (where he could strike you) and never give a steady downward pull on his head while he's rearing, or he may go over backward while trying to resist your pull.

PROBLEMS WITH LEADING

What If Nothing Works?

If a horse continues to rear and is dangerous, you need a professional trainer to help correct the behavior.

RUSHES AWAY WHEN HALTER IS REMOVED

Some horses are so eager to be turned loose that they don't like to wait politely while you take off the halter. They are so busy tugging at you in a hurry to be free, it is difficult to lead them safely through the gate of the pasture or paddock. Some will also kick up their heels as soon as they are released, without regard for the proximity of the person standing next to them.

How to Change This Habit

Examine your own behavior as you lead the horse from his stall to the paddock or pasture to turn him out. Often the impatient horse has been inadvertently encouraged and made worse by a timid handler. A common handler error is to unsnap the lead rope while the horse is going through the gate, hoping the horse will take the few last steps on his own before taking off. This "bad handler habit" leads to less control of the horse. In addition, you should not leave a halter on a horse while he's turned out for safety reasons (there are a few exceptions, such as those I've already described on pp. 55 and 58).

As his handler, you must train the horse to stand quietly beside you while you remove his halter.

• Think ahead and exude a calm, confident manner.

• Make the horse stop and stand still *after* you lead him through the door or gate, and *before* you turn him loose. This may take a bit of practice and patience: You may need to be prepared to wait the first few times, until the horse realizes he's not going to be let loose until he stands still.

- Before you take off the halter, loop the end of the lead rope around the horse's neck. This ensures you still have control over him after you remove the halter. Ask him to stand there a bit longer, and keep him guessing as to when he can go. Wait until a moment when he is calm and relaxed, and then step back and walk away, so that *you* are the one leaving, *not* him.

When the horse is overly exuberant when released in the pasture or paddock, turn him around to face the gate (leave it closed but unlatched so you can slip through it) before removing his halter. Make him wait beside you with the lead rope still around his neck until he is calm. Then, slip the rope off his neck and exit through the gate—so again, *you* are the one who leaves first.

When a horse is so set in his habit that he prances and rears and is uncontrollable in his impatience to be turned loose, walk him to the pasture or paddock and tie him with a secure halter and rope (use a quick-release/manger knot—see p. 75) to a safe tying spot next to his turnout area. He should remain tied until he calms down, at which point, lead him into the paddock or pasture and turn him out as his reward.

PROBLEMS WITH LEADING

What If Nothing Works?

If a horse can't contain himself at turnout time, consider the amount of time he is expected to live in his stall and whether or not he has enough opportunity to socialize with other horses. As mentioned in conjunction with many of the "bad habits" in this book, a diet high in grain can also contribute to out-of-control behavior. A general change in care and management may be the best solution of all.

RUSHES WHEN LED/PULLS AHEAD OF HANDLER

Some horses are always rushing or in a nervous hurry to go faster, dragging you along. They don't pay much attention to your efforts to slow or halt them.

How to Change This Habit

 Do not exert a steady pressure on the halter to try to slow the horse down. If you are constantly pulling back on his head, he responds by pulling harder on the halter. In fact, the horse probably developed the pulling habit in response to being actively pulled on. Try to always give him a little slack in the lead rope, and he'll be more apt to stop the "tug of war." If he takes all the slack out of the rope by increasing his speed, resist his pull passively (don't move your hand) so that only when he lets up on his pull does the halter pressure cease. When he is the one doing all the pulling, he'll usually stop.

>> **Horses often develop the pulling habit in response to being actively pulled on by a handler.**

 If passive resistance doesn't work and the horse continues to go too fast when led in hand, give intermittent short tugs on his halter. This is more effective than a steady pull, as it doesn't give him as much to brace against and is less likely to inspire him to keep pulling back against you.

 When short, intermittent tugs on the halter are not enough to slow him down, use a chain lead over his nose. To attach and use the chain:

- Insert the clip end of it through the ring on the left side of the halter, running it over the nose to clip it to the inside of the side ring on the right side of the halter. All the links over the nose should be touching the horse's face—do not wrap it over the halter noseband.

- Put a knot in the lead rope just behind where the chain begins. Your right hand holds the lead rope where the chain meets it (above the knot).

- Walk beside the horse's left shoulder with about a foot of slack between your hand and the halter. If the horse tries to jerk away, bolt, or go too fast, and the lead pulls through your hand, the slack will stop when your hand hits the knot, causing a jerk on the chain and pressure on his nose. When he stops or slows when the chain puts pressure on his nose, the rope will loosen again and release the pressure. This is the secret to correcting his pulling habit—instant release of pressure when he does the right thing.

PROBLEMS WITH LEADING

What If Nothing Works?

See Prances/Jigs in Hand (p. 66) for other solutions.

STRIKES IN HAND

This is another intolerable form of aggression. Some horses will strike while being led, often in conjunction with a rear (see p. 68). Striking is one of the most dangerous habits, since a horse can be very swift (and it's hard to get out of the way), and the force of a front foot can kill or seriously injure a human.

How to Change This Habit

If a horse tends to strike when he rears, use tactics to thwart the rearing habit first (see p. 68). Be sure to use safety precautions, such as moving back toward the horse's hindquarters as you try to control the rear. Always lead the horse from the side; never walk in front of him. You have more control over his actions when you are at his shoulder and in a safer position if he strikes.

Use a chain lead with the chain over his nose when leading him (see p. 72 for a description of correct use of the chain lead). Use a sharp tug on the chain to reprimand the horse for his misbehavior. If the only time they feel the chain's pressure on their nose is when they try to rear or strike out, most horses will curtail their bad actions.

What If Nothing Works?

If a horse continues aggressive striking behavior when being led, get a professional trainer to help correct the habit—or get a new horse! When you have a personality conflict that can't be resolved, it's best to start over with a horse that has a different disposition.

Problems with Tying

CHEWS/NIBBLES ROPE AND UNTIES HIMSELF

There are horses that chew on and play with the lead rope when tied, nibbling the knot, and sometimes managing to untie themselves. Young horses are very prone to chewing on ropes because they tend to chew on everything, and some continue the habit into adulthood—especially if they've accidentally managed to untie themselves once or twice.

How to Change this Habit

When tying the horse to a stationary object, use a knot the horse can't easily undo while still ensuring quick release in an emergency. Putting the "running end" of the rope through the loop in a quick-release/manger knot, for instance, foils most horses' attempts at untying themselves. Here's how to do it correctly:

- Pass the running end of the rope under and then over the rail, pole, or edge of a tie ring.

- Form a loop in the end of the rope and hold it under the part of the rope just before it passes under the rail.

- Double the end of the rope into a second loop and pass this second loop *over* the rope that goes under the rail, then partly *through* the first loop, just far enough that when you "snug" the manger knot/tie, a free end "dangles" where you could easily grab it and release the knot if necessary.

- As mentioned, you can keep the horse from untying himself by tucking the "loose" quick-release end of the rope into the second loop.

If the horse still manages to pull the running end of the rope out of the knot loop, arrange the knot so the end of the rope is out of his reach. For example, use a rope that's long enough to turn the knot so it's on the other side of the post. Or, after tying one knot, run the end of the rope down the backside of the fence and add a second quick-release tie to a lower rail. A very long lead rope allows you to dally it around one post, then run it down the fence to the next post to tie it—out of reach of the horse.

» **Get creative, finding ways to arrange the tie knot so the end of the rope is out of the horse's reach.**

Tie the horse to a stout overhead tree branch (or another high-up, stationary object he can't reach), so long as you can tie the knot somewhere *you* can easily reach it when necessary. In the tree branch example, you can throw the rope up over the stout branch, and then tie it back around the backside of the tree trunk, out of the horse's reach.

When the horse insists on chewing the lead rope to the point of damaging it, apply a foul-tasting (but nontoxic) product to the portion of the rope he can reach. Tabasco sauce often works for this purpose, and I have suggested other options on p. 46.

» **You can reduce rope chewing by applying a foul-tasting (but nontoxic) product to the portion of the rope the horse can reach.**

What If Nothing Works?

When working with a well-broke horse that plays with his rope but is unlikely to ever pull back, you can use a *breakaway halter* (a leather halter or one with a leather replaceable crown that breaks when extreme pressure is applied) and a lead rope with a snap on each end, of proper length to go from the halter to the tie ring (or around the tie post or rail) and back to the halter to snap into the halter ring. If both ends of the rope are snapped into the halter and there isn't a knot to untie, the horse can't untie himself. Note: This technique should *not* be used with a horse that is likely to pull back or without a breakaway halter as you may be unable to quickly unsnap the rope if the horse panics.

PANICS WHEN STEPS ON A LOOSE LEAD ROPE OR DROPPED REIN

PROBLEMS WITH TYING

A horse that is unaccustomed to the sound, sight, or feel of a dragging lead rope may panic if his lead ends up on the ground or his bridle reins are dropped and he steps on them. The horse's reaction is often to jerk his head up and fight the restraint he feels (caused by his own foot on the lead or reins), and his behavior may injure you if he slams his head or neck into you in his panic, or may seriously injure his tongue if he's wearing a bridle.

How to Change This Habit

SOLUTION 1

Turn the horse loose in a safe, enclosed area—a small field, pen, or corral—free of hazards on which to catch a rope. Outfit him with a well-fit halter and attach a short, strong lead rope to the ring under his chin. Turn him loose. As he grazes and walks around, he will step on the rope. At first he will panic and try to raise his head; during his fight to free his head, he will move the foot on the rope and release himself. As he wanders around, he'll keep stepping on the rope and releasing himself, and eventually, he will figure out that if he moves the proper foot, his head is freed.

Once the horse makes this connection, he'll relax and quit fighting when he steps on the rope, making him a lot safer—both for you and for himself.

What If Nothing Works?

Most horses will grow accustomed to a rope dragging if you use Solution 1 and give him enough time. If you continue to have trouble, seek help from a professional trainer.

PAWS WHILE TIED

Some horses don't like being restrained and paw continually when tied, digging holes with their front feet.

How to Change This Habit

More "tying time" is the best solution. Tie him more often and for longer periods—it will help the horse learn patience so he can relax.

If the horse continues to paw, try fastening a small chain to a padded strap buckled around the horse's leg above the fetlock joint. When the horse paws, the chain will bump and rattle against his foot, which often works to deter the behavior.

You can hobble the horse's front legs when tied to prevent pawing. This solution should only be used on a horse that is well halter broke (not apt to pull back on the rope) and also hobble-trained (already well accustomed to the feel and action of the hobbles).

What If Nothing Works?

When you can't halt the horse's pawing habit, make sure you always tie him in a safe place where he can't get a front foot stuck between two rails or in a net or wire fence. Never tie him with enough slack in the rope that he could get a foot over it. If he digs holes, tie him on firmer ground and/or use an old rubber mat under his front feet at the tie area (secure it on the edges and corners so he can't displace it). The mat is easier on his feet than a concrete slab or packed gravel.

PULLS BACK/BREAKS HALTER OR ROPE WHEN TIED

A horse that pulls back when tied is dangerous to his handlers and to property. He may continually break halters or ropes, and may injure himself if he falls down or flips over backward. Even if you tie him with something strong enough to hold him, he may injure his neck muscles, or at the very least, tighten the rope so much you can't get your tie knot undone.

PROBLEMS WITH TYING

Whichever solution you try, use a sturdy halter and rope the horse can't break, a quick-release knot that won't come loose, and make a routine of tying the horse every day (two or three times a day if you have the time) and leave him tied 30 minutes to an hour—long enough that the lesson begins to sink in, and he realizes he must stand patiently without trying to pull free. The secret to retraining a halter puller is to tie him a lot, so that he resigns himself to the fact that the rope will not break and that it's pointless to pull back.

How to Change This Habit

One way to tie the habitual halter puller with less risk to himself (and less chance for breaking the halter or lead rope) is to use a "body rope" in conjunction with the lead rope. When a body rope is used, most of the strain of the pull is absorbed by his whole body and not just his head and neck, so he's less apt to injure his neck muscles. After he tries it a few times he may also be less inclined to keep pulling back since it puts pressure around his barrel, causing mild discomfort. Note: This method is safest for a young horse that is not yet set in his ways—a foal, weanling, or yearling. An older, stronger, "spoiled" horse may be more likely to injure himself if he pulls back with all his strength.

- Loop the rope around the horse's girth and tie it in a non-slip knot, such as a *bowline knot*. To tie this knot correctly: Form a loop or "eye" with the "standing" part of the rope, and pass the "running" end around the horse's girth. Bring the running end through the "eye," under the standing part of the rope, and back through the "eye," pulling it snug.

- Run the free end between his front legs and through the halter ring under his chin.

- Using a quick-release/manger knot, tie the body rope to your tie post or tie ring (the object to which you tie should be solid so it won't give or come loose when he sets back).

- Tie the lead rope attached to his halter too, but with more slack in the rope so that most of the strain will come on the body rope when the horse pulls back.

 Tie the horse using a deflated tire inner tube. Put the inner tube over a stout post and fasten it securely with a short rope around the tire and the post, then tie the horse to the inner tube rather than to the fence. When the horse pulls back, the tire stretches a little and is not as hard on his neck—and the pull is not as apt to break the halter or rope.

 An inner tube can be used to retrain the puller in another way:

- Attach two strong ropes to two sturdy, neighboring trees at a height above the horse's head.

- Tie the free ends of the ropes to opposite sides of a deflated tire inner tube, stretching the tube taught between them, in the middle of the two trees.

- Tie the horse directly to this "picket line" in a spot where he won't run into either of the trees if he pulls back. Because of the height and flexibility of the line, he can't pull hard enough to hurt his head or neck if he sets back.

- The picket line will need to be adjusted and retightened after a certain amount of time, as the ropes will sag.

SOLUTION 4 Tie a sturdy rope to a high, stout, tree branch or ceiling beam in the barn. Tie a strong metal ring to the free end of the rope that hangs down—at a height you can reach that is also safe to use for tying a horse. Any time you tie your horse to something higher than his head, you make it more difficult for him to pull back and he is less apt to hurt himself. At this angle, he also raises his front end off the ground every time he pulls back, which means he loses some of his leverage power, and he soon learns it's futile to pull.

PROBLEMS WITH TYING

» **Any time you tie your horse to something higher than his head, you make it more difficult for him to pull back and he is less apt to hurt himself.**

SOLUTION 5 Another way to safely tie the horse that pulls back is with a "belt" around his neck to absorb some of the strain.

- Place a string cinch around the horse's neck with the ring ends coming together under his neck, behind the halter.

- Instead of clipping the lead rope to the halter, run it through the ring under his chin, up along his jawbones, and out through the back of the throatlatch.

- Tie the lead rope to the cinch rings with a bowline (non-slip) knot, or snap it to them, and tie the other end of the lead to your post or tie ring using a quick-release/manger knot. This way, if he pulls back, the force is distributed on a wide area of his neck instead of just the halter strap that runs behind his ears. When a horse is always tied with something that he cannot break, he will usually stop his pulling habit.

For those with time and a friend to assist, you can use reward and self-punishment. For this solution to work, you need to incorporate the lesson into the schedule every day until the horse no longer pulls back.

- Tie your horse in a safe way to a sturdy, stationary object.

- Stand near the front of the horse, and ask your helper to stand behind and to one side of him holding a broom parallel to the ground with the bristle end pointed toward the horse's rump. The broom bristles provide a "prickly" extension of your helper's arm so she can remain a safe distance away.

- When the horse stands quietly (not pulling back), praise and rub him.

- When the horse pulls back, your helper should adjust the position of the broom so he runs into the bristles with his rump. This usually makes the horse step forward, and he should then be immediately rewarded by the person in front. Most horses eventually decide it's better to stand quietly and be rewarded than to pull back and feel the poke of the broom bristles.

What If Nothing Works?

Most horses can be retrained to tie and respect the restraint of halter and rope, but some have such a phobia that they are never trustworthy. There are also some horses that for no apparent reason occasionally pull back.

For these two types of halter pullers, it's best to never tie them solidly. This is a nuisance because it means you can't leave them unattended, but there are ways in which you can reach a "truce" with such a horse. He may stand at the hitching post or grooming area patiently and quietly while you groom or saddle him if you just dally the rope around the tie rail or post a few times, or slide it through the tie ring without knotting it. This ensures there's always some give to the rope and the horse doesn't feel trapped, so he won't pull back.

There are also commercial tie rings and tie clips that can be used effectively: The lead rope goes through them and they put some tension on the rope to hold it in place, but if the horse pulls back, the tension is released, allowing the rope to slide so the horse does not hurt himself. Since these rings/clips allow the rope to "give" when the horse pulls strongly, the horse is less apt to panic about having his head restrained and may quit pulling.

PROBLEMS
WITH TYING

WON'T STAND STILL WHEN TIED

Some horses are so nervous they can't stand still when tied, fidgeting around and making it difficult to groom or saddle them. They are always bumping into you or stepping on your toes.

How to Change This Habit

The best solution for the horse that's not at ease with being tied is *more time being tied*. This does more than any other method to help the horse learn patience and discover that he might as well relax and stand still rather than wasting his energy in nervous fidgeting, whinnying, or stomping. Tie him as part of his daily routine, leaving him tied as you do chores or other tasks nearby.

If the horse is extremely nervous or upset about being tied, try tying him in his stall, pen, or paddock—a familiar place where he feels at home. (Note: When trying this lesson in a pen or paddock, he should be the only horse in the pen so herdmates cannot take advantage of him while he's tied.) If the horse regularly lives at pasture with other horses, tie him where he can still see them, or put one of his buddies in a pen or paddock next to him while he has a tying lesson, so he doesn't think he's been deserted by the herd.

Once the horse becomes comfortable with being tied in a familiar place, tie him in different locations around the barnyard and leave him tied for an hour or so each day while you are nearby doing chores and working with other horses. This way, he'll get used to all kinds of activity and resign himself to being patient (and standing still) wherever he is. Don't tie him in the same spot every time, or he might think that's the only place he should be tied, and will still be nervous in other locations.

What If Nothing Works?

If you don't have appropriate places to tie the horse regularly for periods of time (and therefore can't spend the time necessary to condition his mind and change the habit), you may have to live with his fidget habit—or have someone hold him for you to keep him still when you groom or saddle him.

Problems with Grooming and Management

AFRAID OF BLANKETING

It is more common for a horse that isn't used to wearing a blanket to be skittish about having one put on, but even a horse that's been blanketed a lot may develop an avoidance habit, trying to move away from you or resist your efforts to swing it over his back and buckle it on.

》 **Even a horse that's been blanketed a lot may try to move away when you try to swing the blanket over him.**

How to Change This Habit

SOLUTION 1

Try to figure out *why* the horse is skittish. He may have been frightened in the past by a blanket slipping or another blanket-related situation that spooked him. To get him over his fear, you may have to start over: Treat him as if he is a young, green horse that's never had a blanket put on.

• During the following "retraining" steps, hold the horse or have a helper hold him so he does not feel "trapped"—tying him is not a good idea because he may panic and pull back.

- Start with something small, like a folded towel, and rub it over his entire body.

- Once he is at ease with that, unfold the towel so it is larger, and again move it all over him. If he becomes alarmed or "goosey," fold it smaller again, and keep rubbing him with it until he relaxes.

- Once you can rub the horse's back, hindquarters, and belly with the unfolded towel, try a folded blanket. Again, only unfold the blanket after he's at ease with it at a smaller size. Slowly progress to having the whole blanket unfolded and on the horse.

» **Hang a blanket on the horse's stall door or paddock fence so he can check it out while you do chores nearby or groom him.**

Select a well-worn blanket that already smells like a horse (this makes it less frightening). Hang it on the horse's stall door or paddock fence so he can check it out while you do chores nearby or groom him, but don't let him nibble on it—he might pull it off and scare himself when it falls to the ground. Let the blanket become part of his daily surroundings so he gets completely over his fear or suspicion of it. Then use gradual steps—similar to Solution 1—taking as many lessons/days as needed.

- Start with the blanket folded into a small "package," and hold it out for the horse to smell. If he backs away, wait until he relaxes before holding it close to his nose again.

- Once the horse realizes the folded blanket won't hurt him, rub his neck with it (keeping it folded small so it doesn't flop around). Then rub it over his shoulders and back, down his front and hind legs, on both sides.

- Drape the blanket over his withers. After he's comfortable with that, slide it slowly over his back and rump, keeping out of kicking range. Keep a good hold on the blanket so it won't slide off and startle the horse if he moves. (If it does fall off before you make it all the way down his back and rump, start over again at his front end.)

- Once he's calm about the blanket sliding over him, secure the straps together so they won't dangle and alarm him, fold the blanket over itself so you can set the front of the blanket over his withers, then slowly unfold the rest of it over his back and rump, leaving it correctly in place on his body. Fold it back up and remove it. Repeat several times until he no longer resists. Only when he is perfectly calm about this process should you fasten the straps around his body.

» **Only when the horse is perfectly calm about the blanketing process should you fasten the straps around his body.**

SOLUTION
3

Tarp training can help any horse that is skittish about a saddle blanket flapping or a stable blanket being put on. Use a small tarp to desensitize him over several days, if necessary.

- Leave the horse loose in a round pen or small corral or paddock with a tarp lying on the ground so he can check it out at his own pace. Most horses will eventually get close enough on their own to smell the tarp and realize it isn't so scary.

- Once the horse will walk up to the tarp on his own, longe him in the pen so he must travel around it, and eventually over it.

- When he will walk over the tarp on the longe line, spend time rubbing him all over with the tarp, working up to laying it over his back. Take as many lessons as needed to get him used to having the tarp moving around and over him. Once the horse is okay with a tarp on his back, a blanket is easy! (Note: Never leave a horse unattended for long periods of time with a sack or tarp loose in his pen, particularly if he is shod as a shoe could catch the material and drag it when the horse moves. He may also start chewing on it.)

What If Nothing Works?

See Afraid of Blanket Removal (below).

AFRAID OF BLANKET REMOVAL

Some horses are well-behaved when you put a blanket on but skittish when you take it off. They may have developed this habit because a blanket "hung up" once when someone was taking it off, or it slipped down under his belly, or twisted around his flanks or in front of him, causing him to panic.

A blanket may sometimes produce static electricity as it's pulled off, causing the horse to experience a mild shock. The horse may then anticipate an uncomfortable or scary sensation and become jumpy when you start to remove the blanket, which only makes the process more difficult for you to complete.

>>   **A blanket may sometimes produce static electricity as it's pulled off, causing the horse to experience a mild shock.**

How to Change This Habit

You can help make sure the blanket is not causing him discomfort and doesn't create static electricity as it moves across his hair coat by spraying the blanket before use with anti-static spray. Or, you can use a cotton blanket (or an under layer or liner that's 100-percent cotton) since it's less likely to create static.

SOLUTION 2 Always undo every strap and surcingle before you start to remove a blanket. Proceed slowly and carefully, keeping the blanket close to the horse with nothing flapping. Fold the blanket as you go, making the total area smaller and less scary before pulling it off: Fold the front part back over the middle, and then the back part over the middle, and then gently pull the blanket off from the horse's back and barrel area, just as you would pull off a saddle.

What If Nothing Works?

When a horse has an unreasonable phobia about blankets, try desensitizing him with a tarp as described on p. 87. If that doesn't work, change his care and management so you don't have to use a blanket. Let him grow a winter hair coat for natural protection and give him access to shelter. Use fly spray/wipe in summer months instead of fly sheets, and work on other management alternatives to protect him and/or his hair coat without resorting to blanketing.

AFRAID OF SPRAY BOTTLES

Many horses are afraid of fly spray or aerosol applications because of the hissing sound they make when the product is dispensed. Some people make the mistake of trying to apply spray for the first time with the horse restrained (tied up). Unfortunately, if the horse feels trapped in the face of the unfamiliar sound and sensation of the spray, he may panic and pull back. Fear of the sound of the spray quickly becomes a phobia and resistance becomes a habit.

How to Change This Habit

Start over and reacquaint the horse with the spray in a totally nonconfrontational manner. Take as much time and use as many lessons as necessary to get him relaxed about the sound of spray. Work on this in a safe, open area where the horse can't run into anything.

- Stand next to his shoulder, holding onto the lead rope, and spray the bottle far away from him, at first. He may run circles around you, trying to get away from it, but just continue spraying while talking quietly to the horse. If you are not actually trying to spray him, you will also be more relaxed and at ease, not tense and fighting with him to stand still. As soon as the horse stands quietly instead of moving around when he hears the sound, pet him and let him know he's done the right thing.

» **Take as much time and use as many lessons as necessary to get the horse to stay relaxed even when he hears the sound of a spray bottle.**

- Gradually work the spray closer to the horse as he begins to settle down. Repeat the lesson several times a day until he starts to fuss less and relax.

- Usually within a few days the horse realizes it's not going to hurt him—the sound no longer scares him—and you can cautiously start applying the spray to his body. The key throughout the process is to not restrain him so he doesn't feel trapped. If he's free to move around you in a circle, he gets over his fear more quickly. (He's also less apt to try to kick at you when he's moving.)

If the horse is really nervous and scared, take a lot of time to reacquaint him with the spray. Enlist the help of a friend so one of you can hold him while the other starts spraying well away from him, gradually getting closer. Bring the spray a little closer and then take it farther away again, alternating proximity so he knows it won't "get him." Give him a chance to think about it, allowing him to circle if he wants to. When he does stop and stand still, rub his neck and withers to help relax him—rubbing this area tends to calm a horse because this is where his dam nuzzled him when he was a foal.

A horse always "thinks" more rationally when he is calm than when he's scared and upset, so your job in the process is to get him calm, rather than try to force him to accept the spray.

What If Nothing Works?

When a horse absolutely won't stand still for a spray, use an alternate method for applying insecticide or other spray products. Spray onto a soft cloth and then wipe it on the horse. If it's a medication, find a way to dab it on instead. Seek alternative product choices, like roll-ons and ointments..

DIFFICULT TO BATHE/HOSE OFF

Some horses are afraid of having water poured or squirted over their body. They resist your attempts to bathe them or hose off sweat after a workout or on a hot day.

How to Change This Habit

If the horse is sensitive or skittish about cold water, start with warm water in a bucket and sponge it on him, then pour it gently over him as he gets used to it and realizes the water is pleasant. Start with a small container of water at first, filling it from the bucket, since a small amount is not as spooky. As he grows accustomed to the water being ladled over him, you can begin to use cooler and cooler water until he's accustomed to the temperature of water that comes out of your hose. Note: Don't bathe or hose the horse with cold water on a cold or windy day, however—you may chill him, as well as discourage him from liking the bathing process.

» **When training/retraining a horse to accept the hose, start with warm water in a bucket and sponge it on him.**

If the horse is afraid of the hose and the way it squirts, first spend some time getting him used to the hose without any water running out of it.

- Move the hose around just like you would if you were bathing him, but without the water turned on. Repeat this lesson several times before actually trying the water: Bring the hose closer to his body (only after he's at ease with it from several feet away), and when he's relaxed about it, let it touch various parts of his body, with more and more contact as he becomes at ease with it.

- When you start running water from the hose, turn it on so low it's barely trickling, and move it around the horse's body (without touching him) just so he can get used to the sound and sight of the water running.

- After he's at ease with the sight and sound of the water, let him smell the trickling water or lick at it if he's curious, so he knows what it is and isn't afraid.

- Let the water trickle over one front foot, then the other, gradually moving up the legs after he quits moving around and stands still for it. Let his reactions tell you how quickly you can progress: It may take just one long session or several to get him to where you can move the hose higher and wet his belly, chest, hind legs, neck, and back, and eventually his head.

- After the horse is used to a trickle of water from the hose all over his body, you can increase the flow.

What If Nothing Works?

If the horse remains skittish about being hosed with cold water (some barn and outdoor water sources are quite cold), it may be best for both you and the horse if you use buckets of lukewarm water and sponge-bathe him instead.

DIFFICULT TO CLIP

Many horses are nervous about being clipped, especially around the head and ears. The buzzing noise and vibration from electric and battery-operated clippers are alarming, and it is natural that horses are inclined to move away from the source. Even some very gentle and otherwise well-behaved horses are difficult to clip because they were over-disciplined when they attempted to avoid the clippers at some point in their life: When the horse moves away or raises his head and is given a rude smack or a jerk on the halter, it is only more likely that whenever they hear the sound of clippers in the future, they will resist. Disciplining a horse for his reactions to discomfort or fear only makes the problem worse, and some horses become irrationally terrified of clippers due to this handler mistake, since they know that when they see or hear the clippers there is likely to be punishment.

> » **Even some very gentle and otherwise well-behaved horses are difficult to clip because they were over-disciplined when they attempted to avoid the clippers at some point in their life.**

How to Change This Habit

SOLUTION
1

First assess the horse's problem and try to understand why he is reacting the way he does. If the horse has a physical problem that causes discomfort when his ears are handled or makes him extra-sensitive around his head or ears, the problem should be dealt with prior to clipping, if possible, and at the very least, taken into consideration during the process. If he has an injury or infection, ear ticks or warts, or any other abnormality, do not try to clip his ears (or even any part of his head) until the condition is treated. And be aware that some of these kinds of problems may leave a lasting discomfort or fear of having the head/ears handled.

The cause of the horse's aversion may have been impatient or inappropriate handling that convinced the horse that he must try to protect his ears at all costs (that is, keep people from grabbing them). As mentioned, if he equates clipping with discomfort and punishment, it will take very patient retraining to enable him to realize that clipping won't hurt.

Evaluate the clippers you use, especially those you use on the horse's head. Large, heavy-duty clippers designed for body clipping or for thick hair may cause discomfort or irritation when used on the finer hair and more sensitive areas of head and ears. Not only are they large and cumbersome (more awkward when you are trying to do a precision job around the head, and thus more likely to bump and annoy the horse) but they also make more noise. Smaller, quieter models are less intimidating to the horse, and more easily run over the bony contours of his head without causing him discomfort.

Also check the blades of all the clippers you use to make sure they're not getting dull and pulling on his hair.

» **Heavy-duty clippers designed for body clipping or for thick hair may cause discomfort or irritation when used on the finer hair and more sensitive areas of the horse's head and ears.**

To train a horse to accept clippers, or to retrain a horse that has become afraid of them, start slowly and take as much time as needed. Proceed step by step, progressing at a rate that's comfortable for that particular horse. If you try to do too much too soon, or trim him all at once, you are bound to have problems. If you need to clip the horse in preparation for a show or special event, start working with him well ahead of when you actually need him to look his best. A few sessions spent getting him used to clipping in a nonconfrontational way (*before* the day you *really* need to clip him) will pay off, making him much easier to clip in the future. Remember, you are trying to build trust.

For all training sessions, have someone hold the horse rather than tying him (or drape the lead rope over your arm if there isn't a friend available to help you), so he never feels trapped.

- Before you start using the clippers, make sure the horse is comfortable with all parts of his body being handled and brushed. If you can't brush his legs or rub his face and ears without him being sensitive or ticklish, you won't be able to clip him in those areas. Spend time getting him used to being touched and rubbed until he is relaxed about having your hands all over his body.

- If the horse is not accustomed to clippers, let him see and smell them while they are turned off.

- Next let him listen to the sound of the clippers when they are on, but from a distance. If he is already afraid of clippers, it will take more time to desensitize him—you'll want to let him hear them running from some distance away for several sessions (until he's no longer jumpy about the noise) before you bring them close to him.

- For the inexperienced horse (new to clipping), after he's comfortable with the sound of clippers from a distance, turn them off and run them over his body so he realizes they don't hurt.

- For the horse that is already afraid of clippers, just the sight of them may upset him, even after becoming more comfortable with the noise from a distance. Substitute another item, like a brush or cell phone—anything that is about the same size and shape of the clippers. First let him smell the object, then go through the motions of running it over his body and and neck and finally—as he comes to accept the substitute object—his head and near his ears. If at any time he becomes tense or resistant, go back to the areas he feels most comfortable with and slowly work toward the problem area again. Once he's at ease with the substitute object, repeat the process using the turned-off clippers: Get him used to having them all over his body. This may take several sessions—don't try to do it all in one day. If the horse is still nervous, end the lesson on a good note: Rub the clippers over a place he accepts, or go back to the substitute item if need be, knowing you can work on it again later.

• After the horse is at ease with having turned-off clippers run all over his body, start them up and let him become at ease with the sound in closer proximity than earlier in the training/retraining. Again, begin at a distance, and if he's not afraid, gradually bring them closer. Approach an area of his body he's not defensive about. Work around the area as if you were clipping, but don't let the clippers actually come into contact with his body. Turn the hand holding the clippers over and lay the back of it against the horse's shoulder or withers (for example) so he can feel the vibration through your hand.

• After the horse is at ease with the up-close sound and feel of the clippers, start clipping his body and neck. If he stands quietly for this, give him a treat. This is when having a helper to hold him is of great benefit: She can help keep him relaxed by talking and humming, and occasionally handing out the treat (a bite of green grass, a horse cookie, or whatever your horse likes best) as a reward for standing still. Continue to clip as long as the horse is at ease. If at any point he becomes tense or nervous, go back to an area he tolerates, and save the rest (such as the legs and head) for another day or days. Be sure to end on a good note, and plan on repeating several lessons before actually clipping his ears or head.

- When you do make your way to the horse's ears, touch and rub them with your hands (but not with the clippers) while the horse listens to the sound. If he tolerates this, give him praise and a reward and end the lesson. Repeat several sessions where you hold the clippers next to his ears and rub and massage the ears with your other hand, but do not actually clip them, until he is fully at ease with this situation.

- When you determine your horse is ready for you to start clipping his head and ears, trim the area around the ears first, such as the bridle path, so he grows accustomed to the feel of the clippers. Then venture to one ear, touching it first with your hand before you do with the clippers. Do as much as you can with the horse remaining calm: Even if you are only able to clip part of an ear, you are better off ending the session on a good note than trying for the whole thing and losing ground if the horse grows impatient or starts to react adversely. Short successful lessons make more progress in the long run.

 If the horse is still bothered by having the clippers close to his ears, but is not ear shy (p. 98) otherwise, it may be that he can't handle the sound. You might try gently stuffing toilet paper or cotton into his ears to help muffle the buzzing.

 If a horse objects to having the long hairs (whiskers) around his muzzle clipped, use a safety razor (for humans) and stroke it gently downward (with the lay of the hair) to trim them. This makes no noise or vibration, and the horse generally won't object.

» **Substitute another item, like a brush or cell phone—anything that is about the same size and shape of the clippers—and go through the motions of running it all over his body.**

What If Nothing Works?

If the horse is irrationally afraid or uncontrollably ticklish, and if even patient handling and attempts to retrain him don't work, seriously evaluate the need to clip him. Keep in mind that even though clipping is traditionally desired for the show ring, you are actually doing the horse a disservice by depriving him of the protection of ear hairs (they help keep insects out and prevent debris from falling into the ear canal) and the whiskers around his muzzle (important to him for feeling the ground or his feed tub, or the stall wall in the dark, since he can't see the end of his nose).

HEAD SHY/EAR SHY

Some horses are extremely sensitive about having parts of their face or head touched, especially around the eyes and ears. Some won't let you touch their ears at all, jerking their head away or raising it up so you can't reach.

How to Change This Habit

First determine if there's a physical reason for the bad behavior (ear ticks, ear warts, or another problem that's making the ears sensitive or painful). If you suspect this is the case, have your veterinarian examine the horse so you can deal appropriately with the condition.

If there isn't a physical issue, the horse has probably developed this habit because his ears have been roughly handled in the past, or he may have had a bad experience having his ears (or eyes) treated for a medical problem. The result is that he doesn't trust anything coming near his ears, or he is fearful of any movement close to his head, and the best solution in this case is to carefully and consistently touch and rub the nearby areas that the horse *will* accept. Gradually over time, come closer and closer to the areas (the ears, face, or eyes, for example) he wants to protect.

» **When a horse's ears have been roughly handled in the past, carefully and consistently touch and rub the nearby areas that the horse *will* accept.**

SOLUTION 3

When the horse is ear shy, rub his neck at a spot where he's comfortable with your touch, and gradually work up the neck and closer to the ears. Rub in circles, and as each circle comes closer to the ears, gently brush against them lightly in passing. Stay in tune with the horse's attitude; don't start touching the ears—even in this mild way—until he is ready (more relaxed and less evasive). If he realizes you are not hurting his ears as you rub your hand in circles, lightly touching the base of the ear, he'll come to accept your gradual progression to gently touching *more* of the ear, and then rubbing the *whole* ear. Do it all matter-of-factly, staying relaxed yourself and softly talking or humming to help the horse stay calm. If you are tense or nervous, he will be also. Note: As the horse comes to accept having his ears touched, be sure to handle both ears, and do it from both sides his body, as well as in front of him.

SOLUTION 4

If the horse is sensitive around his eyes, gently rub other areas of his face that he accepts, starting around his cheeks or muzzle and gradually working upward. The key is to stay relaxed—don't worry if you don't make immediate progress. Just handle his head and face as often as possible, in a very nonchalant way, coming closer and closer to the eyes until he is no longer so guarded. Over time he'll realize there's no reason to be afraid, especially if you never try to force him to accept your touch.

» **Don't worry if you don't make immediate progress—just handle his head and face as often as possible, in a very nonchalant way.**

What If Nothing Works?

If a horse remains head shy or ear shy in spite of everything you do (perhaps because of a deep-seated phobia from an earlier bad experience), and you have to handle his ears, eyes, or face for medical purposes, you may need to have an experienced person help you and use a *skin* or *lip twitch* (see p. 138). In addition, I personally have found the Stableizer® Equine Restraint and Training System, when appropriately used, to be effective in these situations. If your veterinarian is attempting to treat the head-shy horse, he or she may resort to the use of a tranquilizer.

RESISTANT TO BRUSHING/SENSITIVE-SKINNED

Some horses have sensitive skin or ticklish areas and don't want to be touched. When you try to groom them, they move around, fidget to avoid you, swish their tail in annoyance, or are actively resistant (pulling back, stomping, or kicking).

How to Change This Habit

 When the horse moves around and won't stand still, try to determine if he's fidgety because of nervousness and sensitivity, because he has learned he can get away with it, or because he has never been taught to stand still. If he has a particularly sensitive area he doesn't want you to touch, make sure there isn't a physical problem—like an injury or skin disease—that needs medical attention.

 If he's stepping on your feet, or swatting you in the face with his tail, or pushing you against the wall or fence "on purpose," be firm and consistent in demanding that he stand still. When he crowds into your space, make it uncomfortable for him: Position a stiff brush or curry comb so he bumps into the sharp bristles instead of you. Praise him when he stands still; reprimand him when he doesn't.

If the horse moves around because he's ticklish and sensitive, his behavior requires a totally different tactic. Don't reprimand, and don't get impatient with him, as it will just make him more nervous. Try to get him to relax. Start your grooming session without tools: Merely rub him with your hand. It will upset him least if you start at his withers. This is the area a mare nuzzles her foal, and most horses are at ease with being touched and rubbed here (it tends to relax them). Talk to the horse as you rub gently, using a soft voice, or a quiet humming or whistling sound, to help relax him. Monotonous and continuous low sounds will soothe a nervous horse.

PROBLEMS WITH GROOMING AND MANAGEMENT

When the horse allows you to rub his withers, gradually expand your gentle rubbing to other parts of his body—work up the neck and back down again, along his back, around his rump, under his abdomen, and down his legs. If you come to a sensitive area and the horse resists, go back to areas where he's comfortable and gradually work toward the sensitive part again.

Once the horse is relaxed about being touched by your hands, try a soft cloth, then a soft brush. If he's sensitive about his face, don't use a brush there—just a soft cloth. After he finds you aren't hurting him, most horses will accept simple grooming with a brush, and will come to enjoy being rubbed or brushed in certain areas—particularly those hard-to-reach itchy spots.

What If Nothing Works?

Some horses remain very sensitive about certain parts of their body; you might never be able to use a curry comb (even the rubber kind) or stiff bristled brush on those areas. Just continue to use a very soft brush or soft cloth on those spots: Don't ever try to groom a sensitive horse roughly or use stiffer/harder tools in certain areas that cause him discomfort, or he may resist *all* grooming.

Problems with Tacking Up

AGGRESSIVE TOWARD HANDLER WHEN SADDLED

Some horses resent the saddle so much—because the girth or cinch causes them discomfort when tightened, or they have a sore back, or they equate saddling with long rides and hard work that they'd rather avoid—that they reach around to nip when you are saddling up. A few go so far as to take a swat at you with a hind leg when you reach under to take hold of the girth or cinch.

How to Change This Habit

First, make sure the saddle and its related equipment are not causing the horse discomfort. The saddle may not fit him properly and cause pain. Chronic back pain or even any kind of minor irritation caused by the way the saddle presses against the muscles and bones of his back may make the horse grouchy. You may have to change saddles and/or have one properly fitted to his back, as well as treating any chronic pain, before you can resolve this problem.

If the horse is touchy about the girth area, cinch up slowly and gradually (to make sure you don't pinch the tender skin), and don't finish tightening the girth/cinch until you are ready to mount and have led the horse forward a few steps. Never tighten the girth or cinch excessively. As is the case with a sore back, if the problem is a raw or tender area at the girth, it should be addressed medically.

» **Pain or discomfort caused by the way the saddle presses against the muscles and bones of the horse's back may make him grouchy.**

When there isn't a physical problem, or if there was a physical problem in the past, but it has been treated and is not painful anymore (and the horse is just being grouchy out of habit), he needs to be reminded of his manners.

Nipping should be discouraged in the same manner that you'd deal with it at any other time (see also p. 149). He should learn that it's not pleasant to nip you, and the "punishment" should be instant. Slapping at him is ineffective because he'll merely jerk his head away, and he's likely quicker than you are—and it may become a "game" to him to see if he can grab you and jerk away before you can smack him. It's much more effective to use *self-punishment*: Ignore his antics (don't get mad or yell or try to hit him) and simply position your elbow so it's the first part of your body with which he comes into contact. Hitting his muzzle on your elbow will be uncomfortable, and he may decide it isn't so fun, after all. If the horse bites hard, wear a light jacket while saddling, and attach (duct tape works) a relatively sharp object (like a dog grooming comb) to the portion of your sleeve closest to him on that side. If you consistently make sure he hits the the dog grooming comb every time he tries to bite you, he'll usually give it up.

If the horse tends to take a swat at you with his hind foot as you reach under his belly to grab the girth or cinch, use a long, blunted hook (a coat hanger can be taken apart and reformed as a long rod with a hook at the end) to snag the end of the girth/cinch and pull it over to you. Reprimand the horse if he picks up his foot to kick.

To get him over the kicking habit, spend some time practicing with the girth or cinch so that he realizes you are not hurting him and there's no need to protect himself.

- Before saddling the horse, fasten a short strap (a lead rope with snap end works well) to the near-side end of the girth or cinch.

- With the saddle on, pull the end of the lead rope under the horse to his near side. Now you can hold on to the lead rope and use it to bring the girth/cinch toward you (you don't have to bend under the horse).

- Keep lifting the girth/cinch up toward the horse's belly and then let it "retreat" again: Lift it up and let it down; gently touch his girth area with it, then let it drop away. Repeat over and over again until the horse realizes it's not hurting him, and it's pointless to kick at it every time.

> » **Spend some time practicing with the girth or cinch— pulling it snug, then releasing it again—so the horse realizes it won't hurt him.**

What If Nothing Works?

If a horse continues to bite or to kick viciously when you try to saddle him, there is either something physically wrong that you haven't been able to diagnose, or he has a very bad attitude about being handled or ridden. When a horse is dangerous to saddle, he needs medical help or you need help from a professional trainer.

"ANTSY"/FIDGETS WHEN SADDLED

If the horse moves around as you try to saddle him, he may step on your feet or bump into you, or he may move at the wrong time as you are placing the saddle on his back so it ends up in the wrong place. The latter can cause an accident if the saddle irritates him or slides to one side and spooks him; he may then jump around and the saddle might fall to the ground and scare him more.

PROBLEMS WITH TACKING UP

How to Change This Habit

If the horse is in the habit of fidgeting when saddled and there isn't a physical reason for his evasiveness (the saddle fits and doesn't cause pain, and his girth is not sore) go "back to basics" and teach him to stand still when asked. More tying lessons (working with him tied for an hour or so every day or several times a day) may be helpful to teach patience.

> » **Go "back to basics" with the fidgety horse, and teach him to stand still when asked.**

Do more groundwork with a focus on lessons on stopping and standing still. The horse needs more handling so he knows he must stop and stand when you tell him "whoa." If he moves forward or back or to the side when you say "whoa," reposition him, and ask again for him to stand still until you give him the signal to move forward again. Reward him with praise when he stands for a few minutes. Stand for longer and longer periods—until he knows that whenever you tell him to "whoa," he must stop moving, and then he must not move until you tell him to. If necessary, go back to the round pen or the longe line and make him work hard for a few minutes, with many changes of direction, until he is glad for a chance to respond to your cue to stop and stand still. Once his "whoa" is solid, go back to saddling lessons, which he should now accept quietly.

If the horse is skittish and fearful when being saddled, he probably had a bad experience with the process in the past. Maybe someone carelessly flopped a saddle onto his back and the off-side stirrup flipped down and hit him, or he was startled in some other way.

Whatever the reason for his jumpiness, the best way to resolve it is to "start over" and saddle the horse as carefully as you would a young inexperienced animal.

- Have a friend hold him rather than tying him for saddling lessons. This way, he won't feel trapped, and the person holding him can help keep him calm by praising him when he stands still (giving a treat when the horse is scared or nervous can encourage him to relax and stand) or gently reprimanding him when he moves around.

- Stay calm and confident. If *you* are relaxed the *horse* will be more apt to relax. (If *you* are nervous, the *horse* will think there's something to be afraid of and less apt to stand still.) Start by brushing and touching the horse all over his back and girth area. There's no point in saddling him up until he's at ease with you touching his body. If he's ticklish about the girth area, spend a lot of time in that area.

- Once he's relaxed with your grooming, slide a saddle pad on and off his back slowly and carefully, without any extra movement that might startle him. If he's "goosey" about the pad, use a folded towel (so you can keep the total area of it very small) first, and slide it up and down his side and onto his back before moving on to the pad again.

- When he's at ease with you putting on the saddle pad in a slow and careful way, begin the lesson again, but this time put it on and take it off in a "normal" fashion—use a little more motion, and lift it higher as you put it on, like you would do with a saddle.

Repeat this from both sides until the horse accepts the pad and realizes it won't hurt him.

- Next, introduce the saddle. Start with a lightweight saddle: If you ride English, use a child's saddle first, and Western riders can use an English saddle. A light saddle is easier for you to hold on to and set on his back slowly and carefully without bumping him. It also won't alarm him as much. Reduce loose, flopping parts by running the stirrup irons up the leathers on an English saddle and hooking the off-side stirrup bow over the horn on a Western saddle. Lay the girth or cinch across the saddle seat so it won't flop down on the off side, or detach the girth/cinch from the saddle altogether, and do not buckle it on to either side until the horse accepts the saddle on his back. If there's little that can startle him, the horse will have less reason to be nervous and jumpy.

- Set the saddle on the horse's back and take it off again several times. Make sure he'll stand still and be calm and relaxed with what you are doing before you go on to the next step. Once he stands quietly while you swing the saddle on and pull it off, and he doesn't fidget around, go ahead and fasten the girth/cinch—slowly and carefully.

PROBLEMS WITH TACKING UP

What If Nothing Works?

If a horse absolutely won't stand still for saddling, even after you've patiently revisited basic work as I've described in the solutions, you can hobble his front feet to keep him from moving around (only if he's already familiar with wearing hobbles).

BUCKS WHEN SADDLED

A few horses are so "goosey" or uncomfortable with the saddle that they may try to buck it off before you can fasten the girth or cinch, or they may "hump up" when the cinch is tightened and try to buck the saddle off when you lead them forward a few steps before mounting.

How to Change This Habit

In this scenario, there is often a physical problem involved—either currently or at some point in the horse's background he experienced pain related to the saddle and he remembers it with aversion. An ill-fitting saddle that's causing serious discomfort may make even the quietest, most gentle horse buck. Your saddle should be checked for fit, a broken tree, or another problem, such as a nail or screw working down through the fleece, and possibly changed to one that fits the horse properly and does not cause him pain. If this does not help, a thorough examination by an equine veterinarian (with particular focus on his back and/or girth area) is imperative.

If the saddle fits and there isn't a physical problem (that is, whatever caused the horse to react to saddling this way is no longer an issue), extensive and careful retraining, starting over with grooming and saddling step by step, may help solve this problem (see my solutions for "Antsy"/Fidgets When Saddled, p. 105). Once a horse realizes he won't experience pain or discomfort, he may quit trying to buck the saddle off.

What If Nothing Works?

A few horses, for whatever reason, never get over the habit of resenting/resisting the saddle. If this is dangerous, rather than merely annoying, you are better off spending your efforts on a different horse. Any time a horse has a habit that poses a safety issue to you or to himself, and when you can't find a way to resolve it readily and easily, it's wise to get a new horse.

GIRTHY/CINCHY

Many horses are at ease with saddling, until you start to tighten the girth or cinch. They protest by humping up their back, trying to move away to avoid the tightening, or taking a deep breath and holding it so that when they exhale, the girth/cinch is no longer tight. Some horses are so sensitive about having the girth/cinch tightened that their front legs buckle during the process (perhaps from a nerve being pinched).

How to Change This Habit

SOLUTION 1

First make sure there isn't a physical reason for the horse's sensitivity and protest. The girth area may be sore from a ride the previous day, or it could have tender areas or scar tissue from past rubbing or pressure (from a girth or cinch that didn't fit well). An old injury in the girth area, which is rubbed or pressed when the cinch is tightened, may cause the horse discomfort.

>> **Some horses are so sensitive about having the girth/cinch tightened that their front legs buckle during the process.**

SOLUTION 2

Take more time and care when tightening the girth or cinch. Never jerk it tight (which can pinch the tender skin) or tighten it all at once. Fasten and tighten it *just enough* to keep the saddle in place so it won't slip or shift position, then wait a moment before tightening it a little more. Lead the horse around a few steps before tightening it more, and then tighten it a final time (only if necessary) just before you mount. When the horse is in the habit of "blowing up" (taking a deep breath and holding it), this step-by-step tightening will ensure that the cinch is not dangerously loose when you start to mount.

SOLUTION 3

The girth/cinch only needs to be snug enough to keep the saddle in position. The girth/cinch should be loose enough to slide a couple fingers between it and the horse at all times. The horse's withers are actually what keep the saddle from turning to the side. A horse with good withers will not need a tight girth/cinch. When you have a horse with low withers that won't hold a saddle well, use a breast collar or breastplate to help keep the saddle in place so you won't have to make the girth so uncomfortably tight, and use a mounting block so you are not pulling the saddle to the side as you get on.

» **The girth/cinch only needs to be snug enough to keep the saddle in position.**

If the horse has very sensitive skin and is ticklish about having anything touch his girth area, spend some time gently rubbing and brushing near the area, using an advance-and-retreat technique to gradually put him at ease. Gently massage his barrel, moving your fingers lightly and in a circular motion closer and closer to the girth area until you are rubbing the sensitive spots and he remains relaxed. Then run a lead rope over his back, reach under to take hold of it as you would a girth or cinch, and rub the rope gently around his girth area. Tighten and release the rope, as well, taking as many sessions as you need to get him over his fear.

What If Nothing Works?

The horse may have a physical problem that is difficult to diagnose that makes him extra sensitive in the girth area. Try changing saddles and girths/cinches to find tack that fits his shape better and is more comfortable for him.

PUTS TONGUE OVER BIT

Occasionally you'll encounter a horse that is hard to bridle. This bad habit is usually due to lack of proper training or bad experiences from early in the horse's life, such as a bridle that didn't fit (a painful bit or headstall that rubbed) or poor bridling techniques (pinched ears, clanked teeth, or some other mishandling that left an unpleasant memory). The horse that has made up his mind that bridling is traumatic can try to avoid it in a number of different ways. For example, a horse that continually mouths the bit and gets his tongue over it may soon learn that by doing this he can avoid bit control.

» **Being hard to bridle is usually due to lack of proper training or bad past experiences.**

How to Change This Habit

Make sure the bit and bridle fits the horse. Usually the bridle is too loose if the horse can put his tongue over the bit. You may have to use a tighter headstall for a while so the bit rides a little higher in his mouth and he can't get his tongue over it. Once the horse becomes accustomed to carrying the bit as he should, he won't try as hard to put his tongue over it, and you can then loosen the headstall a little again so he can safely move the bit around with his tongue and put it where it's most comfortable.

Sometimes a different type of bit may help solve this problem. Horses' mouths are not all the same in shape and depth. Tongue thickness also varies. Another style and/or shape of bit may be more comfortable for the horse, and therefore he will not fuss with it as much.

What If Nothing Works?

If the horse continues to play with the bit and insists on putting his tongue over it, you may want to try using a bitless bridle or a hackamore.

RAISES/TOSSES HEAD WHEN BRIDLED

Some horses don't like their ears handled, while others raise or toss their heads for other reasons, such as a tooth problem that causes them pain when bridled.

How to Change This Habit

Check the bit and headstall for proper fit to see if they are causing discomfort. When fit is the issue, a change in tack may help resolve the problem, but you will probably have to spend some careful, patient sessions with the horse to reassure him that the bridle will no longer hurt him.

> » **Check the bit and headstall for proper fit to see if they are causing discomfort.**

If the bridle and bit fit properly, make sure there aren't any physical problems that are causing the horse to be head shy or ear shy (see p. 98). Have your veterinarian check the horse's head, ears, and mouth. The horse might have a wolf tooth (in the interdental space, right next to the first cheek teeth) that is being bumped and irritated by the bit, causing pain. (This problem can be resolved by having the wolf tooth removed.) Or, the horse might have a cut tongue, sore poll, or an ear problem. Always try to see if there's a current reason for the horse's avoidance of the bridle, and correct any problems that may exist before attempting to resolve the bad habit.

Make sure you have a good bridling technique and are not causing the horse alarm or discomfort by the way you handle him.

- Stand beside the horse's neck on his left side, facing the same way he is, with the bridle headstall lying over your left arm. Use your right hand to slip the lead rope over the horse's neck (reaching under and over the neck) so that you can hold him with the rope while removing his halter and bridling him. If you wish, you can also temporarily rebuckle the halter around his neck for additional security.

- Since you are working behind the horse's line of vision, move slowly so as not to startle him. Raise the headstall in your right hand to the height of the horse's forehead while guiding the bit with your left hand up under his mouth. Gently slip your thumb or one finger into the corner of his mouth to encourage him to open it as you raise the bit. Don't hit his teeth with the bit; wait for him to open his mouth. If the bridle has a curb strap or chain, use your fingers or thumb to guide it behind his chin and out of the way of his lips.

- As he opens his mouth, raise the bit and slip it into it, then finish raising the headstall and pull it gently over the horse's ears, one at a time. It's usually easiest to slip the far-side ear in first, and then the near one. Fasten the throatlatch (and curb chain, if there is one and it's not already fastened), and make sure the bridle is properly adjusted for the horse's comfort. All straps should be snug and smooth so they don't rub the horse. The throatlatch should be just loose enough for you to slip your hand between it and the horse's throat.

» **When working behind the horse's line of vision, move slowly so as not to startle him.**

SOLUTION
4

If the horse is extremely sensitive about his ears (either due to an earlier physical problem or fear of having them hurt because they've been mishandled in the past), use a bridle headstall that can be unbuckled at the side and put on the horse without going over the ears. If need be, don't use a browband or throatlatch and just loop the headstall over the horse's head behind his ears, without touching them at all. Note: Most ear-shy horses are not bit shy, so they are not hard to bridle if you can find a way to avoid the ears. Do some patient ear-handling sessions (working toward being able to touch the ears) at other times, when you are *not* trying to bridle him (see p. 98 for guidance in this area). Many ear-shy horses will get over the bridling bad habit once they realize that having their ears touched doesn't result in pain.

Some horses habitually raise their head just to thwart a child or short handler who is trying to bridle them. These horses are not afraid of having their ears touched or the head handled—they have merely discovered a way to take advantage of someone and get out of being bridled. In this scenario, a little more firmness may be all that's needed.

For a horse that raises his head (and maybe clenches his teeth, too—see p. 115) so you can't get the headstall high enough to bridle him, grasp the bridle headstall midway up (rather than at the top) with your right hand. Wrap your right arm under and around his head, and use the right hand holding the headstall to press on the bridge of the horse's nose. This discourages him from raising his head so high. Then you can use the left hand, as usual, to slip the bit in his mouth before pulling the headstall up and over the horse's ears. You can prevent his "devious" actions when it comes to bridling with gentle firmness—more lessons on relaxing and lowering his head on cue can also help.

» **Some horses are not afraid of having their ears touched or the head handled—they have merely discovered a way to get out of being bridled.**

Teach the horse to lower his head in response to pressure on his nose and crest (see p. 59). When it is time to bridle the horse, hold the headstall in your right hand, ask him to lower his head, and slide your right hand forward from the crest over the horse's forehead to keep him from raising his head. Gently guide the bit into his mouth with your left hand.

What If Nothing Works?

If you are short and your horse is gentle, you can try standing on a stool while bridling him; however, some horses move around and make this awkward. It is best to take the time to teach the horse to lower his head on cue.

WON'T OPEN MOUTH WHEN BRIDLED

Some horses clench their teeth and won't open their mouth for the bit, often raising their head, too, so it's harder for you to reach (see p. 112).

How to Change This Habit

 As with the other bad habits we've discussed in this book, first make sure there isn't a physical problem that is causing the horse's resistance. A dental checkup is in order.

 If there is nothing causing him pain and the horse is merely refusing because he doesn't want to be bridled, encourage him to open his mouth by poking your thumb or finger into the side of his mouth to press on his gum (in the interdental space where there aren't any teeth). This will make most horses open up for the bit. However, when the horse is still evasive about receiving the bit, spend time working with his mouth at times other than bridling. Stick your finger in the side of his mouth every day during routine grooming. Play with his lips and chin, and make handling his mouth a matter-of-fact thing rather than something that only happens during bridling.

 If the horse clenches his teeth and won't open his mouth, or if he fights you by raising his head, rearing, or using some other evasive tactic, try using a reward system to change his habit.

• Coat the bit with molasses, honey, or another sweet treat that he likes.

- Get the horse "softened up" by letting him lick the sweet treat off your hand, without the bit present.

- Once he readily licks your hand, hold the bit—coated with the good stuff—and let him lick the bit. Don't even try to raise the headstall or put it into his mouth. (And, if you are working with a horse that is really problematic when it comes to bridling, offer him *just the bit* at first, without the headstall attached.) It may take several sessions for him to get over being apprehensive, so don't even try to bridle him until he is relaxed and comfortable about licking the sweet treat off the bit.

- Only after the horse is comfortable with licking the bit should you go ahead and slip the bit into his mouth and pull the headstall over his ears. Continue to put the "sweet stuff" on the bit prior to every bridling until the horse is completely over his phobia or aversion.

An alternative method, if he likes horse cookies, is to hold a treat in the palm of your hand and let the horse eat it, then slip the bit in while he's chewing (and therefore doesn't have his teeth clenched). If he comes to realize that every time he is bridled he gets a treat, the horse will be more willing to open up for the bit. Soon you can progress to the point where he can be bridled first, and only then rewarded with a cookie.

» **If he comes to realize that every time he is bridled he gets a treat, the horse will be more willing to open up for the bit.**

Always avoid picking a fight with the horse. Plan to have your retraining sessions when you are relaxed and not in a hurry. Never tie the horse when trying to bridle him—he will feel trapped and be more apt to resist and pull back. If he's quite evasive, have a friend hold him while you work with him.

What If Nothing Works?

On rare occasion you'll encounter a horse that is adamant about not accepting a bit in his mouth. Rather than fight with the horse or become totally frustrated in your retraining efforts, try a bitless bridle.

WON'T STAND WHILE BRIDLE IS REMOVED

Some horses are fearful of having the bridle removed. They fling their head up or rush backward when you start to take it off. This makes it impossible to remove it without clanking the bit on his teeth—which only reinforces his fear of unbridling.

How to Change This Habit

 Ensure you are taking the bridle off properly. If you bump the horse's teeth with the bit, he will automatically raise his head to try to avoid pain. With his head raised, the bit can't slip out of his mouth easily—it catches on his lower incisors and causes even more pain. Only remove the bridle when the horse's head is lowered and he's relaxed, so you can let him "spit out" the bit. Don't ever try to pull the bit out of his mouth; wait for him to release it. Use the following steps for proper removal of the bridle.

- Stand beside the horse's neck—a little behind his head, facing forward—and undo any straps on the bridle that need to be loose or free for it to be safely and easily removed: The throatlatch, noseband, and/or curb chain should be unfastened.

- Then put your right hand up around the other side of the horse's neck, or rest it on his neck as high as you can reach and ask the horse to lower his head (see p. 59).

- As you start to take the headstall off, using your right and left hands, bring it forward over the horse's ears, one at a time, and make sure the bit stays well up in his mouth (support it with slight tension on the headstall, or place your left forearm across the horse's face so it contacts the sidepieces of the bridle and gently holds the bit up) until he opens his mouth and starts to spit it out.

If the horse is wearing a halter under his bridle, you can hold on to it with your left hand to steady his head and keep him from raising it as you gently remove the headstall with the other hand.

Never pull the headstall straight off over his ears—rather than over one ear at a time, as described above—or it will catch on the muscles at the base of the ears and cause the horse pain.

 If he doesn't already know how, teach the horse to lower his head on cue to make it easier to remove the bridle. Teach this lesson in sessions *without* the bridle, encouraging him to respond to pressure/release by realizing he can get relief from pressure by lowering the head (see p. 59 for step-by-step instructions). Another way to teach him to relax and lower his head for bridle removal is to rub on his forehead.

 Use a treat to teach the horse to lower his head and open his mouth to release the bit. Place a horse cookie in the palm of your hand, and hold it below his nose so he has to reach down for it. The treat and the action of reaching for it will take his focus off his phobia and encourage him to open his mouth.

What If Nothing Works?

If a horse has such an unreasonable phobia that you can't use progressive lessons to prevent him from flinging his head up every time the bridle is removed (making it impossible to unbridle him without causing him pain), use a bitless bridle that also unbuckles on the side of his head so you don't have to pull it over his ears.

Problems with Longeing

AFRAID OF THE LONGE WHIP

Many riders and trainers utilize *longeing* as a training method. It is also commonly used to give a horse exercise, or as a way to warm him up before a ride. Some horses are difficult to longe, but this is usually due to lack of proper training. Poor longeing habits are primarily a sign that incorrect methods (on the handler/trainer's part) have been used in the past, and the horse has either not learned how to longe properly or has been allowed to get away with inappropriate behavior while on the longe line.

When longeing the horse, the longe whip is used merely as an extension of your arm—to point direction or touch the horse to encourage him to move. The whip should be about 5 feet long with a 6-foot lash, enabling it to make a loud pop if you snap it, which can be used to encourage the horse to go forward or move faster. You should *never* hit the horse with the longe whip.

Due to lack of correct training or misuse, some horses are afraid of the longe whip. When this is the case, the horse may be so upset by the whip that he won't pay attention to what he is supposed to do. He may bolt, rush backward, or become skittish and inattentive if it is pointed toward him.

How to Change This Habit

Spend time getting the horse used to the whip before you ever try to longe him. Let him see and smell it. If he's already afraid of the whip, be prepared to spend several sessions using advance-and-retreat techniques (start with the whip at a distance he accepts, then bring it a little closer, taking it away again when he shows any sign of anxiety, and advancing again only when he is relaxed). Consider giving a cookie reward for staying calm. If he can equate something good (the treat) with having the whip near him, he may lose his fear sooner.

» **If the horse is already afraid of the whip, be prepared to spend several sessions using advance-and-retreat techniques to desensitize him.**

When you can bring the longe whip close to the horse's body, move it slowly and gently over his back. Use several training sessions, if needed, to get him used to having it touch him on various parts of his body.

If the horse is calm when he sees the whip and is okay if it touches him, work around him while carrying and moving the whip. Let him realize you can raise it or wave it and it will not hurt him. Do this in gradual steps, progressing to bigger movements only as he loses his fear of smaller ones.

What If Nothing Works?

If you must longe a horse that has an unreasonable fear of the whip and your attempts at retraining fail to gain ground, don't use a whip when you longe him. Experiment with other ways to encourage him to move forward or move faster. The best way is to teach him voice cues (walk, trot, whoa) in hand on the lead rope, and if you are consistent with how you give these commands, they will translate to working on the longe line.

Instead of a standard longe line, you can use a long rope with a leather "popper" on the end to longe your horse. If you need to encourage your horse to move faster or with more enthusiasm, you can swing "your" end of the rope, and use the "popper" as necessary to reinforce voice commands.

Another trick you might try when working a horse that is a bit lazy out on the longe line is to carry a sack of small, round pebbles in your coat pocket. When necessary (the horse is not responding), you can reinforce a "forward" voice cue by tossing a pebble against the horse's hindquarters. This will impress upon him the fact that you *can* reach him from a distance—even without a whip—and he will respond appropriately to your voice commands.

BUCKS OR KICKS OUT WHEN LONGED

Many young horses, and some older ones, want to buck and play when longed, especially if they are confined in stalls much of their day and don't get enough exercise. They use the longeing session as an excuse to express pent-up energy.

How to Change This Habit

Make sure the horse has adequate opportunity to get out of his stall every day. Longeing should not be his only outlet for burning off high spirits and energy. More turnout time might be the answer to this problem.

If the horse is bucking and playing because he hasn't learned to control himself and mind his manners while being longed, go back to earlier steps in the longe-training process, making a smaller circle in a smaller pen or arena until he learns to respect your cues.

Work in a large round pen *without* the longe line: "Free longe" him by having him do many circles around you at a canter, in both directions. If he wants to buck and play, keep driving him forward until he tires of going fast and settles down. Lots of groundwork in a round pen will teach him control, and he will be more willing to "listen" to you at other times, such as when he is on the longe line. This practice also teaches you how to direct his speed and direction by changing your position relative to his, as he circles around you, which is very useful for controlling the horse on the longe line.

» **"Free longe" the horse in a round pen to teach the horse to mind his manners and listen to you.**

What If Nothing Works?

When a horse is too obnoxious to safely longe, try another training method for teaching him self-control and to respond to commands, such a lot more groundwork while being led (in-hand work) or driving in long lines. If you longe him to provide a means of exercise, consider teaching him to pony from another horse on cross-country excursions.

CUTS CORNERS

Some horses learn that they can avoid working as hard on the longe line if they cut corners and don't stay out on the circle. They keep making smaller and smaller circles around you and won't keep the longe line taut, making it hard to longe them without risk of a tangle.

How to Change This Habit

Keep the horse out at the edge of the circle by pointing the longe whip at his hindquarters and encouraging him to move forward. Some horses insist on trying to cut in on the circle, and in these cases you must be more forceful, threatening more strongly with the whip or the "popper" on the end of your rope (see p. 120).

Work him at a faster pace. A little speed will tend to cause him to make larger circles. The horse that cuts corners is usually being lazy, going slower as he drifts in toward you.

>> **Work the horse that cuts corners at a faster pace to keep him on a larger circle.**

What if Nothing Works?

Get help from a more experienced horse trainer.

PULLS AWAY

Some horses are rambunctious and want to go too fast or make bigger and bigger circles, and some are always trying to pull away from you. It's difficult to longe them because they are not always under optimum control.

How to Change This Habit

 Use proper equipment so you have adequate control over the horse. A longeing cavesson works better than a halter. The cavesson has a heavy, padded noseband, and the longe line is snapped to the center ring on top of the noseband. When pressure is applied to the longe line, the noseband pulls against the soft cartilage on the horse's nose, and he pays more attention to its pressure than that of a halter. This gives you more control to slow or turn him when he wants to go too fast or pull away from you.

Use a flat, nylon longe line rather than one made of rope. The flat nylon webbing is less likely to slip through your hands if the horse tries to pull away. Wear gloves so you'll have better grip on the line and it won't burn your hands; you'll have more chance of hanging on and not letting him pull away.

Always longe the horse in a small pen at first, rather than a large arena or an open area, until he learns respect on the longe line and to stay under control, so he can never pull away from you and get away. It is helpful to use a round pen rather than a square one so the horse can't head into a corner. If you only have a square pen or ring and have problems with the corners, block them off with ground poles or cavalletti.

Make sure you are always in the proper position in relation to the horse. You must keep him moving between the hand holding the longe line and the hand holding the whip, with your body at the center of his circle. If you get too far behind him, he has enough leverage to pull or rush forward and be out of your control.

Revisit earlier groundwork lessons to ensure he knows what "whoa" means. If he insists on pulling and making bigger and bigger circles, or if he wants to go too fast on the longe line, go back to leading in hand and refresh his memory that "whoa" means *stop*. Going back to basics to reinforce voice cues and the meaning of "whoa" will help any horse that tends to get out of control or that won't stop on command while being longed.

Using body position to reinforce your cues, make the horse change directions much more frequently, stopping and turning toward the center of the longe circle, then going the other way. Frequent change of direction puts you in control so he can't keep going faster and faster around the circle.

What If Nothing Works?

If a horse is so headstrong that he does not respect the longe line, you need help from a more experienced horse trainer. In some instances you may prefer to dispense with trying to longe him, and concentrate on other methods for working with him.

TURNS TO FACE YOU (WITHOUT BEING ASKED)

Most horses don't understand that, when being longed, they must move around you in a circle; they must be taught how to do this. When early longeing lessons were inadequate, or if the horse finds out that he can avoid having to move around and around you if he turns to face you, it becomes impossible to longe him.

How to Change This Habit

First make sure conditions are optimal for helping the horse understand what you want him to do: He shouldn't be confused or distracted. Use proper equipment and a round pen rather than a square one (if possible). If he's inexperienced on the longe line or has learned to avoid longeing by stopping and facing you, lead him in a circle both directions before feeding out the longe line and putting him on the circle on his own. Pay particular attention to leading him from the right (off) side: Some horses don't lead very well from their right side and are easily confused when you longe them in that direction.

As mentioned previously in this book, the secret to successful longeing is your position in relation to that of the horse. You should be "holding" him between the whip (which should always be somewhat behind him) and the line to have complete control over his movements and speed. If your body position is too far forward, he will slow down or stop and face you. Have him travel in a small circle around you at first, so you can easily stay in proper position somewhat behind him and driving him forward. As he gets the idea, you can gradually play out more line so he's making a larger circle.

If your horse habitually turns to face you, at first you may have to walk in a circle just slightly smaller than his, so you are almost walking behind him—as if you are driving him in a larger circle around you—until he resigns himself to the fact he must keep moving instead of stopping and facing you.

If the horse is exceptionally stubborn or doesn't seem to "get" the idea that he should continue circling around you (rather than stopping and facing you), have an assistant walk to one side and a little behind him with the longe whip as you urge him on from your position in the center of the circle. The helper's job is to encourage him to keep moving forward, reinforcing your voice commands with a pop or a flick of the whip. Your assistant shouldn't have to actually touch him with the whip once he knows what he's supposed to do—merely pointing it at his flank or hindquarters, or popping it, should be an adequate cue to keep moving.

If at any point the horse regresses and again stops to face you instead of moving forward, examine your position. When a smart horse (that's also a bit lazy) begins stopping and facing you when he's out on a large longe circle (realizing you are too far away to reach him with the whip), you are probably in front of his center. Make sure you are always slightly behind him so you can "drive" him forward. Go back to making smaller circles for a while so you can stay behind his center and touch him with the whip if necessary, or use the "popper" on the end of the rope (see p. 120). You may have to get more aggressive in your insistence that he needs to keep moving, until he figures out that if he slows, stops, or turns to face you without being asked, he will have to work harder for a while.

What If Nothing Works?

If you continue to have trouble with this bad habit, request assistance from an experienced horse trainer.

Problems with Foot Handling

FALLS OVER/LOSES BALANCE/WON'T HOLD ONE LEG UP

Some horses willingly pick up their feet, but then have trouble keeping their balance or won't stand patiently holding one leg up.

How to Change This Habit

Begin by making sure there isn't a physical reason for the horse to struggle to keep his leg up. He may have a neurological problem (interfering with his balance) or painful joints that make it hard for him to comfortably keep one foot off the ground very long. If you suspect any kind of physical problem, schedule a veterinary examination.

Check that you are not holding his foot or leg at an awkward angle and causing him to lose his balance. Be sure he's able to stand comfortably on the other three legs before you pick up a foot, and then try to help him keep his balance by allowing him to adjust his position a little if he needs to, while you still keep hold of the foot.

If the horse is nervous and tense when you pick up one foot, try to keep him calm and relaxed (so he is more willing and able to work with you in trying to keep his balance) rather than making him more tense by fighting with him. If he is insecure about holding a foot up, punishment and force may only aggravate the problem, convincing the horse that having his feet worked with is scary or unpleasant. Then he'll be more adamant about wanting to keep all four feet on the ground.

One way to keep the horse calm, happy, and cooperative is to have a helper stand at the horse's head and feed him a cookie as reward for holding his foot up. If he's praised and rewarded when he cooperates, he may come to realize that having a foot held up is not so bad, after all.

What if Nothing Works?

See Pulls Foot Away/Rears/Kicks (p. 129) for other recommendations.

LEANS ON FARRIER

Some horses make it hard for the farrier to trim or shoe them because they won't balance themselves; they lean on the individual working on their feet.

How to Change This Habit

Try to determine whether the horse doesn't know *how* to balance himself (has trouble finding his balance) or is leaning "on purpose" as a way to make you (or the farrier) put the foot back down again. If the horse has trouble keeping his balance, make sure he's always in a good position (standing squarely on even footing) before one foot is picked up. If much of his weight is on the leg of choice to begin with, encourage him to change his position *before* you attempt to pick up the foot. Then help him keep his balance by not pulling the foot or leg too far out of its natural position.

In the case of the "spoiled" horse that deliberately leans on you or the farrier, sometimes the only effective way to change the habit is to make it uncomfortable for the horse to put so much weight on you. How you do it should depend upon the horse's personality: The reprimand should fit the situation and not be too extreme. You don't want the horse to react adversely or you've merely created another problem.

For some horses, a jab in the belly with your elbow (when holding up a front foot) is adequate. With others, the best way to impress on them that they must not lean on you is to suddenly release the foot and let them nearly fall down. This gets their attention because horses don't like to feel vulnerable to falling.

What if Nothing Works?

When a horse absolutely won't quit leaning and his habit makes it miserable or impossible to work on his feet, a professional trainer is needed.

PROBLEMS WITH FOOT HANDLING

PULLS FOOT AWAY/REARS/KICKS

If the horse actively takes his foot away, refuses to let you hold on to it, or reacts by rearing or kicking if you try to hold on to it, there is a serious safety need to overcome the problem.

How to Change This Habit

When a horse won't let you (or the farrier) work on a foot and tries to pull it away, there may be a physical problem causing him discomfort. If he is especially sensitive about having one foot or leg handled, you should suspect a physical reason, and have your vet examine him. Note: The pain might not be in the leg he "favors," but the opposite one (the one he is standing on), so your veterinarian should do a thorough exam.

>> **When the horse is especially sensitive about having one foot or leg handled, you should suspect a physical reason behind the bad habit.**

If it is an older horse that is displaying the bad habit, he may have arthritic joints. If you hold a foot up very long or try to force the leg into an awkward position, it may be painful for him. In the case of the older horse, or any horse you suspect to be stiff or arthritic, don't hold the foot very high off the ground or for an extended period of time. Work on each foot swiftly and only for a few seconds, then put it down again. Go on to the next, and come back to finish the first one, if necessary, after that leg has had a sufficient positional rest.

Don't pull this horse's leg out at an awkward angle—keep it under the horse so you don't put extra stress on the joints. Some farriers pull the leg they are working on too much to the side (especially tall farriers working on short horses) and this may cause pain, resulting in the horse trying to take the foot away.

If the horse is reacting out of inexperience, fear, or suspicion (perhaps due to a bad experience in the past), go back to basics.

- Handle his legs and feet every day as part of his routine grooming. Run your hand down each leg often, until the horse is not afraid of nor resents having it touched.

- Encourage the horse to pick up each foot and hold it up briefly, then put it down again. Time everything so *you* are giving the foot back, rather than *him* taking it away. If he does manage to jerk the foot away from you, pick it right back up again. Offer praise and reward (the "cookie system" works for most horses) if he allows you to hold it for even a few seconds without protest. Then, gradually increase the time you hold it. Never punish a timid horse for taking his foot away. Be patient and persistent and keep working with his feet until he realizes that foot handling is not scary or painful.

- When the horse lets you hold his foot without putting up a fight, start doing things with it: Use a hoof pick to clean it; gently tap the hoof with the hoof pick; take a couple quick swipes with a rasp, and so on. "Work" with the hoof for just a few seconds and then put it back down, gradually increasing the time you handle it as he becomes more at ease. Imitate the actions the farrier will take with the foot in a nonconfrontational setting (a training session rather than the actual moment when the horse must be trimmed or shod). If you do this every day, he will soon be more at ease with the process.

In conjunction with retraining the horse to be more at ease with (and more cooperative about) letting you work on his feet—that is, he doesn't jerk them away, rear, or kick—strategic use of a reward system (having an assistant hold the horse and give treats for good behavior) is often very helpful. The horse can associate foot handling/trimming/shoeing with something pleasant and is less apt to continue fighting.

PROBLEMS WITH FOOT HANDLING

What If Nothing Works?

If the horse is very aggressive in refusing to have his feet handled for trimming or shoeing, he may need a more drastic method to convince him that he *can* hold his foot up. Enlist the help of a professional horse trainer.

WON'T PICK UP FEET

An inexperienced or "spoiled" horse may refuse to pick up his feet at all. He may feel threatened because he hasn't learned to balance on three legs, he may be uncomfortable with a leg held up, or he may have developed this habit of resistance because he's gotten away with it in the past.

How to Change This Habit

The horse may have a physical reason for not wanting to pick up his feet. Soreness or lameness—laminitis (founder), navicular syndrome, or arthritis, for example—may make him uncomfortable putting extra weight on a particular foot. He might be reluctant to pick up one foot because it puts more weight on the opposite one. Rule out a physical problem before you go forward with training the reluctant, inexperienced horse or retraining the "spoiled" one.

» **The horse may feel threatened if he hasn't learned to balance on three legs.**

Make sure the horse is standing in a position that enables him to balance himself easily on the other three legs. Reposition him if necessary by asking him to take a step forward or back, until he is standing more squarely. Never try to pick up a foot that he's already putting most of his weight on. Backing up a step can help him be more ready to pick up a certain front foot; stepping forward a little may take the weight off his hind end.

If the horse is not at ease with balancing himself on three legs, lean against him a little (his shoulder, or his hip) to help encourage him to shift his weight off the leg you want to pick up. Run your hand down his leg and gently pinch the back of his tendon at the fetlock joint, or press into the soft area between the cannon bone and tendon. This will generally encourage him to pick up that foot. When working with a foal or young horse, tickling the back of the heel also works; with an older horse, pressing into the back of the heel is an alternative.

» **When working with a foal or young horse, tickle the back of the heel to ask him to pick up his foot.**

If you are unsure about how the horse will react to having the back of his cannon pinched or his heel pressed, and you don't want to bend down where you are more vulnerable to being kicked or hit by a foot, try pinching the chestnut on the inside of that front leg or the point of the hock on the hind leg. You can also pinch the tendon just below the back of the knee or hock. This creates a reflex action that causes the horse to pick up his leg without putting your head and face in harm's way.

Establish a reward system, praising the horse and giving him a treat or horse cookie when he promptly picks up a foot for you.

What If Nothing Works?

PROBLEMS WITH FOOT HANDLING

If a horse is so spoiled or has such a phobia that he won't pick up his feet, consult an experienced horse trainer for help changing the bad habit.

WON'T STAND STILL FOR TRIMMING/SHOEING

Some horses make it difficult for the farrier to work on their feet just because they fidget and keep moving. And if they try to move while a foot is being worked on, they may lose their balance and want to pull away.

How to Change This Habit

Fidgeting is a sign of bad manners and lack of training; the horse needs to learn to stand still. Start over with this aspect of handling, and teach him the meaning of "whoa." Make his lessons a part of his routine handling and leading, often asking him to stop and stay stopped. Whenever you groom him or clean his feet, insist that he stand still, and be consistent about it.

» Fidgeting by the horse while you are handling his feet is a sign of bad manners and a lack of training.

 Handle the horse's feet every day during routine grooming so that he is at ease with the process and not so apt to fidget from nervousness.

 Leave him tied for a while each day while you do chores nearby so he learns to be patient and stand quietly, rather than fussing (see my tying solutions on p. 83).

What If Nothing Works?

Patient training will improve the manners of most horses, but if you continue to have trouble persuading your horse to stand still for trimming or shoeing, seek the help of an experienced horse trainer.

Problems with Veterinary Care/Treatment

DIFFICULT TO ADMINISTER INJECTIONS

Some horses have a phobia about needles. They won't stand still for injections, or they may react violently if they think you are going to give them a "shot"—rushing backward, rearing, striking, or kicking. This habit is usually due to a vet or handler's poor injection techniques in the past that were painful for the horse.

How to Change This Habit

 First, you must make sure your injection technique is totally painless to the horse: He should not feel the needle at all. Here are a few suggestions:

- Use a new, sharp needle of the smallest possible diameter that will still carry adequate flow for the liquid being injected. Never use anything larger than an 18-gauge needle for intramuscular injections (for most vaccinations a 20-gauge needle is used) as a larger size causes more discomfort and leakage. A very sharp needle goes in more easily and so causes less pain than a dull one.

• If the horse fidgets or resents intramuscular shots in the neck, inject into the pectoral (chest) muscle(s). The horse is not very sensitive in this area and is less apt to feel the needle. This is also a preferred location if a horse tends to develop swelling or soreness after an injection. A sore or swollen neck affects the horse's movement more (causing stiffness in turning) and also makes it painful and/or difficult for the horse to lower his head to eat and drink. For a large shot, note that the pectoral isn't a big enough muscle to absorb it; split it into two doses (one in each pectoral muscle). It is preferable to choose a site close to his front end so you are better able to control him or move with him if necessary. You are more apt to be kicked if you are trying to inject into the area below his buttocks, for instance (even though that can be a good site for a large intramuscular injection due to the heavy muscling).

• Detach the needle from the syringe. Press firmly on the area where you'll put the needle (with your thumb or the side of your hand), to temporarily desensitize the area, then slip the needle in quickly. Some people thump the area a couple times with the side of the hand holding the needle, or give a slap against the side of the neck, which also works to desensitize the area, but if the horse is "needle shy," he's probably already experienced this technique and will become suspicious. Firmly pressing the spot may be less likely to arouse suspicion.

• Another way to desensitize the skin and mask the prick of the needle is to pinch or twist the skin just before you put the needle in. This works well when using the neck or pectoral muscle because the overlying skin (especially on the chest) is loose enough to pinch between your fingers. Press the area firmly, then twist the skin, and the horse will rarely feel the needle—especially if you routinely do some pressing and pinching during ordinary grooming and handling.

- Insert the needle (as mentioned, detached from the syringe is best) quickly with one swift motion. The mistake some people make is not pushing forcefully enough. The faster the needle goes in, the less it will hurt the horse. The advantage of putting the needle first, before attaching it to the syringe, is that you can then wait a moment if the horse jumps or moves. Once he's settled down and calm, you can quietly attach the syringe and proceed with the injection. Note: Always make sure the needle hasn't gone in to a blood vessel. If blood starts oozing out of the inserted needle before you attach the syringe, take it out and try again, using a slightly different location.

 In order to give a shot to a suspicious horse (one that has had bad experiences with injections in the past), you must trick him so he doesn't know or suspect that he's about to get one. The best solution is to provide some kind of distraction so he's not thinking about the shot and therefore won't react adversely in anticipation. One of the best distractions is food.

If he's in a stall or paddock without access to green grass, often the best thing to offer him is a big bouquet of lush green grass. Have a friend hold the horse and hand-feed him plenty of grass to keep his attention as you give the injection. Other options include grain or treats/horse cookies. Whatever you use, it must be something he's eager to eat so he'll be completely focused on the food.

 When the horse cannot be distracted with food, try using a blindfold. If he stands quietly while blindfolded, you can rub him on his neck and withers for a while until you have him calm and relaxed, and slip the needle in only after desensitizing the area with your rubbing and/or a skin tweak (see Solution 1, p. 136).

PROBLEMS WITH
VETERINARY
CARE/TREATMENT

Have an assistant hold the horse rather than tying him (he will be less likely to throw a fit if he doesn't feel trapped) and use a "shoulder twitch" (or "skin twitch") if need be to keep him distracted and still. A shoulder twitch consists of grasping the loose skin on the horse's shoulder and pulling it tight with the hand, rolling it a little over your knuckles. The pull on the skin stimulates endorphin release, which helps calm the horse.

What If Nothing Works?

If a horse still has an unreasonable fear and is dangerous to vaccinate, you may have to consider using a "lip twitch" (loop of rope or chain on a long handle or metal clamp that squeezes the horse's nose/upper lip and is believed to stimulate endorphin release) or a Stableizer® to keep him calm so you can slip the needle in without causing him pain or risking your safety.

DIFFICULT TO APPLY EYE OINTMENT/ TREATMENT

Most horses are very sensitive about their eyes, and putting medication into an eye can therefore be a difficult challenge. Even a gentle horse that trusts you may resist and throw his head in the air or rush backward when you attempt to treat an eye.

How to Change This Habit

 Spend a lot of time working with the horse's head and face in your daily interactions and training sessions. Rub the areas around both eyes (but not too close to them), using advance-and-retreat techniques (going closer, then backing away to an area where he was comfortable with your touch before coming closer again). Work toward the horse allowing you to gently cup your hand over each eye without touching it. If he raises his head to avoid your touch, work on lessons for lowering his head (see p. 59) giving him treats, if necessary, as a reward. Take your time and be patient. When *you* are tense or in a hurry the horse is more likely to become upset.

» **Work toward the horse allowing you to gently cup your hand over each of his eyes.**

If the horse accepts having your hands near his eyes, consider your technique when applying the ointment.

- Stand facing the side of his head and slide your hand (the one nearest his neck) under the cheek piece of his halter, so that if he moves your hand will move with him.

- Place the tube of eye medication in that hand, and point it toward the front corner of the horse's eye. Hold the tube parallel with the eye so it won't be so apt to bump the eye if he moves.

- Rest the wrist of your opposite hand against the side of the horse's nose/face and put the thumb of that hand against his lower eyelid near the front corner of the eye.

- Use this thumb to roll the lower eyelid down and your index finger to push upward on the upper eyelid to keep the horse from shutting his eye tightly.

- Gently place the tip of the medication tube in the corner of his eye and draw it carefully along the inside of the lower eyelid as you squeeze out a string of ointment, depositing it along the membrane of the inner lower eyelid. With good luck, the horse cooperates and you can release the eyelids so he can close his eye following this application.

- Use your thumb to gently massage the lower eyelid to help spread the medication around.

PROBLEMS WITH
VETERINARY
CARE/TREATMENT

If necessary, squeeze the proper amount of medication onto your clean finger (or wear a surgical glove if you don't want it in contact with your skin). Repeat the process described in Solution 2 for holding the upper and lower eyelids open. Once the lower eyelid is exposed, gently transfer/scrape the ointment from your finger onto the inner part of the lid and release the lid, allowing the horse to close his eye and spread the medication around. This method is often less confrontational to many horses and so they are more apt to stand still.

》 **You can squeeze the eye ointment onto your finger and then gently transfer/scrape the ointment from your finger onto the inner part of the horse's eyelid.**

What If Nothing Works?

When the horse is too touchy about his eyes to stand still enough for applying necessary medication, consider having an assistant help you and using a shoulder or nose twitch or a Stableizer® (see p. 138).

DIFFICULT TO CHECK HEART RATE

Some horses resent it when you check their heart rate because they don't like the feel of the stethoscope pressing against their rib cage. They fidget and move away to try to avoid it.

How to Change This Habit

Spend time getting the horse used to having a small, firm object pressed against his rib cage in various locations, including the sensitive girth area. If you do this during routine grooming, using advance-and-retreat tactics (see p. 120), most horses come to accept it over time.

If the horse remains ticklish in the girth area and fidgety when the stethoscope makes an appearance, use an alternative method to check heart rate. Place your fingers on any large artery and you can feel it pulsing, enabling you to count his heart rate. One of the best places to press is the lower jaw: If you run your fingers along the underside of the jawbone, you'll find a large artery (it feels like a small firm cord). Another easy location is the lower leg: An artery runs under the fetlock joint on both sides, and with practice you can find it.

To measure his heart rate, press the artery slightly and count the number of "pulses" in 15 seconds, then multiply that number by four. The horse's average resting heart rate should be between 32 and 44 beats per minute.

» **Place your fingers on any of the horse's large arteries, and you can feel it pulsing, enabling you to count his heart rate.**

PROBLEMS WITH
VETERINARY
CARE/TREATMENT

What If Nothing Works?

If you continue to have trouble checking the horse's heart rate, seek assistance from an experienced horse person or trainer.

DIFFICULT TO DEWORM OR GIVE ORAL MEDICATION

Some horses refuse to let you put anything into their mouths and are hard to deworm or medicate by oral syringe. They flip their heads up, rush backward, or may rear or strike. Every young horse should be trained to accept having things inserted into the corner of his mouth (your finger, an oral dose syringe) as part of routine handling, but when your horse has already developed the avoidance habit, it makes your job harder. Especially if the only things you ever put into his mouth taste nasty.

» Every young horse should be trained to accept having things inserted into the corner of his mouth as part of routine handling.

How to Change This Habit

When dealing with an older horse that already has a fear of the deworming process or oral medication, start over with mouth handling basics. Rub and massage the horse's head/face and muzzle area every time you handle him. If you routinely rub the sides of his mouth in a neutral setting (that is, you're not trying to give him any kind of medication) most horses will become at ease with your touch. Once the horse is relaxed about your hands on his muzzle, start putting a finger into the corners of his mouth every once in a while. If this alarms him, smear a little molasses or applesauce on your finger so he'll be more willing to have it in his mouth. When he is comfortable with the finger going in, start wiggling it around in the interdental space between the incisors and molars (where teeth do not grow from the gums). Use advance and retreat: If at any time the horse becomes tense or alarmed, go back to an earlier step that he's comfortable with.

When the horse is at ease having your finger in his mouth, accustom him to the feel of a small syringe (finger-size), slipping it into the corner of his mouth. Fill it with a molasses/water mix or some runny applesauce, and make sure there's some of this "treat" on the outside of the syringe, as well, so it smells and tastes good as you stick it into his mouth. Even if he protests at first, if you can squirt a little of the "good stuff" into his mouth before he dislodges the syringe with a flip of his head or by rushing backward, he'll start to reconsider. Once he realizes that a syringe in his mouth means he's going to get something that tastes good rather than bad, he will change his behavior.

Work with the horse so he grows accustomed to a large syringe over a number of training sessions—a well-washed dewormer syringe is a good choice. Give the horse a squirt of "good stuff" (see Solution 2) by large syringe on a routine basis so he begins to expect a treat rather than suspect dewormer or medication. Use anything he really likes as a semi-liquid treat—for example, molasses and warm water, Karo syrup or pancake syrup, applesauce, or brown sugar and water.

To persuade a very unwilling horse, give him a "syringe treat" (see Solution 3) daily—or even twice a day—for a few days before you plan to deworm him. When deworming day arrives, give him a syringe full of "good stuff" first, just before you give him the dewormer (be sure to smear some of the molasses or syrup on the outside of the dewormer syringe), then give him a "chaser" of "good stuff" after he has swallowed the dewormer. Most horses will forgive you for occasional deworming if they can have a few mouthfuls of sweet treats in conjunction with it.

PROBLEMS WITH VETERINARY CARE/TREATMENT

When you have to give bad-tasting medication by mouth (such as phenylbutazone or "bute") always sweeten it with a treat, such as molasses or syrup. Medication in the form of pills can be crushed, then mixed with molasses and water, thick syrup, applesauce, or yogurt (whatever your horse likes best) before being readied in the oral syringe.

Whenever giving oral medication, use the right technique:

- First make sure the horse's mouth is empty of feed (so he can't "wad" the medicine around the feed and spit it out). Do this by sticking your finger into the corner of his mouth and wiggling it around until he moves his tongue and spits out anything that happens to be in his mouth.

- Place the oral syringe into the corner of his mouth and as far back on the tongue as possible. The farther back you deposit the medication or dewormer, the less the horse can taste it, and the less able he'll be to push it out again with his tongue.

- Tip his head up until he swallows the mixture or paste, so he can't spit it out.

- Reward him for his good behavior by giving him a syringe full of "good stuff" after you are sure he's swallowed all the medicine or dewormer (see Solution 4).

What If Nothing Works?

If a horse continues to fight oral medication/deworming in spite of retraining efforts and the use of treats, you may have to use a "lip twitch" to help immobilize him during the process (see p. 138).

DIFFICULT TO TAKE TEMPERATURE

Many horses are reluctant to have their temperature taken rectally. They may clamp their tail so you can't get the thermometer in, and if you persist, they may kick.

How to Change This Habit

Spend some time working with the horse's tail before you try inserting a thermometer. Brush his tail each time you groom him, and touch all around the tailhead (dock), rubbing alongside it with your hands or a soft cloth rather than a brush (the hairless area under the tailhead is sensitive). Most horses enjoy having the sides of the tailhead rubbed because this is a place that's hard to scratch if it itches, and if you begin gently, they rarely protest. Even a horse that vehemently resists a thermometer will generally come to accept tail rubbing as a pleasant part of his daily routine.

» **Brush the horse's tail each time you groom him, and touch all around the tailhead (dock), rubbing alongside it with your hands or a soft cloth.**

Check your technique. When you are experienced in taking a horse's temperature, you can slip the thermomenter in almost without the horse knowing it. Technique is most of the secret to retraining a horse to allow his temperature to be taken without a fuss. If you practice a few times with a thermometer (before you actually have to take the horse's temperature), taking your time, you'll be less tense and nervous about it, and this will help keep the horse relaxed when it matters.

- Stand on the left side of the horse, next to his hindquarters, facing toward the rear, with your body touching his hip. If you are pressed up against his hip and stifle, he can't kick you because you are too close, and if he moves, you can move with him.

- Put your left arm over his rump and gently rub his tail area with your left hand until he relaxes. As discussed in Solution 1, most horses like to have the tailhead rubbed and will relax and be cooperative if you don't rush, especially if you have been handling the area ahead of time during daily grooming (see p. 144).

- When the horse relaxes, he raises his tail instead of clamping it down, and he may even lift it and move it toward you in an effort to encourage your rubbing. Wait until he lifts his tail before attempting to put the thermometer into the rectum.

- Always lubricate the thermometer (to reduce friction) so it will slip in without rubbing and irritating his rectum; a dry thermometer is more abrasive. You can lubricate it with petroleum jelly or with some saliva (spit into the palm of your hand and roll the thermometer in the saliva prior to insertion).

PROBLEMS WITH VETERINARY CARE/TREATMENT

- Insert the thermometer into the rectum with a spinning motion. This helps it go in easily, causing less rubbing and irritation. Aim it slightly upward so it won't poke into the side of the rectum. If the horse clamps his tail, gently rub it and move it to the side; don't try to pick it up, or he'll clamp down harder. Leave the thermometer in place for the recommended length of time (a mercury thermometer needs at least three minutes, while a digital may work in less than one). A horse's normal body temperature is 99 to 100.5 degrees Fahrenheit.

What If Nothing Works?

Almost every horse can be trained to accept a thermometer if you are patient, but in the case of a horse with a true phobia (perhaps from a bad experience or an old injury in the tail area), you may need to seek an alternative method for taking his temperature. There are some new devices that work well—ask your veterinarian for recommendations.

RESISTANT TO LEG/FOOT SOAKING

After a foot or lower leg injury, follow-up treatment may involve daily soaking during the first few days of the recovery period. A puncture wound, for instance, may need a hot water soak for 15 to 20 minutes once or twice a day, while a severe bruise may require soaking in ice water. If the horse has never had his leg soaked or has an aversion to standing with a foot in a tub or bucket because of a bad experience in the past, this necessary part of the healing process can be a challenge.

How to Change This Habit

Spend a little time getting the horse used to having his foot in an empty tub or bucket *before* an injury requires soaking. Start with a shallow rubber feed tub. Don't use a metal or plastic bucket, as it is less flexible (more apt to cause discomfort to the horse if he bumps or crashes down on it) and also more noisy and likely to spook him. Pick up one foot and put it down gently into the empty tub. Be patient if he is nervous about it and lifts it right back out again. Give him a treat if he stands still for a moment. If he picks up his foot again, take hold of it and guide it gently back down into the tub.

Only after he is at ease with having one foot in a shallow tub should you progress to a taller bucket, and after that practice washing his foot. Add only a little water at a time until it reaches the proper level. You'll only need a couple inches of water when soaking a puncture wound on the bottom of the foot, but more if the injury is above the hoof. Length of time the injury must soak will vary, so practice standing for longer and longer lengths of time. (Note: When using a bucket rather than a rubber feed tub, use one without a handle so the horse won't catch his foot if the bucket tips over.)

If your horse is nervous despite working with his feet in a tub or bucket as described in Solution 1, or if he won't stand still as long as your veterinarian has prescribed the soak, it helps to have a friend to help: One of you can hold the horse and feed him treats to keep him happy during the procedure, and one of you can monitor the foot. The "foot monitor" can grab the foot if the horse picks it up and guide it back down into the tub. She can also try to help the horse keep his weight balanced squarely (so he won't want to pick up that particular foot).

In some instances it may help to hold up the opposite foot so he'll stand on the one that needs soaking.

What If Nothing Works?

If a horse absolutely refuses to stand with his foot in a tub or bucket, invest in a soaking boot that you can fill with warm water, a poultice, or ice water.

PROBLEMS WITH
VETERINARY
CARE/TREATMENT

RESISTANT TO WOUND CARE

Some horses do not trust people enough to let you handle an injured leg or inspect a body wound. If they are in pain or your touch causes more discomfort (even inadvertently), they instinctively pull away or resist.

How to Change This Habit

The goal here is to alleviate the horse's fear and get him to relax enough that you can handle the leg or get close enough to the body wound for examination and treatment. First, you must stay relaxed yourself: If you are tense or panicked because your horse is hurt, he definitely will be more afraid. Rub and handle him in areas of his body that are not hurting, and gradually work toward the area you need to deal with, using an advance-and-retreat technique to help him relax.

The best insurance regarding ability to "doctor" a horse when necessary is a basic state of trust. This means patient handling and routine training *before* a situation arises in which you need to deal with an injury. If the horse trusts you and respects you as his partner in your everyday dealings, he is much more likely to allow you to handle and treat an injured area.

If the horse won't let you treat the injury, consider using a "lip twitch" (see p. 138) or a Stableizer® to help calm him and keep him still.

What If Nothing Works?

When an injury is so painful that the horse will not tolerate what needs to be done, or the injury requires attention that you cannot give due to your horse's behavior, you need veterinary assistance. The veterinarian can sedate or tranquilize the horse to allow for treatment.

Ground Vices

BITING/NIPPING

Young horses often nibble, sampling you just like they do everything else in their surroundings. They want to chew on your clothing or your arm or hand when you handle them. This kind of *nibbling* should be discouraged, however, or it may progress to *nipping*, which is a form of play when young horses interact with one another. You *do not* want a horse to think of you as an equal or playmate; the roughhouse games of rambunctious young horses are dangerous. Instead, the youngster must learn that *you* are dominant (just like a herd member that's higher in the pecking order) and to be respected at all times—and that means *no nipping*.

In some horses, especially stallions, nipping progresses to biting as they mature (biting is their natural action when fighting another stallion or when courting a mare). Other horses develop a habit of biting because they don't respect people and have found they can intimidate others with their teeth. Any horse that bites a human is out of line, however, and needs to be taught that the behavior is unacceptable.

> » **Young horses often nibble, sampling you just like they do everything else in their surroundings.**

How to Change This Habit

SOLUTION 1 If a horse that previously did not nip or bite starts the habit, examine your own actions to see if anything you are doing is a cause of irritation or pain.

A horse may nip in self-defense when you jerk the cinch or girth too tight or too fast, pinching the tender skin, for instance. He may bite at you if you groom a tender area too roughly. A horse with a nervous tendency may bite if he feels trapped or threatened by what you are doing to him, or if he feels frustrated or stressed. A medical condition may cause pain or irritation that makes the horse grouchy about being handled in certain ways. Try to identify if there is a specific reason the horse feels he must protect himself, and work to correct the underlying condition or cause of his discomfort first.

>> **An underlying medical condition may cause pain or irritation that makes the horse grouchy about being handled.**

For the overly friendly horse that nuzzles and nibbles in play, it's wise to discourage the behavior before it becomes biting. Most young horses go through a nibbling stage, but it can transform from harmless to dangerous as they get older and bolder. One nonconfrontational way to halt the nuzzler/nibbler's bad habit is to discourage him from putting his nose near you. Every time his nose nears, put both hands around his muzzle and give it a vigorous rub—not hard enough to "hurt," but enough to make him uncomfortable. He'll learn that whenever he gets his nose too close to you he gets a "Dutch rub" ("noogie") on the muzzle, which he will soon tire of and so stop trying to nibble.

When a horse has developed the habit of biting and uses this defense any time he wants to show his displeasure or attempt to gain dominance over you, be firm and consistent in discouraging him. Do not "punish" this horse with a slap on the face or the nose, as it just becomes a game to him: The horse will come back at you and try to see "who is fastest." It's too easy for him to get in a quick nip and jerk his head away before you give him a smack.

Slapping a horse that bites usually just makes him sneaky or head shy (see p. 98). Punishment needs to be instant and consistent, not a moment after the fact, and it is most effective if the horse does it to himself (self-punishment)—for example, reaching for your arm but meeting a grooming brush, hoof pick, or your elbow with his nose or teeth instead. Whenever you do bump him in the nose or mouth as a "No!," do it calmly so he will think he's bumping himself. Don't get angry or jab at him. The most important thing is to stay alert so you catch him every time with instant self-punishment.

SOLUTION 4 Most biting habits can be changed by being more conscientious in the way you handle the horse. Do not give him a reason or opportunity to bite. Horses often "try you out," and many will do whatever you allow them to do, pushing to see what else they can get away with. Often the worst biters are not "mean" horses; they are spoiled pets that have had their own way. Horses with a dominant personality quickly take advantage of a timid or easy-going person, so you must be consistently firm. For example, if a horse puts his ears back and makes threatening gestures and you instinctively back away from him, he will think you are the submissive one in the relationship. Soon he may not only pin his ears, he may take a bite at you or even lunge toward you—like he would a herdmate he was bullying.

If you don't firmly reprimand the horse at the beginning of an effort to be dominant in your "herd," he will continue this kind of bad behavior. You must impress upon him that you must be respected. He needs immediate, firm, consistent discipline every time he tries to bite, just like *he* would *receive* in a herd situation from a more dominant horse. He needs to know it's *not* a game. If self-punishment hasn't worked (see Solution 3), a swift smack on his shoulder (as mentioned, *do not* try to connect with his head when reprimanding him), coupled with a verbal rebuke or something more startling, like a loud growling yell, may convince him he made a mistake and should not try biting you again.

When a horse is a persistent biter, it may take several sessions with a squirt gun—casually squirting him in the face each time he turns to nip at you—to change his habit. The trick is to devise something startling or uncomfortable as a reprimand to the behavior, and to time it right in order to convince the horse it's *not* fun to try to bite you.

 When a young horse is becoming so aggressive that he's hard to handle, and if his biting has become a real problem, often the best solution is to let him live in a paddock or pen with an older, more dominant horse that won't tolerate his aggressive bossy attitude. The discipline he will get from the older, dominant horse will help him realize he's not such a tough guy. When he's learned to submit to another horse, it will be easier to persuade him to submit to you.

What If Nothing Works?

For stallions (or any other horse that bites frequently and bites hard), you may need to put a muzzle on the horse when you groom him or perform other procedures in which he's likely to try to bite. If the horse is truly dangerous, however, it's best to move on to a safer partner.

KICKING

Kicking is a defense mechanism and usually employed by a horse that is afraid or insecure. A horse that kicks in an attempt to hurt you has generally been mistreated at some point in his life; he kicks because he doesn't trust the people that enter his personal space. This habit is very dangerous and best dealt with by a professional horseman. But many nervous, insecure horses merely kick as a reflex when they are startled, and this bad habit can be retrained with patient handling.

>> Many nervous, insecure horses merely kick as a reflex when they are startled.

How to Change This Habit

Remember, horses have a fight-or-flight reflex: If the horse is startled, afraid, or uncomfortable and can't flee, he may kick in self-defense. For this reason, avoid startling a horse. Let him know you are nearby, using your voice, before you approach him physically. Don't come up behind a horse that might kick; approach him from the side or front.

Some horses are touchy about their hindquarters, but with patient handling, they may learn to tolerate the kinds of situations that once caused them to kick. The horse must first learn to trust people, so what he used to perceive as threatening is no longer scary. If he is jumpy about having his hind legs bumped or handled, for instance, provide patient lessons in gentle touching and brushing, using advance-and-retreat techniques—handle the areas he's comfortable with, then venture closer to his touchy spots, returning to the "okay" spots if he gets anxious.

During retraining the habitual kicker should be properly restrained (which may mean using a chain over his nose—see p. 65) so he can't avoid the lessons, and it's safest to have an assistant hold him rather than tying him, so he doesn't feel trapped. It can help to position him with a wall or solid fence on one side so he can't move away from you.

>> When working to desensitize a kicker, position him with a wall or solid fence on one side so he can't move away from you.

With a nervous or insecure horse you may make faster progress if you bribe him with treats. Chewing something tasty diverts his attention and helps him realize that having his hind legs brushed and bumped is not such a bad thing. Reward the horse for standing still and when you've handled a touchy spot without him kicking. It's amazing how quickly some horses figure this out.

If the horse is too fearful or defensive to begin by handling his hind end and can't be swayed by treats, use a far more gradual desensitization program. As in Solution 2, have a helper hold him alongside a wall or fence.

- Begin with an old saddle pad, hand towel, or anything soft and familiar the horse is not afraid of. Rub him with it, beginning along his back, then gradually progressing to his neck, under his belly, and eventually his rump.

- If the horse gets nervous, retreat to his back area and rub there again for a while before trying again with the advance-and-retreat technique. Tell him "whoa" if he tries to move. Praise him when he stays calm.

- Rub the saddle pad or towel more quickly over him and let it flop against his belly and hind legs. Do this from both sides.

- When the horse is at ease with the saddle blanket flopping against his body from all angles, swap the blanket for a crumpled paper bag, or something else that makes a little noise, and repeat the process. If he gets jumpy or threatens to kick, slow down again. Always remember that you are trying to alleviate fear, not elevate it.

Using a soft rope, move it over his body (as in Solution 4) and then dangle it over his rump. Loop the rope around each of his hind legs. Slide it back and forth around each one at various heights, especially down around the cannons and pasterns. This training session not only helps teach him not to kick (since he loses his fear of things

touching his hind end and hind legs) but may also prove very benefi-
cial if he ever gets tangled in a longe line or fence wire: He'll be less
apt to panic because he'll have experienced the sensation already
and will know it won't hurt him.

SOLUTION 6 You can use a long whip—a dressage or driving whip, for example—
to reach out and touch the horse's hind legs, getting him used to
contact, while you remain out of kicking range.

- Let the horse smell the whip, then slowly and gently rub and
  touch him with it all over his "upper" body—over his sides and
  rump and along his flanks.

- When he is at ease with the whip rubbing against his body, move
  down to his legs, gently brushing the whip around his hind legs
  and between them. It may take several sessions of this form
  of gradual desensitization before the horse realizes that having
  his hind legs touched is not scary and he doesn't have to kick in
  self-defense.

» **When the horse is at ease with the whip rubbing against
his body, move down to his legs, gently brushing the
whip around his hind legs and between them.**

SOLUTION 7 As mentioned, some horses kick not because they are afraid, but
because they are headstrong and spoiled. A horse with this attitude
has found that kicking puts him in control because humans back
off—just as a subordinate herd member would back off when he
kicks or threatens another horse out in the field.

This habit is more difficult to deal with because the horse thinks he
is dominant. Your first challenge is to establish your authority over
the horse so he accepts *you* as leader rather than thinking *he* can
be the boss. One way to do this is to work with him in a round pen,
giving him lessons in paying attention to a handler while establish-

ing trust and respect. Loose in the round pen, the horse doesn't feel trapped and is not restrained and "punished" in a setting where he can't get away. He can make his own choices as the lesson progresses, and is thus, in some ways, teaching himself.

Since the horse can't leave the pen, he has two options—to move around the pen or stand still. Your goal is to teach him to stand and face you whenever something frightens or irritates him. This impresses upon him that *you* are dominant and can make him move or stop. The horse also learns that when he behaves properly he is allowed to relax, but when he behaves badly (moves away from you or turns his hindquarters toward you) he will have to run around the pen some more.

Once the horse responds to your presence with respect and trust via lessons in the round pen, you can then progress to specific lessons to desensitize his hind end, such as those the previous solutions in this section suggest (brushing his hind legs, touching them with a whip, and so on). He'll be less apt to kick during his retraining because you will have established your authority over him.

> » **Once the horse responds to your presence with respect and trust in the round pen, you can progress to specific lessons to desensitize his hind end.**

What If Nothing Works?

Some habitual kickers never become trustworthy, and in these cases, you are better off getting a new horse. (Note: Never sell a kicker without warning the prospective buyer of his dangerous habit.)

-3-

Bad Habits
Under Saddle

Some horses have phobias or bad habits when mounted and ridden. Most of these problems are due to lack of training or mistakes made by the handler/rider during training. In many cases it is harder to undo a bad habit than it would have been to build a good habit in the first place.

Mounting problems may vary from minor to serious. The horse that fidgets and moves around is not as dangerous as the one who bolts, spins, or tries to buck, but any mounting problem should be addressed and corrected. A horse that moves at just the wrong time can get the rider in trouble.

Some horses, due to their laid-back personality, lack of training, or because they have learned that they can avoid work by being slow and unwilling develop the habit of laziness. Others have the opposite problem and are always in too big a hurry. They can't stand to follow another horse and always want to be in front of a group, or they jig impatiently on the way home, rooting and pulling at the bit, or even trying to bolt. Both of these bad habits in horses can be a constant frustration, and a frustrated rider usually only aggravates the problem by picking a fight with the horse.

Some horses don't "steer" well, either due to lack of training or because they've learned that they can get out of work by being sloppy in their turns and responses to rider cues. Many horses don't want to leave the security of home or other horses. Others do fine when ridden by themselves but have bad manners when ridden in company. And then there are horses that balk at every new experience or unfamiliar obstacle.

The potential bad habits under saddle are too numerous to count, but in many cases, patient retraining and a rider who is willing to improve his or her own position or technique can lead to a positive result.

Problems with Mounting

BACKS UP DURING MOUNTING

The horse that backs up while being mounted may have a physical problem that makes him uncomfortable when you put your weight in the saddle. Or he may have gotten into this habit because a rider checked him too much with the reins in an effort to keep him from moving forward. Others may back up to avoid being mounted because they want to get out of work.

> » A horse may back up while being mounted because a rider once checked him too much with the reins in an effort to keep him from moving forward.

How to Change This Habit

SOLUTION 1 First make sure there isn't a physical problem causing the horse's reaction. An examination of his back and your saddle and related equipment can help ensure there isn't a source of pain or irritation that's at fault.

SOLUTION 2 Check your mounting technique and make sure you are not inadvertently pulling on the horse's mouth as you mount. Give him plenty of slack in the reins.

SOLUTION 3 When mounting, position the horse so his rump is in a fence corner so he can't back up. Make sure the

corner is constructed of safe, solid fencing that won't hurt him, or collapse if he backs into it. Practice mounting and dismounting in this corner, trying to make the experience as pleasant as possible for the horse. Once his ability to back up is literally "closed down," he may give up this dangerous habit altogether.

» **When mounting, position the horse so his rump is in a fence corner so he can't back up.**

If the horse continues to back up when you try to mount him out in the open, have an assistant stand behind and to one side of him with a broom held with the bristles toward the horse's rump or training whip held so the blunt-ended handle points toward his rump.

- Do not mount the first time: Act like you are preparing to get on, then back the horse in hand until he runs right into the bristles of the broom or blunt end of the whip. The horse *should not* be hit with the broom or whip, he should merely be allowed to run into it on his own.

- The horse may startle at the contact and jump forward (which is why you shouldn't actually mount the first time).

- Repeat, but this time, actually get on. Most horses will soon realize that it's not so pleasant to back up into something that pokes them in the behind.

What If Nothing Works?

Most horses will get over this behavior once they realize that mounting is not causing discomfort and that they can't back up without getting a prod from behind. When a horse still insists on backing up whenever you get on, you may have to always position him with his rump toward a fence or wall corner (see Solution 3).

BUCKS AS RIDER GETS ON

This is the most serious aversion behavior, signifying that the horse definitely does not want you to get on his back, either because having a rider in the saddle causes him pain or reminds him of past bad experiences.

PROBLEMS WITH MOUNTING

How to Change This Habit

SOLUTION 1 As with other bad habits, confirm that there isn't a physical problem causing the horse's anxiety or stubborn resistance. A painful back or poorly fitting (or broken) saddle may trigger this kind of vehement reaction. If the horse is generally well-mannered, there must be a reason for his behavior. He should be checked by a veterinarian.

SOLUTION 2 Make sure you are not inadvertently causing the horse pain or annoyance by the way you mount. A sensitive horse may be irritated or alarmed if you always poke him with your toe, brush your leg over his rump, or plunk down hard in the saddle. For some, this kind of sloppy technique can inspire bucking.

SOLUTION 3 If the horse's bad attitude about mounting is merely the reaction of a spoiled, timid, or nervous horse that has learned that this is a way to avoid being ridden, go back to basics with mounting lessons. Have a competent helper hold the horse for you, standing the horse so he faces a safe and solid fence corner so he knows he can't move very much. Note: If you have a helper holding the horse, make sure the helper holds the horse by the halter (if the horse is wearing a halter under the bridle) or by the cheek pieces of the headstall—not by the reins. You want the horse's mouth left alone so there's not an accidental pull on the bit when he moves. You don't want the bit causing him pain just as you are mounting, as it would create a bad mounting experience for the horse instead of a good one, defeating the purpose of the lesson.

In the case of the timid or nervous horse, use patience and bribery (such as your helper feeding him a horse cookie when he stands still as you mount), until the horse relaxes as you progressively put weight in the stirrup and then on the saddle, and then swing yourself on board.

 If you don't have a friend to help you with this problem and must deal with it alone, use a Western saddle during mounting lessons, and leave a halter on under the horse's bridle. Tie the lead rope from the halter to the saddle horn, leaving the horse just enough slack for comfortable head movement, but not enough that he can get his head down far enough to buck.

 Sometimes it helps if you exercise the horse a little first—before saddling and/or mounting. Thirty minutes to an hour of vigorous exercise on a longe line or being ponied may take the edge off his resistance and improve his attitude. Work on mounting lessons after the horse is warmed up or a little tired (and not so apt to be "cold backed").

 If you are agile and able to get on a horse smoothly and quickly, try checking and circling him as you get on:

- As you prepare to mount, reach forward with your left hand and grab his headstall (or the left rein, up close to the bit) and pull his head toward you as you put your foot in the stirrup and swing on. It is physically impossible for the horse to buck while he's making a tight circle, so continue to apply pressure to the left rein, spinning him to his left several turns after you are in the saddle and before you ask him to move forward.

What If Nothing Works?

Any horse that continues to try to buck you off during mounting despite your attention to a possible physical cause, your technique, and mounting practice, is dangerous. You need a professional horseman to help with his training, or a new horse.

STEPS SIDEWAYS AWAY FROM RIDER

Some horses evade the rider by stepping away as you start to get on.

How to Change This Habit

 As with other bad habits, make sure there isn't a physical reason the horse does not want to be mounted: Check for possible causes of pain or irritation related to his back or the saddle.

>> **When the horse is merely being evasive out of habit, incorporate retraining sessions in his daily routine.**

 If the horse is merely being evasive out of habit, incorporate retraining sessions in his daily routine. Practice mounting him in a safe and stable wall or fence corner so he cannot move away as you mount. Your goal is to keep him relaxed about the process—if he stands nicely (because he can't move away in the fence corner), reward him by ending the lesson after just a few successful tries. Repeat this process for a few days until the horse realizes that mounting is not unpleasant.

What If Nothing Works?

If the horse still insists on stepping sideways (away from you) as you mount, continue to place him next to a wall or fence so he cannot step away. You can also try some of the solutions provided for the other bad habits listed in this section.

TRIES TO RUN AWAY

Some horses are so impatient they won't wait until you are all the way in the saddle—they take off as you try to put your foot in the stirrup, and they are part way down the road before you can swing your leg over. This dangerous habit often starts because the rider was sloppy and did not insist that the horse stand still for mounting. The horse may have moved only a step or two forward at first, and the rider didn't bother to make him halt because it didn't seem like such a big deal. Before long, though, the horse was taking off before the rider could put a foot in the stirrup. As you can see, this bad habit can quickly escalate from a minor annoyance to a dangerous problem.

How to Change This Habit

 Check your technique: Make sure you are not accidentally causing him to move too soon by poking him in the belly with your toe as you put your foot in the stirrup or bumping your leg on his rump as you swing into the saddle.

 Make it a habit of your own to always insist that the horse stand still for mounting.

- If he starts to move as you prepare to mount, stop, check him, and make him stand before trying again.

- Put your foot in the stirrup but don't actually mount: Ask him to stand, and if he doesn't, wait until he stands still before you try to pull yourself up. If necessary, work with him in his paddock or some other enclosed area where he can't really go anywhere, and face him into a safe, strong wall or fence so he can't move forward.

- Mount and dismount many times, every day, without actually letting the horse move off. Sit on his back a moment and then dismount again.

- Even after you have retrained him to stand still, make a habit of asking the horse to stand for a moment every time you mount, so he doesn't get right back into the habit of moving off too soon. A horse with a nervous or impatient tendency can quickly revert to taking off as you try to get on if you let him.

» **Make a habit of asking the horse to stand for a moment every time you mount.**

 Have a helper hold the horse for the first retraining lessons. Work in an enclosed area so the horse realizes he can't run off. As in Solution 2, begin by putting your weight in the stirrup and getting up and down without actually mounting. Progress to mounting and dismounting, and then having the horse stand still as you sit on him. Once the horse has taken this lesson on board, go through all the steps again without the help of your assistant—you don't want him to get into the habit of having to be held for mounting. Stay in the enclosed area until he can stay relaxed and not try to take off when you get on. When you do move on to mounting him out in the open, face him toward the barn or a safe, strong fence corner at first, just to make sure he continues to stand still.

 If the horse is always so energetic and overeager that he has a hard time standing still for mounting, practice mounting at the end of long rides or workouts when he is a little tired. Most horses are more willing to stand and relax at the end of a ride because they burned off the extra energy and are ready to stay home. As the horse progresses in your retraining efforts, do more mounting at other times as well—such as in the middle of the ride. Eventually, his ability to stand still will apply to the beginning of the ride, as well.

» **Most horses are more willing to stand and relax at the end of a ride because they have burned off extra energy.**

What If Nothing Works?

See other possible solutions offered in this section. If the horse is so set in his ways that he always takes off when the rider starts to mount, you may need a professional trainer to help retrain him.

WON'T STAND STILL/FIDGETS

There are many horses that are simply nervous and don't like standing still, or that fidget around during mounting because they've never been taught to stand still. Others may not want to stand still because mounting causes them discomfort.

How to Change This Habit

First try to determine whether the horse is reacting from pain or discomfort, or simply lack of training. If the saddle shifts to the side as you put your weight in the stirrup to mount, or if it puts pressure on a sore back or rubs a tender spot on the horse's back or girth, he will be evasive. Check his back and girth area to make sure there isn't a physical cause for his behavior.

Don't tighten the horse's girth all at once before mounting. If he's sensitive in the girth/cinch area, the sudden pressure could make him fidget. You should tighten the girth/cinch in gradual increments as you lead him around, before you mount (see also Girthy/Cinchy, p. 109).

Examine your mounting technique. Are you causing the horse any discomfort as you mount? Are you inadvertently pulling on the bit, poking the horse in the belly with your toe as you get on, or dragging your foot across his rump? Are you coming down hard in the saddle instead of easing into it? Are you pulling the horse to the side as you pull yourself up and making him lose his balance? If any of your actions are startling, uncomfortable, or annoying to the horse, he may begin to fidget in anticipation of mounting.

If you are heavy or awkward in your mounting technique, you may be twisting the saddle against his back as you get on or pulling him to the side as you mount, causing the horse to take a step or reposition his feet to keep his balance. First correct your mounting methods and then work on his bad habit.

PROBLEMS WITH MOUNTING

If it is hard for you to mount gracefully (and without pulling and twisting on the saddle as you swing on) when standing next to his shoulder facing to the rear, try mounting from a position just slightly behind the saddle, facing forward. This doesn't take as much effort and does not pull on the saddle so much (with less twisting and sideways motion). It is also less apt to pull the horse off balance because you are behind his center of gravity and keeping your weight along his "long axis" (front to back) instead of twisting your body 180 degrees across his "short axis" (side to side). You can also use a mounting block to ease the process for both you and your horse (see Solution 4).

If the horse is tall and you are short, or there is any other reason that it's difficult for you to get into the saddle quickly and easily without bumping him or pulling the saddle to the side, use a mounting block. A mounting block makes it possible for you to ease into the saddle, is thought by many to be the preferable way to get on the horse in order to prevent back and saddle problems, and is especially helpful when you are a heavy individual or have trouble getting on your horse. Note: A mounting block works nicely with a well-trained horse, but can be problematic, and even dangerous, when working with a nervous or "devious" horse that does not stand still for mounting. Prior to using a mounting block, the horse must learn to stand still on command, and stand still next to the block (see below).

The mounting block should be something the horse is not afraid of and easy to lead him up to. If you don't have a "real" mounting block, even a bale of hay or straw works fine—as long as it is solid and stable. Get the horse used to standing beside the mounting block before you ever try mounting from it. Lead him around it, then next to it, gradually getting him closer, and finally asking him to stand quietly beside it.

Don't hurry these lessons or the horse will become nervous about approaching and standing next to the mounting block. Praise him for each small increment of progress (or give him a treat when he stands quietly), until he is content to stand patiently in proper position next to the block. Next get him used to standing still while you are on the block, touching him all over, leaning over him, and putting weight on the saddle. Once he is at ease with you standing and moving around on the block, you can use it to advantage to mount him without causing him discomfort or loss of balance.

If there aren't any physical/mechanical problems involved, and the horse just needs to learn better mounting manners, start over in his training and work on "whoa" during leading and longeing lessons so he understands that when you want him to stop and stand still, he needs to do it. He must learn that he can't fidget and move around when he's asked to stop or told to stand.

Once he respects and obeys "whoa" when he's being handled or led, progress to some mounting lessons and apply what he's learned. Ask him to stop and stand as you prepare to mount. Do not tolerate *any* movement. If he starts to move forward or sideways, check him and say "whoa" to remind him of his earlier lessons. Get on and off repeatedly, without going anywhere, just asking him to stand still while you do it. Once this lesson is initially in place, it's up to you to be consistent each time you mount, making sure that he continues to stand still before you get on. Most fidgety horses become that way because they are allowed to do so by an inconsistent rider.

SOLUTION 6

If the horse is a very nervous individual and worries a lot, or if he is very impatient to be "off and going," take extra time to keep him relaxed and calm during the mounting process. Do a lot of mounting and dismounting in a quiet, enclosed area where he feels at ease, such as in his paddock. Don't let him move after you get on; just sit there a moment and get off again, and then do it all again. After he stands quietly without fidgeting a time or two, reward him by ending the lesson on a good note.

PROBLEMS WITH MOUNTING

SOLUTION 7

Try bribery to refocus the horse's thoughts and take the edge off his nervousness. If he stands still as you mount, reach forward and give him a treat or horse cookie after you are settled into the saddle. Most horses come to expect the reward for good behavior and stand still, waiting for their treat. (Note: You can also use a helper at his head to give the horse a treat once you've gotten on.)

SOLUTION 8

Accustom the horse to hobbles on his front feet (padded leather hobbles around his front pasterns or figure-eight gunny sack hobbles around his front cannon bones), letting him wear them while he is groomed, for instance, while also being held by an assistant. Once the horse is "hobble trained," put the hobbles on after he's been saddled, and use them as an aid in teaching him to stand while being mounted. Get on and off him while he's wearing the hobbles, telling him "whoa" each time you get on. Once he learns to stand still for mounting, you can dispense with the hobbles.

What If Nothing Works?

Almost every fidgety horse can be retrained to stand still while you mount. If the horse is absolutely too nervous to stand still, and it's difficult for you to get into the saddle, use a mounting block and have a helper hold the horse as you get on.

Problems with Not Enough Energy

CUTS CORNERS

Some horses won't make a nice turn under saddle. This problem might be due to lack of training or to the rider letting the horse get sloppy in his schooling. A "lazy" horse (one with a tendency to *not* have a lot of energy) may start cutting corners if he's allowed to get away with it.

How to Change This Habit

SOLUTION 1 The horse could have a physical problem that makes him stiff and unwilling to take his corners smoothly. If he wants to cut them instead of bend around them, he could have a back problem, arthritis, or a neurological issue that interferes with his ability to execute a nice turn.

SOLUTION 2 If the horse is green or not well trained, spend more time working on turns and teaching him the proper way to follow his head around the curve without cutting corners. Use your legs as well as your reins to guide his body. Horses move away from pressure, so leg pressure at the appropriate time in the course of the turn can keep his body in proper position.

Be more consistent in your own riding technique, and never letting the horse cut corners. Keep his body out in the circle by using your inside leg and asking him to bend around it. If you insist on him staying out in the circle, he will be less likely to cut the corners.

Set up an obstacle course for the horse to maneuver through, using cones or milk jugs filled with sand or pebbles (to keep them from blowing away), and work your horse around the markers several times a day. If he tries to walk over the cones rather than bend around them, use taller obstacles, such as barrels. Going around obstacles will help him begin to respond to your legs better, and you'll eventually be able to school him in corners without the obstacles to help promote bend.

PROBLEMS WITH NOT ENOUGH ENERGY

What If Nothing Works?

If you still have trouble getting the horse to bend and turn properly, ask an experienced trainer or advanced rider to observe you and the horse and provide input as to what you might be doing wrong, and additional suggestions for solving the problem.

DRIFTS OFF THE RAIL

Some horses won't work in straight lines along the rail when schooling in the arena; they start veering/drifting away from it.

How to Change This Habit

Make sure the horse doesn't have a physical problem that hinders him from traveling straight.

Check your own riding technique to make sure you are not inadvertently giving mixed signals to the horse or are inconsistent in your leg/rein actions.

If the horse is merely being inattentive or lazy, spend more time going up and down the rail, focusing constant attention on your leg aids. Proper use of your hands (good communication through the bit and reins) in combination with attentive leg pressure should catch the problem before it starts, pushing him back on line whenever he starts to drift.

If the horse is not paying attention to you because he's sour, the solution is *less* ring work instead of *more*. Take him out every day for a long ride outside the arena. Get him on the trail with other things to see and do besides circles in a riding ring. This can give him a fresh approach and more willing attitude when you go back to his arena lessons again.

What If Nothing Works?

Examine your riding skills and horsemanship and consider investing in a few lessons to strengthen your seat and aids.

PICKS UP INCORRECT LEAD

Some horses prefer one canter or lope lead over the other and are very "one-sided" when ridden, always taking the same lead even when asked for the other (see my discussion of "right-" and "left-handedness" on p. 181).

How to Change This Habit

Check that there isn't a physical reason for the horse to take the wrong lead. Perhaps he doesn't want to put extra stress and weight on a certain leg. Consider the potential causes of soreness and stiffness.

Take a good look at your canter cues and verify you are giving the horse an adequate signal; he may not understand what you want.

Go back to basics with training. Experiment with different ways to signal for a certain canter lead to find out which way works best for your particular horse. Then, make it easier for him at first by always signaling for his weak lead as you make a turn in that direction—since it's a horse's natural tendency to lead with his inside legs to help balance himself, he'll be more inclined to canter off correctly. As you signal for the turn with your legs, ask him to pick up the canter, using strongest leg pressure with your outside leg to help him know you want him to continue turning while changing gaits. The horse's inclination is to *move away* from pressure: Your leg pressure on that side also stimulates him to push hardest with his outside hind leg (the one furthest away from the center of the arena), which is what he must do in order to then reach farther forward with his inside (leading) legs.

» **It's a horse's natural tendency to lead with his inside legs to help balance himself.**

To make it easier for him take the correct lead when you go into a canter from a trot, squeeze with your outside leg as his outside hind leg is moving forward and just about to strike the ground—this encourages it to push off more strongly and thus propel the horse into the proper lead.

You can time yourself to the horse's trotting strides: His diagonal legs are working in unison, which means that his outside front leg and inside hind leg are moving forward together, as are the inside front leg and outside hind leg. If you squeeze with your outside leg when your horse's outside front leg is on the ground, this means his outside hind is moving forward, readying to strike the ground.

PROBLEMS WITH NOT ENOUGH ENERGY

When posting at the trot ("standing" and "sitting" on alternating strides), you should be on the "outside diagonal" (rising in the saddle when the outside front leg is in the air and sitting as it hits the ground). This makes it very easy to give the cue to canter as you settle into the saddle, pressing with your outside leg at the same time the horse's outside front foot is on the ground.

» **To cue the horse to pick up the correct lead, press with your outside leg at the same time the horse's outside front foot is on the ground.**

Another combination of cues that helps some horses pick up the correct lead is to turn the horse's head slightly to the outside of a turn (away from the center of the circle or arena) while leaning your weight back very slightly (rather than leaning forward) and squeezing hard with your outside leg. Turning his head to the outside tends to hinder the forward action of his outside shoulder (by moving his weight to that side), enabling the inside shoulder to move farther forward so he can lead with the inside leg. If you watch a horse running loose in the pasture, he tends to tip his muzzle to the outside of a turn when he picks up a canter, and this natural, slight redistribution of balance is what you are trying to mimic. Don't tilt his head *too* much, however, or you'll put him *off* balance and he'll take the wrong lead.

Press hard with your outside leg against the horse's barrel as you come through a turn, pushing his hindquarters a little to the inside (toward the center of your circle or turn) as you ask him to pick up the canter. This helps him lead with his inside hind leg while stimulating his outside hind leg to push off more strongly.

» **Push the horse's hindquarters a little to the inside (toward the center of your circle or turn) as you ask him to pick up the canter.**

What If Nothing Works?

Get help from a more experienced horseman or trainer.

REFUSES TO CANTER OR LOPE

Some horses are reluctant to break into a canter or lope and prefer to trot: They pick up the trot when you try to go directly from a halt or a walk into a canter, and merely trot faster when you ask them to go from a trot to a canter.

PROBLEMS WITH NOT ENOUGH ENERGY

How to Change This Habit

 There could be a physical cause of the horse's reluctance to canter. He may be uncomfortable or in pain due to an injury, stiffness, or a poorly fitting saddle. Make sure the horse is healthy and sound before focusing on reschooling.

 Another reason for a horse's reluctance to canter may simply be due to inadequate training. A green horse that has not been cantered very much may not understand the canter aids yet. When the cause is likely a training issue, you need to spend more time working on trot-to-canter and walk-to-canter transitions.

» **A horse's reluctance to canter may simply be due to inadequate training.**

 Work on your technique: Your cues need to be extra clear so the horse will get the idea he's supposed to canter rather than just trot faster.

- Work on your leg and rein signals for speeding up and slowing down so you have better control over transitions from walk to trot and back again.

- When the horse is responsive to these signals, give him a cue to canter while at the trot by squeezing/driving him harder/faster with your legs. When he starts to trot faster, "check him" lightly with the bit to control his energy and "bottle it up," so to speak. Pushed between your legs and the bit signal, he will find that he can't trot faster and will break into a canter. Immediately release pressure on the bit and give him a little slack in the reins so he knows he did the right thing and can stride forward.

 Ask him to pick up the canter on a slight turn or corner while applying your outside leg very strongly (those with a secure leg position can wear spurs and add a touch of the spur at this moment). Lean slightly forward to encourage the horse to move faster and restore his balance, and to help convince him to "shift gears" into the faster gait.

 If the horse is exceptionally lazy, carry a riding crop or whip in your outside hand and apply one or two firm smacks behind your outside leg to enforce your cues to canter. If applied decisively and with good timing, one or two smacks should be enough to get the horse's attention and drive him forward. You do not need to be excessively harsh or overly timid (you don't want to be a tyrant, nor do you want to be a nag). Be prepared for a startled or annoyed reaction; some horses may give a bit of a buck prior to picking up the canter.

> » When a horse is exceptionally lazy, carry a riding crop or whip in your outside hand and apply one or two firm smacks behind your outside leg if he ignores your aids.

What If Nothing Works?

Get help from a more experienced rider or trainer.

REFUSES TO MOVE/BALKS

Most horses will balk at something they don't want to do or come to a halt when approaching something they fear. Balking at scary obstacles will be covered later in this book (see p. 240), but the horses that stop or balk for no apparent reason are the hardest challenge.

How to Change This Habit

(see p. 240)

On occasion a horse has some kind of physical problem that causes pain or discomfort when saddled and ridden. The horse may not be lame, per se: He may move out freely without a saddle or any weight on his back, yet be reluctant to move when someone is riding him. If the horse is balky and stubborn when first starting a ride and then seems to "warm out of it," you should suspect a physical problem as the cause, such as a sore back or arthritic joints.

>> **If the horse "warms out of" balkiness or unwillingness, you should suspect a physical problem as a cause of the behavior.**

When the horse refuses to move because he doesn't want to do something—such as go through a gate—the easiest way to get him moving is to convince him that he's not being made to do the thing he doesn't want to do—in other words, change his focus. For example, you can turn the horse in another direction and reapproach the gate, or back him up through it. This solves the immediate problem, and then you can work on the larger issue with progressive training to teach him to go through gates over many training sessions.

The horse that halts for no apparent reason (there isn't an object or obstacle that seems to be the cause) and refuses to move in spite of coercion is harder to deal with. It's often as if he suddenly decides he's had enough (of whatever you've been asking him to

PROBLEMS WITH NOT ENOUGH ENERGY

do while being ridden) and his mind shuts down. Even if you kick him or use spurs or a whip, he still refuses to budge. Punishment is usually counterproductive in this scenario and makes the horse's mind shut down even more. The best way to get him to move is to make him take a step to the side by getting him a little off balance.

- Pull his head abruptly around toward you and use your leg strongly on the opposite side.

- Lean into the turn you are asking the horse to make to encourage him to move away from the leg pressure and to rebalance himself—he will have to take a step or two with his front feet.

- Using this technique, spin him around one way and then the other. This usually breaks his mindset and you can get him moving forward again.

SOLUTION 4

Some horses that stop and refuse to go forward will still back up when asked. If this is the case, back the horse until he gets his mind off balking, and he will then be likely to go forward again when you request it. Note: This solution should only be used when you are riding in an arena free of hazards. In addition, it is important to recognize that the last thing you want is for the horse to develop a habit of rushing backward blindly whenever he doesn't want to go forward—someday he could back right off a mountain or into a ditch. It is best to use the back-up tactic when you can back him into a safe but solid object, such as the arena wall or board fence. The "bump" from the wall or fence will make him want to go forward again. You can also have a helper stand behind and to one side with a bristle broom as you back him up. Have her point the bristles at his rump—when he runs into them, he will be ready to go forward again.

What If Nothing Works?

If the horse balks when you are riding and you can't get him to move at all, get off and lead him for a few minutes before mounting again. If he refuses to move forward when led, turn him in a tight circle by pulling his head toward you to unbalance him and make him move his front feet.

RELUCTANT TO MOVE OUT/SLUGGISH

Some horses are very lazy walkers and won't speed up (or only hasten their gait temporarily) even when you kick or use spurs or a whip.

PROBLEMS WITH
NOT ENOUGH
ENERGY

How to Change This Habit

SOLUTION 1 The lazy horse has found that he'd rather endure your kicking than speed up his walk. Constant kicking is a form of nagging, and soon the horse becomes immune to it (tunes it out, so to speak) and does not respond as he should. When a horse won't respond to leg pressure anymore, try a different approach so he'll pay more attention. Instead of constantly kicking or squeezing with your legs, just use them periodically, and if the horse does not respond to the single squeeze, immediately follow up with a sharp rap from a crop or whip on his barrel, just behind your leg. He'll discover that he'd rather respond to the gentle squeeze by moving faster than feel the smack of the crop or whip.

SOLUTION 2 The easiest way to teach or retrain a horse to walk more swiftly is to use your legs alternately and with proper timing to stimulate each hind leg to push off harder. This makes him take longer strides and thus creates a faster walk. Squeezing with your left leg stimulates his left hind to push off with more energy and squeezing with your right leg stimulates his right hind. For best results you must squeeze *just* as the leg is preparing to push off; once it is in the air, you are too late.

You can find the proper timing for your alternating leg squeezes by watching the horse's shoulders, since his left front leg moves forward an instant before the right hind does, and his right front moves forward an instant before his left hind. So: Squeeze with your left leg as the horse's right shoulder comes forward and with your right leg as his left shoulder comes forward. There's a natural body rhythm to it, and once you get the feel of this movement you don't have to watch his shoulders—just swing a little at the hips as he moves, rolling your weight a bit in the saddle as you alternately squeeze with your legs.

When you "walk with the horse" like this, pushing him faster with your body, legs, and seat, you use a more effective kind of urging (and it is also easier on you) than constant squeezing or kicking. If the horse responds too much and breaks into a trot, gently check him with the reins to contain the extra energy in the walk.

What If Nothing Works?

If the horse doesn't respond to your solutions, examine your horsemanship, especially your leg and hand cues and coordination. You may need to improve your riding skills with instruction from an experienced rider or trainer.

WON'T CHANGE LEADS

This problem may not be as much a lack of energy or laziness as it is a lack of training (or sometimes a physical problem), but there are a few horses that stubbornly refuse to change leads just because they've become sour.

How to Change This Habit

 First determine if there's a physical reason the horse doesn't want to take a certain lead. He may have a subtle lameness issue, stiffness, or pain. If he took both leads willingly at an earlier time (changing leads readily at your cue) and now refuses, suspect a physical problem is the culprit.

>> **A subtle lameness issue, stiffness, or pain can cause
a horse to refuse to change leads.**

Most horses prefer one lead over the other. They take either lead
when running loose in the pasture in order to balance themselves
on turns, but become one-sided when ridden and must be taught to
take either lead, in either direction. This is partly due to the fact that
most horses are not ambidextrous: They are "right-" or "left-handed,"
just like humans.

Many horses prefer to take the left lead when ridden because they
are actually "right-handed," preferring to push off hardest with the
right hind leg when going into a canter. And since it's more natural
for them to take the left lead, they may prefer to *stay* in that lead
rather than perform a "simple" or "flying change" (switching canter
leads, either by slowing to a walk or trot first, or while remaining in
the canter) when you ask them.

Horses that are strongly right- or left-handed need more work at
the canter, going back to the basics and teaching them to take a
specific lead when asked to canter, and working on lead changes at
the canter only when they are ready. Most horses change leads automatically when working at speed doing something in which they
can anticipate and predict the change of direction (such as when
chasing a cow or galloping cross-country), but they may refuse to
change leads for you in an arena when they aren't always sure about
what you are going to ask of them next. Try to communicate better
with the horse so he knows the direction you'll be taking, and make
sure you always give your cues in a consistent and timely manner.

>> **Most horses change leads automatically when working
at speed doing something in which they can anticipate
and predict the change of direction.**

PROBLEMS WITH
NOT ENOUGH
ENERGY

To work on lead changes, practice large figure eights at the canter, making sure the horse is on the proper lead as you make the first circle in the figure. (If he has a preferred lead, make the circle in that direction.) If the horse has been trained to do flying changes (switching leads at the canter) give him the cue for a lead change as you change direction in the center of the figure eight and begin to make the second loop. If the horse doesn't "get it" or is just learning to switch leads, do a simple change: Drop to a trot for several strides just before you ask for the change in the new direction.

Make sure the horse's body is straight before you ask him to bend in the new direction at the point of the lead change. You don't want him bent in the direction of the old circle when you ask him to start the new circle. A few trotting strides can help him get in better position to make the switch. Gradually reduce the number of trotting strides between circles, until you can eliminate them completely.

When the horse is ready to try flying changes again, check him very lightly with the bit for a split second as you finish one circle and begin the new one, immediately giving him the cue for a lead change, using your (new) outside leg more strongly. Squeeze with your legs at the phase of his stride when your weight is pressed down farthest in the saddle, and he should be able to make the lead change in midair during the elevated phase of his canter stride.

Once the horse can perform lead changes in a figure eight, you can progress to asking for lead changes while he's cantering on a straight line. Regardless of where you are asking for a lead change, your cues should remain consistent.

What If Nothing Works?

Get help from a more experienced rider or trainer.

Problems with Too Much Energy

AVOIDS BIT PRESSURE/GOES BEHIND THE BIT

Some horses attempt to avoid control by getting "behind the bit" or becoming overbent. If you try to "check" the horse with the reins or give him cues through the bit he merely tucks his head and flexes his neck to where his chin is almost touching his chest. Without a light and "alive" contact through the bit, you have little control. Some horses learn this habit as a way to avoid bit pressure or have developed it after experiencing pain from a bit or rough hands.

PROBLEMS WITH TOO MUCH ENERGY

How to Change This Habit

SOLUTION 1

A horse that resorts to this tactic in order to avoid the bit may have had a bad experience with a heavy-handed rider who pulled at or injured his mouth with the bit. Therefore, quite often the answer to this problem lies in less reliance on the bit and less pulling on the reins. Use the mildest bit you can and a very gentle touch.

SOLUTION 2

Go back to basics and work the horse in simple training exercises, practicing better use of your hands and concentrating more on body and seat cues rather than depending so much on the bit and reins.

For instance, cue the horse to slow down or stop by shifting your own weight back a little. The horse's natural inclination is to alter his speed in response to weight changes and balance shifts; changes in your body position are as much or more effective than cues given through the bit. Once the horse realizes he is not going to be hurt by the bit, he will be less inclined to try to avoid it.

» **The horse's natural inclination is to alter his speed in response to the rider's weight changes and balance shifts.**

What If Nothing Works?

If the horse is an overeager, highly energized individual, and you can't control him adequately without relying heavily on the bit, change to a hackamore or bitless bridle. Then you can work again on the basics of retraining him, encouraging him to extend and collect without overbending, since you'll be leaving his mouth completely alone. Without the pain or irritation from the bit, he can regain confidence in moving forward and responding properly to your cues.

DIFFICULT TO STOP/HARD MOUTHED

The "hard-mouthed" horse does not pay attention to the bit, often tightening his jaw and pulling on the reins. Lack of response to bit cues because of a hard mouth is usually the result of poor riding (constant or improper use of a bit and/or heavy or inconsistent hands) that damaged the nerves in the bars of the mouth—the interdental space where teeth do not grow. If the horse lacks feeling in this interdental space, he may find that he can march right through the rider's rein aids and keep going, even when the rider asks him to slow or stop.

>> A hard mouth is usually the result of poor riding.

How to Change This Habit

Go back to basics in the horse's training so you can employ *all* your cues (leg aids, weight shifts, voice) and do not have to rely so much on the reins. Revisit groundwork (leading and longeing) to teach him voice commands. If he learns to stop every time you tell him "whoa," it can prevent a lot of problems when you are riding. Once you can control him with subtle body and seat language, and the horse becomes more responsive to *all* your cues, his insensitive mouth will not be such a big issue.

When you cue the horse with a rein aid, be subtle and gentle. He's more apt to clamp his jaw and pull hard if you demand something from him by giving a hard pull on the reins. A vibrating give-and-take is much more effective: Not only can he feel and respond to it, it's also less confrontational, so he's less apt to pull in response. Always reward the horse when he does respond to an aid by ceasing your cue and giving instant relief from any pressure or bit vibration so he will keep his mouth relaxed.

>> A vibrating give-and-take on the reins is much more effective than a steady pull.

PROBLEMS WITH TOO MUCH ENERGY

What If Nothing Works?

If the horse is so hard-mouthed that he's difficult to ride with a bit, try riding him in a hackamore, bitless bridle, or side-pull.

DIFFICULT TO SLOW DOWN

Some horses always want to go faster than you do. They may lunge into the bit and make it hard to keep them at the controlled rate of speed you desire.

How to Change This Habit

Never give the horse a chance to lean into the bit. Always use a give-and-take action when you are trying to slow the horse. He pays a lot more attention to a vibrating, moving connection via the bit than a steady pull, and it gives him less to brace against if he's the sort that likes to set his neck muscles and pull back.

Use your body language and seat, as well as your reins, to cue the horse to slow down or stay at a slower gait. Lean back a little instead of forward, and he's more apt to slow his speed or remain at a slower gait to try to stay in balance.

Start working on better collection, which will help the horse control his energy and direct it into a more animated (but slower) gait rather than one that relies on extension and speed. You'll have a lot more control over all the horse's actions and movements once he has learned to alternately collect and extend at your cue. Western riders who regularly ride in a snaffle may want to transition the horse to a mild, short-shanked curb, which with proper use can help encourage the horse to flex at the poll and "give," allowing the rider more control over his movement and his speed. The curb bit requires a rider with "light" hands—see p. 197 for more on this.

Practice transitions between all gaits, and between collecting and extending each of those gaits, so you have precise control over his movements (which will also work to great advantage when you wish to tell him to slow down). Transitions are one of the keys to transferring the horse's weight from his forehand to his hind end, gradually enabling him to become more collected for longer periods of time. Keep your hands light and rely on your body language, seat, and legs.

You'll have a lot more control over all the horse's actions and movements once he has learned to alternately collect and extend at your cue.

What If Nothing Works?

You may need a rider or trainer with more experience and finesse to ride the horse for a while and teach him to respond better to the aids.

PRANCES/JIGS

The horse that prances, jigs, and won't settle down and walk is usually a hyper, nervous, insecure horse that finds it hard to relax. This habit may develop just because the horse has too much energy or because the rider always lets him get away with jigging instead of consistently making him walk.

PROBLEMS WITH TOO MUCH ENERGY

This horse may also get into the habit of tossing his head or rooting at the bit if the rider tries to hold him down to a walk. Many of these overeager horses also may contain themselves fairly well when leaving home (on a trail ride, for example), but get very impatient when heading back to the barn or pasture, becoming annoying and frustrating to the rider, who often loses his or her temper and punishes the horse, making matters worse.

>> **Many hyper, nervous, or insecure horses get very impatient when heading back to the barn or pasture.**

How to Change This Habit

 SOLUTION 1

Some horses have too much nervous energy because of the way they are managed. When the horse is fed grain or other high energy, concentrated feed, and confined in a stall or small paddock without room to burn off all that extra energy, he's like a coiled spring, bursting at the seams and ready to explode every time you ride him. Often the best way to take the edge off his exuberance is to feed less (or no) grain and more forage. If he is confined, give him more room to self-exercise so he can burn off some of that energy on his own. The best solution is 24-hour-a-day turnout.

SOLUTION 2

Longe the horse for 30 minutes before you ride, to help use up some of the excess energy.

SOLUTION 3

Take some lessons and otherwise educate yourself to become a better rider. The horse that jigs and prances is not paying enough attention to your cues and body language, and you are not getting through to him properly. Most riders dealing with a prancing horse make the mistake of pulling on the reins and trying to control the horse through the bit. Constant pulling on the reins simply inspires the hyper-energetic horse to pull back or root at the reins, and it becomes a contest of wills and a tug of war.

When your horse won't relax and stop prancing, rethink your tactics—especially your hands and body language. You need a lighter touch on the reins and finer-tuned cues. If you punish his mouth by pulling on him, he will become even more fretful and insecure. "Checking" with the reins should be a gentle give and take. As mentioned on p. 185, the horse will respond better to a bit that is vibrating with subtle cues and communication.

> » **Most riders dealing with a prancing horse make the mistake of pulling on the reins and trying to control the horse through the bit.**

SOLUTION 4

Stay calm yourself (and relax). Make a continual conscious effort to be patient, and don't let yourself get angry. The hyper horse that can't relax and walk is often made worse by *your* emotions and corresponding physical actions: Your tenseness and frustration aggravate the horse's feeling of worry, nervousness, or panic. This type of horse needs understanding and reassurance, not punishment.

Your role is to communicate confidence and a sense of calm so the horse can start to trust your judgment and calm down himself.

Gradually your calm and relaxed attitude will be transmitted to the horse and help him settle down and pay more attention to you and your aids. The communication between you will improve. But if you let yourself get frustrated or angry, the horse may construe your attitude as threatening, confrontational, or even frightening—and he'll just be harder to control.

In addition, when you are tense and stiff you inadvertently punish the horse's mouth with the bit and also tend to drive him forward with your body language because your seat and legs are rigid. Loosen up. Lean back a little and try to become as relaxed as a rag doll. If you are leaning back a little instead of forward, your body weight acts as an anchor, dragging a little behind the horse's center of gravity, and he'll tend to slow down. Be careful not to hang on to the reins for balance; keep your touch on the bit very light.

PROBLEMS WITH TOO MUCH ENERGY

When the horse starts to relax because you are relaxed, you can begin to trust him and let him go a little more "on his honor" without having to "check" him much at all with the bit. When you reach this point, your progress toward proceeding at a walk rather than a prance will come swiftly. Give him his head more and more often, keeping some continual slack in the reins, and making only very gentle contact in which your hands are totally giving and following his head movements.

At first, you may only be able to do this for a few strides, or when things are in your favor and the horse is a little more willing to walk instead of prance—for instance, after you've taken the edge off his bursting-at-the-seams energy with several miles of brisk riding (let him do an extended trot for several miles before asking him to settle down and walk) and he's become a little tired.

>> **Lean back a little instead of forward, so your body weight acts as an anchor, dragging a little behind the horse's center of gravity.**

If you can't take the horse out across country or on the trail, do some arena work and start the session by having him work at an extended trot for a while, but do not let him canter or lope. When you sense that his attitude may be changing and he's ready to relax a bit, ask him to slow to a walk. Try to keep him walking calmly on a loose rein. If he starts prancing again, push him back into an extended trot and keep him trotting until you again sense he might be ready to slow down, and ask him gently to come to a walk. If every time he starts prancing he is made to trot and work harder, he will usually start to rethink his need to hurry and be more content to stay at a walk.

End the lesson as soon as the horse responds by walking nicely for a good distance—once all the way around the arena, for example. Dismount and lead him back to his stall or paddock so he doesn't have a chance to prance again, and you can end the training session on a good, calm, positive note. After a few days of this type of work, in which he is rewarded by being able to walk calmly with no pressure, he most likely will begin to jig less and walk more. Once he walks nicely in the arena, try short rides outside it, gradually lengthening the amount of time you ask him to walk without prancing.

The biggest challenge when riding the horse that jigs and prances is figuring out how to handle the times he *insists* on going too fast. As we've discussed, when you have to check him a lot with the bit, he will likely continue prancing in frustration. Keep striving for a cooperative moment, and the best way to do that is to *encourage him to do the right thing* instead of punishing him with more bit pressure. Praise him for each tiny hint of a walk and "give" to him in that moment, releasing pressure. When he finds that you won't pull on his mouth when he cooperates, he may try a few more calm walk strides.

It may be hard to believe, but if you let him go more and more on a loose rein, the horse's nervous, charge-forward compulsion will ease and disappear. Slowly you'll be able to extend those calm walking moments. The secret to retraining and relaxing the nervous, prancing horse is feeling calm and self-assured enough (and confident enough in your seat) to use *less restraint*. Eventually this helps you develop the trust and cooperation that will enable you to let him go on a slack rein the majority of the time.

» **Encourage the horse to do the right thing instead of punishing him with more bit pressure.**

Another way to communicate with (and calm) the horse that's always trying to prance and jig is to keep your rein actions and body language at "walking rhythm." This means that when the horse is trying to trot, make your body and rein cues stay in "walking mode": your hands giving and taking as they would with the horse's head movement at the walk (rather than still and steady), and your seat bones moving vigorously in time with a walking rhythm. It's harder for the horse to trot if your body is moving in different time than his.

Defuse the prancing, excited horse by asking him to work at a variety of tasks and maneuvers. Request lots of turns and circles, and make continual changes of direction. Have him put his energy into serpentines and figure eights to take his mind off rushing around the arena or hurrying down the trail. If necessary, turn him around and head in the other direction. He will soon realize that all this extra stuff is a lot of work—and it is easier to settle down and walk.

What If Nothing Works?

For the horse that won't listen to you at all and is becoming frantic, don't try to hold him back or he may become angry and react by bucking or displaying other bad behavior. If he starts to prance or trot, spin him in a circle to slow him back to a walk again. Then let him continue on, with very little bit pressure. If he starts to prance or trot again, spin him the other direction. Don't fight him or punish him or the problem may escalate; a diversionary maneuver is always more effective, and much safer.

> » **When the horse starts to prance or trot, spin him in a circle to slow him back to a walk again.**

PULLS ON REINS/ROOTS/GRABS AT BIT/TOSSES HEAD

Many hyper or nervous horses are constantly trying to go faster. If you restrain them with bit pressure when they want to hurry home, or when they are following another horse and are impatient to catch up, their reaction is to pull at the bit—rooting or grabbing or tossing their heads in an attempt to get some slack in your tight reins. Some horses continually toss their heads and jerk on the reins, even when they are walking at the proper speed.

How to Change This Habit

A horse that continually roots or tosses his head may have a physical problem, such as a sore mouth. His teeth, gums, and tongue should be checked for potential causes of discomfort or pain, particularly when he has a bit in his mouth. Make sure the bit fits properly and does not bump or pinch his mouth. The headstall should be adjusted correctly so the bit doesn't clank his teeth (too loose) or rub the corners of his mouth (too tight).

Head tossing may be a sign of discomfort or annoyance if the rider continually bumps the horse in the mouth or keeps the reins too tight. The horse will protest such poor riding skills and try to alleviate discomfort or get more slack in the reins by grabbing at the bit and rooting. Check your riding technique to be sure you are not an inconsiderate rider, inadvertently causing pain and annoyance with inconsistent or too strong contact.

» **The horse will try to alleviate discomfort or get more slack in the reins by grabbing at the bit and rooting.**

Remember that it always takes two to have a tug of war. The reaction of many riders when mounted on a nervous, jumpy, or hyper horse that pulls and roots at the bit is to jerk on the horse's mouth or maintain strong contact with the reins in an attempt to restrain the horse. This merely makes the horse more upset and more determined to try to get some slack in the reins as he tries to escape the bit pressure.

The way to resolve a head tossing problem is to give the horse *more* slack, *not* less. Most head tossers develop the habit because their riders are always using a tight rein or bumping them in the mouth. Instead, you need to have gentle hands—and never use a steady pull—and improve all your cues so you are communicating through leg pressure, weight shifts, and body language—not just the bit.

Use a very gentle give-and-take action with the reins when you need to slow or stop the horse, or regain control. Use just a squeeze of your fingers and/or a slight wrist action for a light touch, rather than pulling backward with your arms. Keep the reins a bit slack all the time *except* when you are gently giving and taking to check his speed. This way the horse has nothing to pull against and will eventually stop fighting you. Whenever you do have to "check" the horse with the reins, immediately give him some slack again. If you never give him a set, fixed bit to pull against, he won't toss his head or root.

PROBLEMS
WITH TOO MUCH
ENERGY

What If Nothing Works?

If the horse has a chronic physical problem that makes it painful or irritating to carry a bit, or if the head tossing habit is so ingrained that you can't retrain him with gentler cues, use a bitless bridle or hackamore. This will usually halt head tossing because it eliminates the reason for it: The horse worrying about his mouth. But remember, you should not give a steady pull on a bitless bridle or hackamore, either, or he can learn to brace against it and continue the tug of war you are trying so hard to end.

PUTS TONGUE OVER BIT

Some horses get their tongue over the bit because they like to play with the bit. Others quickly learn that by putting their tongue over the bit they can thwart proper bit action and avoid rider control.

How to Change This Habit

First make sure the bit and bridle fit the horse and are adjusted properly (see Problems with Tacking Up, pp. 110, 112, and 115). A bit that hangs too low in the mouth makes it easy for a horse to put his tongue over it. When the bridle doesn't seem to adjust high enough to keep him from putting his tongue over the bit without becoming too tight, the bit may be too narrow.

>> **A bit that hangs too low in the horse's mouth makes it easy for him to put his tongue over it.**

Some horses, just by the way their mouths and tongues are conformed, are very dexterous with their tongues and can put their tongues over the bit in a properly fitted bit/bridle. For these individuals, a snug noseband (fairly low on the nose but high enough so it doesn't interfere with the horse's breathing) can help keep the horse's mouth closed, making it more difficult for him to put his tongue over the bit.

If you are using a curb bit, you can change to a bit with a higher port. The port takes up more room in the mouth and makes it a little harder (and more uncomfortable) to put the tongue over the bit. Keep in mind, however, that a higher port makes the bit more se-vere. You should be an experienced rider with steady, gentle hands, and even then must be careful how you use it. (You should use a gentle touch with *any* bit, since the actual severity of a bit lies more in the rider's hands than in the construction of the bit.) A really good rider can keep a light touch and never hurt the horse's mouth while using the severest of curbs, while a poor rider may severely injure or ruin a horse's mouth with the mildest of snaffles.

> » **The actual severity of a bit lies more in the rider's hands than in the construction of the bit.**

PROBLEMS
WITH TOO MUCH
ENERGY

RUNS AWAY/BOLTS

A horse that tries to run home or bolt may be insecure and inexperienced, or he may have become hard-mouthed and spoiled, discovering at some point that he is stronger than his rider and can take advantage of that.

How to Change This Habit

Lack of response to bit pressure is a sign of a communication gap between horse and rider. If the horse is green, go back to basics and do a lot of groundwork and work with voice cues before you ride him again.

While working with the horse on the ground, put his bridle on over his halter. When you lead him, ask for turns and changes of direction with the reins as well as with the lead rope. Use this combination of bit and halter pressure when you ask him to slow or stop, so that part of the control is with the halter. This retraining will teach him to pay attention to your cues to stop and turn when you get back in the saddle.

Drive the horse in long lines in a round pen until he responds properly to signals to slow, stop, and turn both ways You can long line the horse using a snaffle bit or a small-diameter rope halter if you want to avoid pulling on his mouth—the latter is often the best choice to keep the horse's mouth "fresh."

>> **Retrain the horse with groundwork that teaches him to pay attention to your cues to stop and turn—it will go a long way when you get back in the saddle.**

When riding, use a halter under the bridle. Snap an extra set of reins to the side rings of the halter (or at the sides of a rope halter) so you can guide him and slow him with pressure on the halter as well as the bit. Note: A rope halter works better than a nylon/web halter because the horse can't feel varying degrees of pressure as well through wide webbing. In all your cues to turn, slow, or stop, put pressure on the halter (in short, sharp, give-and-take pulls) as well as with a light signal on the bit. This helps save his mouth if he wants to ignore your cues and go too fast, while giving extra control to help him make the transition from cues via the halter to cues given through the bit.

If a horse bolts just once—for example, because something frightened him—don't punish him. Pull him around in a circle and stop him. If the situation or object he's afraid of is something he'll have to encounter again (such as a truck on the highway or a bird flying up under his feet) gradually reintroduce him to this scary thing under different and controlled circumstances. Spend some time getting him used to traffic and startling movements. Reassure him and prepare him for future situations with patient training lessons.

If you ride your horse in a snaffle, you may need to consider a bit with stronger effects. Many horses that ignore a snaffle when they've bolted or are running out of control will respond to the greater leverage and additional pressure points offered by a mild Pelham (English riders) or curb bit (Western riders). This does not mean the rider must use such a bit harshly—quite the opposite. You want the horse's mouth to remain light and sensitive, so your rein aids must be light and sensitive—but you'll have the benefits of the stronger bit *should* you need the extra control. Seek guidance in choosing a different bit from an experienced rider or trainer. *And remember, the stronger the bit, the lighter your hands need to be to preserve the horse's mouth.*

> **PROBLEMS WITH TOO MUCH ENERGY**

» **Learn how to stop the horse when he bolts. You don't want his habit for mindless flight to put you in a dangerous situation.**

If a horse makes a habit of bolting, learn how to stop him. Even if he is truly frightened of something, you don't want his mindless flight to put you in a dangerous situation—you need to remain in control.

• When he starts to run, *do not* pull back on the reins, since this merely gives him a chance to set his jaw or take the bit in his teeth and pull against you. Use one rein and quickly pull the horse's head around to that side with a swift action—you need to move quickly before he can set his jaw and neck muscles.

• At the same time bend the horse's body into the turn as you make him circle. The last thing you want him doing is running blindly forward with his head pulled to the side.

- After you get him on a circle, make the circles smaller and smaller until you can stop him.

- If the horse already has the bit in his teeth, take one rein in both hands, reach well forward on it, and give a series of quick, strong pulls to bring his head around. If it's easier, you can brace yourself on the saddle with one hand and use the other to reach forward on the rein and pull him sharply around.

- Another method that works if you can't stop him any other way is to take a firm, short grip on one rein, reaching toward the bit, low along the horse's neck. Bring the opposite rein over his neck and lean all your weight on it. This combination raises the horse's head/mouth so he can't run as fast. The action is hard on his mouth so should only be used in an emergency, but if necessary, it can save you from a serious accident.

To thwart a bolting habit, ride the horse more. Spend several hours a day riding in open country—travel miles and miles. Ride in areas where open space makes it possible for you to pull him in a circle if he does bolt—avoid narrow tree-lined trails or a road between fenced pastures, for instance.

Riding for extended distances cross-country not only gets the horse more used to potentially spooky objects and scenarios, it also tends to take the edge off his desire to run away. Many miles at the walk and trot tire him out and settle his mind so he's less inclined to think up excuses to run.

If the horse does try to bolt, make him circle and put him to work. Canter or lope him in a circle until he gets a little tired, then make him do the same thing in the other direction. Continue making canter circles until he is quite willing to stop when you ask him to stop. If every time he bolts he finds himself in the middle of an intense work session, he may change his mind about wanting to run.

» Traveling many miles at the walk and trot tires the horse out and settles his mind so he's less inclined to think up excuses to run.

Be consistent in always having the horse *walk* home, even if it means taking lots of side trips and doing extra work along the way (circles and other schooling exercises to take his mind off being in a hurry). Never let *any* horse gallop home; always make him walk the last mile so he won't get to thinking running for home is acceptable.

What If Nothing Works?

If you can't stop the horse adequately with a bridle, even after making an effort to retrain the horse and refine your horsemanship, you may have to switch to a hackamore, bitless bridle, or side-pull. With a hackamore, for instance, you generally travel on a loose rein so the horse doesn't have anything to lean into or pull on. Then you can get his attention if he bolts by quickly and suddenly pulling his head to one side and spinning him in a circle. He can't brace against this kind of unexpected action, so you are able to effectively halt his runaway flight without using his mouth. (The pressure points on most hackamores, bitless bridles, and side-pulls are on the chin, nose and poll.)

If the horse still bolts, you need a professional trainer to help deal with the bad habit or a new horse.

PROBLEMS WITH TOO MUCH ENERGY

Problems with Maneuverability

BULGES OUT

Some horses don't follow their heads around a turn and insist on "bulging out" with their barrel and hindquarters. This is generally a training problem due to an inconsistent rider.

How to Change This Habit

SOLUTION 1 Spend more time doing schooling exercises that involve turns in both directions. Be consistent in your rein, leg, and seat cues.

SOLUTION 2 Remember that horses tend to *move away* from pressure. If the horse is bulging out, he may be trying to move away from pressure you are inadvertently putting on his "outside" (the side facing away from the center of the arena). This pressure may come from your leg, seat, or rein on that side. Make sure you are properly coordinating your cues when traveling curves and making turns.

SOLUTION 3 If the horse continues to "lose" his hindquarters in the turn, use your leg on the outside more strongly: Work to "hold" his hindquarters in place as you make the turn.

» Make sure you are properly coordinating your cues when traveling curves and making turns.

What If Nothing Works?

Get some help from a more experienced rider or trainer.

LEANS IN/FALLS IN ON TURNS

This problem is similar to cutting corners (see p. 170). The horse refuses to stay out on the circle or turn and wants to lean too much to the inside (toward the center of the arena or circle) or "take a shortcut."

How to Change This Habit

Be consistent with your leg, seat, and rein cues so the horse knows he should travel straight between your legs on the path of the circle.

Use your inside leg (closer to the center of the arena or circle) more strongly, if necessary, to "hold" his body out in the circle.

If he doesn't pay attention to your leg and you have a secure seat, wear spurs and use a touch from the spur when necessary to give him a reminder not to get lazy with his position during a turn. Never overuse spurs; they are meant to be merely an aid in communication and not a form of punishment. When used appropriately, they can often help an inattentive or stubborn horse remember to "pay attention" to your cue, or remind him to respond to a leg cue quickly and crisply. Spurs can help you cue the horse with more precision— especially if he's become lazy and inattentive to your leg signals. A "tickle" with the spur with your inside leg when the horse starts leaning can be very effective in changing his habits.

PROBLEMS WITH
MANEUVERABILITY

What If Nothing Works?

If you continue to have trouble with leaning in, seek help from an experienced rider or trainer.

"RUBBERNECKS"/WON'T NECK REIN

Some horses won't respond to your cue to turn and have learned they can avoid it by turning their head but not their body. Even though you are turning their head to the left or to the right, they continue on straight ahead. This can be a dangerous habit because you are not in control of their movements.

How to Change This Habit

This may be a training problem (the horse has not yet learned how to *direct rein* or *neck rein* properly) or may be a sign of a spoiled horse that has learned how to avoid rider control. In either case, the best solution is to go back to basics to teach the horse to respond to rein cues on the bit and/or to neck rein properly.

When the problem is a green horse that hasn't learned to respond properly to rein cues, go back to basics and long line him, or work him with a halter and extra set of reins (see p. 196 for more on this technique).

Check your riding technique. Turns and curves involve leg and seat aids as well as rein aids. You may not be applying support aids when you direct rein, or you may be neck reining incorrectly.

• When asking for the horse to bend his body around a turn while using a direct rein, apply a little bit of inside leg at the girth or cinch and slightly more outside leg just behind the girth, shifting your weight to help encourage the horse's body to follow the direction of your rein cue.

- When asking the horse to turn using a neck rein, hold the reins in one hand, above his neck. Press the *indirect* rein (the rein on the outside of the turn) against the side of his neck to "push" his neck in the direction you want him to turn. At the same time use your body language to encourage his body to turn in that direction, too: Lean slightly into the turn and press your outside leg against his barrel.

In either case (direct rein or neck rein), if the horse is responding by moving his neck and head but not following with his body, you are not giving him enough incentive with your outside leg or your weight shift. Lean a little more into the turn and squeeze sharply with your outside leg (or use a touch of the spur if you wear them) to encourage him to move away from your outside leg pressure.

Cues for changes of direction should *always* be given with leg and body signals as well as the reins because this makes it easier for the horse to understand what you want while making it more diffi-cult for an uncooperative horse to avoid your request.

PROBLEMS WITH MANEUVERABILITY

What If Nothing Works?

If you continue to have difficulty, seek help from an experienced rider or trainer.

RUBS RIDER'S LEG AGAINST RAIL/ WALL/TREES

A horse that brushes your leg against the fence rail or moves too close to the trees along the trail is either inexperienced and oblivious to leg aids or has no respect and consideration for the rider. This habit can be very hard on knees!

How to Change This Habit

You need to either teach (for the first time) or refresh some lessons in maneuverability and responsiveness to leg cues. A horse that drifts too close to the rail or a tree needs to learn to move away from leg pressure so that when you squeeze with your leg he readily moves over, *away* from it. Set up some practice sessions in the ring or arena, using a simple pattern of cones or milk jugs half filled with sand, and ride the horse around and through these obstacles. Work on smooth turns and keeping the horse's body exactly where you want it by using a combination of rein, leg, and seat signals. After he becomes more responsive to your legs you will have more control over all of his movements, and it won't be a problem to keep him from "drifting" too close to the rail in the ring or trees on the trail.

Spend some time on *lateral work*, and teach the horse to move sideways in either direction with leg and rein cues. Teach him to *side-pass* (moving directly sideways, crossing both front and hind legs) and to walk on *two tracks* (moving sideways while still travel-ing forward). To help him get the idea, gently "check" him with the bit so he knows he is not supposed to go forward (or should move forward only very slowly) while at the same time pressing with one leg and encouraging the horse to move away from it. When he takes a step sideways, encourage and praise him so he knows he has done the correct thing. With practice he will become much more maneuverable in response to your leg and rein cues.

If a horse is particularly spoiled, stubborn, and unresponsive to your leg use spurs as an aid to reinforce your leg cues and encourage him to move away from pressure. You should have a secure riding position and quiet leg before you use spurs.

Groundwork can teach the horse to move over in response to pres-sure. Work on having him learn the turn on the forehand by holding his head and front end in place with the halter and asking him to move his hindquarters over when you press on his barrel with your hand or fist. Ask for one step at a time, and praise him when he responds correctly.

What If Nothing Works?

If the horse is so insistent on rubbing you against trees and fences that it becomes a real safety concern, you need help from a professional trainer, or you need a new horse.

TRAVELS CROOKEDLY

Like many of the bad habits in this section, this is usually the result of improper training or acquired sloppiness when a horse discovers that he can get away with being imprecise in his movements.

PROBLEMS WITH MANEUVERABILITY

How to Change This Habit

If the horse traveled straight in earlier ridden work but is now traveling crooked, you need to rule out a physical problem. Some neurological diseases can interfere with proper balance and coordination and one of the first signs of trouble may be inability to travel straight. In addition, mild lameness or stiffness that might be difficult to spot can manifest itself in the horse becoming crooked.

» **Some neurological diseases can interfere with proper balance and coordination.**

Examine your riding techniques to make sure you are sitting evenly in the saddle and are giving proper and easily understood cues (and not mixed signals) to the horse. If the horse is not getting consistent direction from you he may get into the habit of being sloppy, lazy, or imprecise in his movements.

SOLUTION 3 If the horse is still green or has become "ho-hum" in his movements due to a training/rider problem, go back to basics and work on lessons in maneuverability and response to leg and rein cues. Be consistent in your aids. Request that the horse travel straight, on both straight lines and curved ones (his hind feet should follow the tracks of his front feet, whether he's traveling down a road or trotting circles in the arena). Use your leg and rein aids in perfect synchronization; use one leg more than the other any time the horse veers too much in that direction. Make him work crisply and on the bit, with a little more collection (see p. 186). You'll have more precise control of his movements when he is collected.

» **You'll have more precise control of the horse's movements when he is collected.**

What If Nothing Works?

If you continue to have trouble with a crooked horse, get help from a more experienced rider or trainer.

TRIES TO GRAZE

Many horses try to grab a bite of grass as you go along the trail or beside the road. Some are so set in this habit that they hardly pay attention to where they're going and what they're doing—reaching for grass when they should be concentrating on something else. They may also try to pull the reins out of your hands to get to a snack. This can be a dangerous habit if the horse is paying more attention to his foraging than to where he's putting his feet.

How to Change This Habit

Most horses will push you as far as they can. They'll try to do as much of what they want to do, that they *can* do—or in other words, *as much as you let them get away with*. A horse with a grazing habit was allowed to grab at grass while being ridden once or twice, and now he thinks he can do it all the time. Many "grass grabbers" have been ridden by children who were not strong enough to keep them from reaching down for a bite, or by inconsistent, sloppy riders.

The best way to change this habit is to be totally consistent when riding the horse, *never* allowing him to eat while you are on him. The only way to do this is to always pay attention. Ride with the horse somewhat collected so you have better control of his actions and can keep his head in a correct position. Sadly, you can't ride on such a loose rein that he can do as he pleases.

» **Many "grass grabbers" have been ridden by children who were not strong enough to keep them from reaching down for a bite.**

PROBLEMS WITH MANEUVERABILITY

If your horse is quite strong and it's difficult to keep his head up when walking through a grassy area, you may have to change bits just until you break this habit. It's not as easy to keep a horse's head up if he's wearing a snaffle as it is when he's wearing a curb. The curb gives you more leverage and the action of the curb chain/strap against his chin tends to make him lift his head.

What If Nothing Works?

Ride in a Western saddle and leave the horse's halter under the bridle. Tie or loop the lead rope over the horn of the saddle, giving the horse just enough slack for freedom of his head and neck during regular movement and ordinary riding maneuvers, but not so much that he can graze.

TRIES TO GRAB TREES/BRUSH ALONG TRAIL

This is the annoying habit where the horse grabs at anything edible within his reach, so even if you are able to keep his head up so he can't grab for grass (see p. 206) you are still fighting to keep him from snacking on foliage.

How to Change This Habit

Try to ride more actively, rather than passively, meaning that you are always thinking ahead to what the horse might do, and are prepared for his actions. This bad habit develops because a rider lets the horse get away with it. In order to change his behavior, you have to impress upon him that it is not acceptable. If you are paying attention and anticipating him you have a lot better chance of controlling this habit.

Keep the horse collected (see p. 186) as this gives you better control over all his actions. Collection requires working on more precision and coordination of your rein and body cues. When riding through brush, trees, or tall grass where the horse can easily grab without lowering his head, keep him actively gathered between your leg and rein cues so he is "on the bit" and paying complete attention to you. This is just one more instance in which you need to polish and fine-tune your communication with the horse. After he becomes better trained and is listening to you, he won't try so hard to grab at trees and brush as he passes by them.

What If Nothing Works?

The horse may be stubborn enough to still try for a snack along the trail, but a good rider can keep him from grabbing at trees and brush by anticipating his movements and keeping him busy. If you can't control him, maybe someone else can. Find an experienced rider or trainer to work with him, or just resign yourself to his occasionally grabbing a bite to eat along the trail.

Problems Riding with or without Other Horses

AGGRESSIVE TOWARD OTHER HORSES

Some horses are "grouchy" when ridden in the company of other horses, or actively aggressive if another horse gets too close in the arena or on the trail. This aggression may take the form of threatening (pinned ears), biting or kicking, for example.

Mares are more likely to be "witchy" around other horses, especially at certain phases of their estrous cycle, but there are also a few geldings who show aggression under saddle. Sometimes it's just a "personal thing" with certain individuals: Your horse may tolerate some horses but take a dislike to others. When riding next to the horse your horse does not like, he may put his ears back or even try to reach over and bite. Or if another horse (particularly one that's not liked) comes up behind your horse, a kick out may result.

How to Change This Habit

SOLUTION 1 Know your horse and be prepared for aggressive actions when riding in company. Always be aware of the proximity of other horses so as not to be caught off guard. You don't want your horse to show bad manners, but you especially don't want another horse or rider injured by your horse. Riders can suffer a broken leg or worse when another horse kicks at their horse.

It is your responsibility to keep good control of your horse and prevent him from biting or kicking at another horse and rider. Maintain a manageable length of rein: Don't ride on such a loose rein that the horse can reach over and bite whoever is next to you. Control your horse's hindquarters with your legs and body language and don't let him get into a position where he can kick. Always warn riders behind you to avoid crowding your horse too closely.

If your horse is behaving aggressively because he is not accustomed to riding with other horses and is feeling insecure (his behavior is a defensive self-preservation tactic), ride more with other people. At first, however, have them keep a little more distance between their horses and yours until your horse can become more used to riding in a group and realizes the other horses are not a threat.

>> **When riding in a group, keep a little distance between other horses and yours until your horse can become more used to the scenario.**

What If Nothing Works?

Some horses, due to their personality, disposition, or hormones, will always be grumpy or aggressive around other horses. When in the saddle, you can usually control the horse's head actions and keep him from biting another horse, but it's not always easy to prevent kicking. When riding in company, always tie a red ribbon in your horse's tail as a reminder to other riders not to "tailgate" (a red ribbon in the tail is a common symbol that the horse will kick).

If your mare gets "witchy" when she's in heat (or coming into or going out of heat), and you ride a lot with other horsemen or are trying to compete in events in which she must be around a lot of other horses, you might consider hormone therapy to keep her out of heat during the showing or riding season.

BARN SOUR/RUSHES HOME

Some horses become "barn sour" because every time they are ridden they are required to work hard or repeat extensive lessons—they soon realize they'd rather be in their stall or pen than ridden in the arena or on the trail. Others are reluctant to leave the barn (or are constantly trying to turn back toward it) because they are insecure and want to stay in a familiar environment. When taken on a trail ride, they might quicken their speed (even to the point of bolting—see p. 195) when you do turn toward home. Whatever the reason for this habit, it is very frustrating because the horse is always focused on trying to get back to the barn rather than paying attention to the rider and her/his aids.

How to Change This Habit

If the horse is barn sour because he equates being ridden with unpleasant or uncomfortable experiences and lots of hard work, take him out of his stall every day (or several times a day, if possible) just to do something pleasant, interesting, and fairly easy. Change his mind by making each outing enjoyable. Go for frequent short rides near the barn or paddock, without bothering with a long training lesson or hard workout. Ride him to a grassy meadow and get off for a while and let him graze. Talk or sing as you ride to keep him relaxed, and stop every now and then (both going and coming) to give him a break and remind him to stand quietly. Use obstacles and cones when riding in the ring to give him a new challenge and freshen the environment.

If every time you ride the horse you immediately unsaddle him and put him away as soon as you get back to the barn, he is rewarded for rushing home (he gets back to his stall/feed/buddies). You are helping perpetuate his pattern. Make a habit of doing more with the horse at the "end" of your ride so you can keep him guessing about when he's actually going to be "done" and put back in his stall or pen. Ride back to the barn, then leave again. Make short loops around the area or practice easy schooling exercises until he begins to relax. Don't get off and put him away until he is quiet and focused on you.

» **Make a habit of doing more with the horse at the "end" of your ride so you can keep him guessing about when he's actually going to be "done."**

Along the lines of Solution 2, always go a little ways past home when you return from a trail ride, or ride back and forth past the driveway or entrance to the barnyard a few times so he knows he isn't going to be put away immediately each time he comes home.

After returning from a ride, tie your horse in a safe place in the barnyard for a while before you put him away. He should not be rewarded for hurrying home; he should stand tied for a period of time before he actually gets to go back to his stall or his pasturemates.

When going out on the trail, accompany another rider on a calm (*not* barn sour) horse. If your insecure horse has a level-headed buddy to be with, he will be less frantic about leaving his familiar environment and more controllable on the way home. Ride every day, so he gets into the routine of going away from home and coming back without becoming worried and anxious. Work on getting him to relax and walk on the way home, whether he's in front of or behind the other horse. Eventually the pattern of good behavior will pay off, and you won't need the other horse for security, especially if you are riding daily.

» **Work on getting the horse to relax and walk on the way home, whether he's in front of or behind another horse.**

Plan for some patient retraining:

- Take many short trips away from the barnyard instead of one long ride in which you have to fight with him.

- Make your daily ride a number of loops around the barn and paddock area, rather than going to the ring or out on the trail. You can create a fairly long ride without actually going very far away from his stall or paddock.

- Use advance and retreat: Start down a road or trail, and turn around and come back again *before* the horse gets very upset. As soon as you are back to the barn, leave again in another direction. Keep making side trips in all directions, and end the ride only after the horse is walking calmly away from the barn, and coming calmly back. Gradually increase the length of your side trips, and ride your various options and directions in a different sequence each day so the horse won't be able to tell where he's going next (or which side trip will be the last one that ends up at home). *You* must be the one who decides when the ride is over—keep him guessing.

Work on achieving a relaxed and consistent walk. First, always stay relaxed yourself. Alternate walking and trotting while on your ride, and if the horse absolutely won't settle down and walk (either when heading out or heading home), make him trot (but don't let him gallop). Do some extended trot sessions to make him work a bit and take the edge off his eagerness, then follow it with a relaxed walk. Try for longer and longer walking intervals between trotting sessions. Do this in all directions during your ride.

When returning from a trail ride, always make the horse walk the last quarter-to-half-mile home, and *do not* bend this rule. The horse should never be allowed to approach his barnyard or come down your lane or driveway at any gait faster than a walk. If he won't walk the last half mile home, circle or spin him a few times, or head him back in the opposite direction at a trot until he settles down. Every time he tries to speed up, jig, or prance, turn him away again until he realizes the only way he can get home is walking on a loose rein (see also p. 187). If necessary, do some loops, figure eights, and serpentines in the road so that he has to concentrate on something else. Sing, hum, or talk to him to keep his mind occupied and focused on you.

What If Nothing Works?

If your barn sour horse tries to bolt back to the barn, spin him in a tight circle. This will slow him back to a walk and also keep him from rearing or bucking if he's so upset he can't contain himself. If he tries to throw another fit, spin him the other direction. Don't fight him. Trying to hold back an angry or frightened horse may incite him to try even harder to run home. A diversion like making him spin or circle is much more effective than punishment or pulling on him (see Runs Away/Bolts, p. 195).

BUDDY SOUR/HERDBOUND

Many hyper or nervous individuals are herdbound and insecure. They don't like being left alone. If your horse has always had other horses for company, he may throw a fit if his buddies leave him or if you try to take him on a ride by himself or ride him away from the group. Some buddy-sour horses are merely insecure and apprehensive when apart from other horses, while others become so frustrated and angry that they may rear, buck, bolt, or try other ways to thwart your control.

Even if you are riding in a group, the herdbound horse may become upset if he *thinks* he's being left behind: For example, if he can't walk quite as fast as the horse ahead of him, he becomes stressed or panics and wants to trot or charge forward to catch up. Or he may become frustrated at your insistence that he remain at a calm walk so he roots and lugs at the bit.

How to Change This Habit

Ride daily with one or two other riders as you try to get your horse over being herdbound. While riding with them, make your horse go a short ways from the other riders but continue to travel parallel to them. Gradually move farther away from them each day (or each ride), extending the distance as your horse becomes more controllable apart from them. Try these lessons in an arena at first, but work your way out to a wide open space in order to fully rehabilitate your horse.

Eventually you should be able to leave the other riders completely and meet up with them again at a chosen spot. While an insecure horse may never get over being nervous when he's apart from other horses (and may keep looking for his buddies when you're riding alone), with patient training he will become more calm and controllable.

» **Ride daily with one or two other riders as you try to get your horse over being herdbound.**

If your horse can't focus on what you want him to do because he's too focused on being with his buddies, try this lesson in an arena to help persuade him he doesn't have to be right next to other horses to be secure:

- Position another rider (on a calm, quiet horse) at one short end of the arena with his horse out a little way from the rail.

- Ride your horse away from the buddy horse toward the far end of the arena (the "buddy" stays where he is).

- As you get to the opposite end, let your horse turn and face the buddy horse. If your horse wants to go back to his buddy, allow him to do so, but make him walk if you can. Don't fight with him, however; jog if you must.

- When you get back to the other end of the arena, have your horse travel in brisk circles around the buddy horse, trotting and cantering. Go both directions and make him work—do not let him slow down until you ask him to.

- Ride him away from his buddy to the far end of the arena again and let your horse stop and stand still. Stay relaxed, and pat and praise him if he stands there quietly. If he'd rather go back to his buddy again, let him, but when you get there make him work in circles as you did before.

- Keep doing this exercise (going to the far end of the arena to let your horse stand and rest, and making him work hard each time he goes back to his buddy) until your horse starts to realize that the only time he gets to rest is when he's away from his buddy, when he has *you* for praise, comfort, and security.

- Once the horse can stay calm for a moment at the far end alone, ride him slowly back to the other horse and let him stand beside his buddy for a moment, then ride away again. Repeat.

- It may take several lessons, but eventually the horse will learn that he can be comfortable when he's not with the other horse. He'll find that he can listen to you and will start to trust you more, gaining a sense of security from you. Patience is always more productive than punishment, because the only way he'll get over his insecurity about being away from other horses is if he can trust *you*—and transfer his dependence from them to you.

» **With patience and practice, the horse will find that he can listen to you and will start to trust you more, gaining the sense of security he craves from you.**

For a horse that can't stand to be apart from other horses out on the trail and is frantic if he's a little ways behind, enlist the help of two other riders (on calm, sensible mounts) and ride with them in an open area or on a back country road that has room for riding side by side. Keep changing places with the other riders: Switch up who is in front, middle, and rear. Take turns having the front rider trot on ahead a short distance, then drop to a walk as the other two riders trot to catch up and pass. Continue switching places—alternating walking and trotting—for several miles.

At first you'll have to accommodate your insecure horse's phobia and tailor the distance that the lead horse goes on ahead to fit your horse's comfort level. Soon, however, you should be able to gradually increase those distances as he realizes the other horses are *not* leaving him and he becomes more manageable. If he insists on trotting to catch up with the horse ahead of him, don't fight with him—just keep asking him to walk. Release all pressure on the reins when he does walk, even if it's just for a moment. Try to stay relaxed yourself.

Continue training with your fellow riders and rotating positions throughout the ride, repeating the lesson daily until your horse becomes more comfortable with having his buddies farther and farther away.

What If Nothing Works?

If a horse is so emotionally insecure that he never gets over being more focused on other horses than on what you are doing with him, he won't be a good candidate for certain group sports and activities, such as some competitive arena events or endurance riding. With patient effort you can probably rehabilitate him enough to keep him under control (if not, you need help from a professional trainer or a new horse).

BULGES/RUNS TOWARD GATE

A similar problem to the barn sour or buddy sour horse (see pp. 211 and 214), and perhaps more common, is the horse that is too eager to leave the arena. This horse wants to avoid all the work being asked of him when he's in a riding arena and go back to his stall or herdmates.

This problem is usually caused by overworking the horse when he's in the arena (or unsettling his mind with too much fast work, competitive games, or drilling for speed events, like barrel racing or pole bending). The only way the horse knows he can avoid the physical and mental discomfort he experiences in the ring is to get *out* of it, and he becomes obsessed with the arena gate. He may run toward the gate, turn his head toward it, or drift toward it each time his activities in the arena bring him somewhat close by.

>> **Bulging at or rushing for the gate is usually caused by overworking the horse whenever he's in the arena.**

How to Change This Habit

First consider what you are doing with the horse in the arena, and spend some time doing something else: simple or relaxing tasks instead of fast or demanding work.

If bulging or drifting toward the gate has become a habit, and the horse is reluctant to go in directions that take him farther from the gate, change his mind by making it *more pleasant* at the far end of arena and *more work* near the gate. Make lots of circles and have him work hard schooling various movements when he's near the gate. Let him stand and relax when he's at the other end. If every time he approaches the gate he has to do more vigorous work (and he only gets to rest when he's far away from the gate), he'll eventually become less interested in being near the gate.

What If Nothing Works?

If none of your retraining tactics seem to help, let the horse live in the arena for several days. If that's not possible, turn him out in the arena for a few hours a day. When the horse is fed and watered in the arena, and he is free to move around the space as he likes, it becomes a familiar and secure place rather than one he feels threatened by.

PANICS WHEN RIDDEN ALONE

An insecure horse doesn't like working by himself, and the rider may not be able to accomplish much when he or she tries to ride him alone. This horse doesn't like to leave the security of his barn- and pasturemates. He whinnies and "screams," and continually tries to turn toward home through the entire ride. He may get so upset about not being home "right now" that he feels to the rider like he's about to explode. His antics can include: sticking his nose in the air; rooting at the bit (to try to get some slack in the reins so he can go faster); shaking his head; traveling sideways instead of remaining straight between your legs; and spooking at anything and everything in this nervous state of mind. His mind is *not* on his rider; he can only think about getting back to his buddies.

How to Change This Habit

SOLUTION 1

Horses are very emotional animals and when their sense of security is involved, it is impossible to "reason" with them. If the horse is "screaming" and whinnying because he's frantic without his buddies, stumbling all over himself in a panic to get home, firmness and/ or punishment won't help. It just convinces the horse that being "out here away from home" *is* a terrible thing, and he'll try all the harder to run back to his buddies. If YOU smack him every time he screams (as some riders do), it just makes him head shy or more jumpy and insecure. *Patience* is the key to dealing with this problem.

Try to find ways to build his trust and confidence in you, rather than fighting with him.

Like the barn sour horse (see p. 211), you must build gradually on his level of security when out alone with you. Take him on short rides, bring him back to the barn, and ride right back out again. Some horses will begin to relax when they realize they really are not far from home and other horses, and you can gradually extend the distance you travel.

» **When the horse's sense of security is threatened, it is impossible to "reason" with him.**

 Ride with a friend on a quiet, calm mount for a while. Go miles and miles cross-country together, and get the horse settled into a routine of daily rides. Once he is more accustomed to regular rides and has learned to pay attention to you (you've built rapport and trust), he may not be so insecure and frantic when you ride by yourself.

Note: Be prepared for insecurity again whenever the horse has had some time off. You may always need to ride with a buddy the first few rides in the spring, for instance, until the horse settles back into his work routine. He must transfer his trust and confidence from his herdmates to you before he can work in a calm and relaxed manner.

 Work on getting the horse to focus on you and pay attention to your cues rather than frantically trying to get back to his buddies. You need to establish a connection and communication with him so he always looks to you for direction. To get his mind back on you, give him lots to do: If you are in the arena, ask him to trot lots of big circles, do transitions between and within gaits, and negotiate changes in direction. Ride over ground poles and weave around barrels, cones, or jump standards. Do serpentines and figure eights the entire length of the ring and keep him guessing which direction he'll be going next. Occupy his mind to take the focus off his buddies.

» **Give the horse lots of schooling exercises to occupy his mind and take the focus off his buddies.**

SOLUTION 4

If you are out on the trail or riding cross-country and he's throwing a fit because he's alone, don't fight with him. Just trot him briskly for a while, but *don't* let him break into a canter. Trotting can help use up some of his nervous energy and is more calming to a horse than cantering or galloping because of the even cadence of the gait. If there's room to get off the trail, trot circles, or trot around rocks, bushes, or fallen branches. If there's an open meadow, trot all kinds of loops and go different directions. Use leg cues to bend him and both the direct and indirect rein so he has so much to think about, he doesn't have any leftover time or mental space to worry about missing his friends.

SOLUTION 5

One way to defuse the horse that can't be ridden alone is to turn him out separately from his buddies for a while. If he's been living in a paddock or pasture with herdmates, move him to a space of his own. *Do not* stop turning him out just to put him in a stall, though. That is like putting a person in solitary confinement. Intensive confinement is unnatural, especially for the horse accustomed to regular turnout, and likely to spawn other unwanted behaviors.

Instead, put the horse in a paddock with safe fencing, by himself, until he realizes he doesn't have to always be *with* another horse. This tactic works best if you can isolate him to some degree—he needs to be out of sight and sound of other horses. During this time, spend a lot of quality time with him so he comes to trust *you* as his herdmate and comes to depend on you. Convince him to stop looking for his horse buddies because *you* are his buddy.

» **Spend a lot of quality time with your horse so he comes to trust you as his herdmate and depend on you.**

What If Nothing Works?

Most horses will become more manageable and less emotional with a lot of patient work and riding, but there are a few that never seem to get over their panic when ridden alone. In the interests of safety you may always have to ride with a buddy when riding this particular horse out in wide open spaces. Be prepared to handle his behavior if he becomes panicked and works himself into an uncontrollable state—see my recommendations on pp. 187 and 211.

REFUSES TO ENTER ARENA/PEN

Some horses get burned out with arena work and try to avoid it by refusing to go through the gate into the training or competition area.

How to Change This Habit

If the horse starts refusing to go through the gate into the arena, it is a sign you've overdone his training or challenged him with too much too soon. Give him a change of pace and scenery: Ride him somewhere else for a while. Take him on relaxing cross-country rides. Let him try a different sport or activity, just for fun. Basically, he needs a vacation from serious training and competition until he gets over his mental burnout.

Don't punish the horse for balking at the gate or try to force him to go through it. This just reinforces his bad attitude (increasing his fear or apprehension) about going into the arena. Dismount and lead the horse through the gate, and don't make him work when he does go into the ring. Instead, turn around and lead him back out again. Spend several sessions just leading him in and out, so he discovers that sometimes he doesn't have to do *anything* when he's in the arena. He will eventually become more at ease with going through the gate.

Plan to do only "pleasant things" in the arena for a number of sessions: easy groundwork that's not too challenging or confrontational and some leisurely riding. If a horse has been overworked in the ring, and then punished and beaten at the gate and has a bad memory about it, regaining his trust and confidence will take time and patience.

Reinforce positive actions with rewards. Spend a lot of time near or at the gate doing nothing but petting and talking to the horse, gradually getting him closer to the gate, and then through it, in subsequent sessions. Give the horse a treat when he stands next to the gate, in the open gate, and when he goes through it calmly. He'll eventually realize that going through the gate results in good things—treats.

What If Nothing Works?

If the horse is so burned out that he doesn't want to go into the arena in spite of your retraining efforts, it's time for a new career. Retire him from serious training and arena competition and use him for something else, like trail riding—any activity where he can get out and work in less stressful conditions.

> » **When the horse is so burned out that he doesn't want to go into the arena in spite of your retraining efforts, it's time for him to have a new career.**

REFUSES TO LEAVE BARN/STABLE

Some horses are so insecure and paranoid about leaving home that they become angry and stubborn, throwing a fit if you try to leave the barnyard. The horse doesn't listen to his rider and may become dangerous, rearing, bucking, whirling, or running backward if you try to ride him away from the barn. When his actions are intimidating to the rider, it accentuates the problem because the rider may decide *not* to ride (and the horse "wins") or may ride the horse less often, which just reinforces the horse's determination to never leave home.

How to Change This Habit

Spend a lot of time working with the horse—patient sessions to make him realize that leaving his stall or paddock is not something to be feared or fought. *Do not* use force or punishment or you'll make the problem worse. The horse will be even more convinced that leaving his secure place is scary and terrible.

- Take the time to bring the horse out of his stall or paddock several times a day just to lead him, groom him, hand graze him, or do easy groundwork lessons in the barnyard—but don't ride him. If everything you do for a while is pleasant and without conflict, the horse will become more tolerant and trusting.

- Gradually increase his time and distance away from the stall or paddock.

- After he is at ease with being led farther and farther way, you can try riding him again, taking very short rides around the barnyard at first, until he gains confidence that you are not going to cause him distress.

- Ride farther and farther from the barn or paddock, making large circles around his comfort zone. If he starts to get nervous or upset, don't fight with him—just make the circles smaller and closer to home for a while until he regains confidence and relaxes.

- Begin to take very short rides away from the barn, but not so far he starts to panic. Halt when you are a short distance from the barn, and take his mind off his insecurity with a reward, such as dismounting and letting him graze along the road, or giving him a treat. This way he'll realize that pleasant things can happen when he's away from the barn. Increase the distance you ride away from the barn, then get off and give him his reward or hand graze him, then lead him home if necessary (if he loses confidence and gets insecure) until he gets to the point where you can halt him, relax for a little while, then ride home again.

- As with other similar bad habits (see pp. 211, 214, and 219), if the horse panics and throws a fit when you start home, make him halt and stand until he's calm again, or ride in small circles, figure eights, and serpentines to take his mind off his anger and frustration. Trot him, if necessary, to help wear him out. Make him work until he can settle down enough to listen to you.

PROBLEMS RIDING WITH OR WITHOUT OTHER HORSES

» **The "spoiled" horse that throws a fit because he thinks he can get out of work by refusing to leave home should not be rewarded for his bad behavior.**

SOLUTION
(2)

Make the horse work hard in his own barnyard. The "spoiled" horse that throws a fit because he thinks he can get out of work by refusing to leave home should *not* be rewarded for his bad behavior—and when a timid (or intimidated) rider decides to cancel the ride, that's exactly what happens. If he won't leave the barnyard, don't try to force him to leave. Instead, make him work hard—right there, as space allows—and ride figure eights, circles, and serpentines; practice backing up; do gait changes; walk and trot over poles on the ground; or create an obstacle course with barrels, cones, and other handy portable objects that you can weave around and through.

Keep the horse working steadily for a while, even when he'd rather rest, then ask him again to leave the stable area and head to the arena or down the road. If he still refuses, make him work hard again. When he does finally leave when you ask, just ride a short distance away, and then let him stop and rest. Come back to the barnyard, and head out again in another direction for a short ways.

Do this daily until the horse discovers that the only place he actually gets to stop and relax is when you've ridden him *away* from the barn. Eventually he'll be more willing to leave whenever you ask him.

What If Nothing Works?

Occasionally a horse is so mentally stressed and phobic that it's very difficult to convince him it's safe to leave his stall or familiar barnyard. If you can't make any progress in changing his mind with the solutions I offer here, you need help from a professional trainer or a new horse.

WANTS TO LEAD A GROUP

Many horses don't like being left behind when being ridden in a group. With some it's more of a competitive thing, however, than it is an insecurity issue. The competitive horse always wants to be in front. He is not happy following another horse and always tries to crowd or pass. Even if you are riding side by side, this horse may keep pushing ahead, perhaps trying to edge over and cut off the other horse in order to get ahead.

How to Change This Habit

Some horses are naturally very competitive (bred to run or race), and it's in their nature to try to be in front of other horses, even if they are just walking. You can't totally change the horse's nature, but you can work with him on paying attention to your cues and body language so he learns to remain at the gait speed you desire. Make a practice of having him follow other horses just as often as he's in the lead, working on his patience and manners so he comes to realize that his position in the line does not matter, but your directions do.

If you have access to a mechanical exercise device such as a "hot walker," in which a number of horses can be exercised at once on a circle, you can use it to help the horse become accustomed to having another horse "lead." A short daily session on the hot walker with several other horses (that are *always* in front of him) may help him realize he doesn't always have to be in front.

What If Nothing Works?

If your horse always wants to be in front when you are out riding with others, practice patience rather than letting yourself be frustrated. Don't resort to pulling on him. If necessary, just let your horse be in front to keep him happy.

Problems with Obstacles

REFUSES TO CROSS BRIDGES

The hollow sound of a wooden or metal bridge may be unnerving to some horses, and they might refuse to cross when confronted by one on the road or trail. If they get away with balking a few times, refusal to cross bridges becomes a bad habit.

How to Change This Habit

 First try to determine whether the horse is balking because he is truly afraid or inexperienced, or whether he is just being stubborn because he's learned he can get away with it. If the horse is refusing because he had earlier bad experiences related to bridge crossings (being kicked or whipped, for example), or he has gotten away with balking for some time, it may be harder to rehabilitate him than it is to reassure an inexperienced horse.

If you think the horse is afraid, make time for step-by-step lessons to give him confidence and reassure him that crossing this obstacle is nothing to be afraid of.

- Do a lot of groundwork in a familiar setting, such as the arena or his own paddock.

- Lead the horse over ground poles and around obstacles,

and polish his leading lessons so that he trusts and respects you, and leads willingly. Use a long whip (such as a dressage whip) to reach back and touch his hindquarters to encourage him to go forward if he's reluctant.

• Create a "model" bridge out of boards or a sheet of plywood on the ground (wooden materials should be thick enough to support the horse's weight without splintering or cracking), and practice leading the horse over it. It may take several sessions to dispel his fear, but ask for one step at a time, and reward him for every try with praise and release of pressure (stop tugging on the lead rope and/or tapping on his hindquarters with the whip if you are using one).

• When you have built trust through the previous steps, try a real bridge again, this time leading the horse across it several times.

• Once he realizes it's not that scary, you won't have any trouble riding him over it.

Have a friend on a calm and willing horse go first over the bridge, and encourage your horse to follow. Providing the lead of another horse often works because your horse will not want to be left behind. Ride back and forth over the bridge several times, following your friend, before asking your horse to go first.

It is important to know your horse: Coercion might work for a stubborn bluffer but might be very counterproductive with a timid, frightened horse. If you deem that firmness is in order, lead the horse across the bridge with a helper following, and have the helper tap the horse's hindquarters with a whip if the horse refuses to go forward. Lead him back and forth several times with your assistant to remind him he needs to pay attention to your cues until you feel the horse "change his mind" about refusing. Lead him across with the helper following at a distance to remind the horse that he can't get away with balking, then try riding him over it.

>> **It is important to know your horse: Coercion might work for a stubborn bluffer but might be very counterproductive with a timid, frightened horse.**

What If Nothing Works?

If you continue to have trouble crossing bridges with your horse, seek help from a professional trainer.

REFUSES TO CROSS DITCHES/GULLIES

Some horses are as fearful about crossing a dry gully as they are about walking through water. Usually this reluctance is due to inexperience (they've lived in a stall or paddock and have not had opportunity or reason to traverse varying terrain), or they have succeeded in refusing such crossings in the past and it is now a bad habit.

How to Change This Habit

 Go back to basics. Incorporate some lessons in ditch and gully crossing in your daily work with your horse. Find a ditch that is relatively easy to cross—where the bank is not too steep and the gully not too deep—and give him lots of time to approach it. Ride him across and back several times until he realizes it's not so scary. Note that it's usually best to stay mounted rather than try to lead a frightened horse across because he may leap the ditch and knock you down if you are on foot. You don't want the horse to try to jump it, and you have more control over his ability to do that if you are riding him than if you are leading him.

 If your horse continues to balk, ask another rider on a willing horse to ride through first. Have the other rider and horse cross the gully and wait for you on the other side where your horse can see them.

You don't want your horse to panic about being left behind and try to bolt through the gully or leap it.

If the horse stubbornly refuses but does not seem to be doing it out of fear, have a helper on horseback "pony" him through the ditch while you follow on foot from behind, giving light taps with a whip on his rump to encourage him to go forward. Go back and forth across the ditch several times to make sure he is now listening to you.

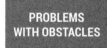

If the horse rushes through the gully, rather than calmly walking across, make him stop and stand for an instant before you start through. Try to keep him at a slow and controlled walk. Make him halt at the bottom of the ditch, and stand a moment so he doesn't charge up the other side, then ask him to walk calmly up out.

» **Try to keep the horse at a slow and controlled walk when going through a ditch.**

What If Nothing Works?

Get assistance from a more experienced horseman.

REFUSES TO CROSS WATER

This is a common problem with horses that grow up in stalls, paddocks, or small pastures without puddles or streams as part of their natural environment. Balking at water crossings may be due to lack of experience, but it can then become a habit if the rider has trouble making the horse go through. In addition, if the horse thinks water is a scary thing and every time he faces it he is kicked and whipped, he's only convinced it's more dangerous and tries even harder to get away from it.

How to Change This Habit

 Spend some lesson time working on getting the horse across a puddle or stream in a nonconfrontational setting, when you don't actually *have* to get across it.

- Start with groundwork, leading the horse around the barnyard or pasture the day after a rainstorm when there are puddles to walk through. If he tries to skirt around smaller puddles (seeing no reason to put his feet into them if he can go around), choose very large ones, or a shallow ditch that has accumulated water. (A gentle stream can work as well—just make sure it isn't too scary.)

- Lead the horse to the water, but don't force him any closer than is comfortable for him. Let him stand near the puddle or stream until he relaxes, realizing you are not trying to make him cross it. If there is grass near the water, let him graze. Take the next steps only as he becomes ready for them.

- If he's reluctant to come clear up to the edge of the puddle or stream, don't rush him. Come back again the next day and let him graze beside the water again and repeat until he doesn't pay much attention to it.

- If possible, bring the horse to a stream when he's thirsty. Be patient until he relaxes and decides to check out the water. He may sniff it or paw at it, then drink. Let him get comfortable with it.

- Once the horse knows the puddle or stream is "just water," encourage him to cross it. Hold out a treat (a handful of grass or a horse cookie) from the other side (don't be in his way, however, in case he decides to jump). If he steps across, immediately reward him with the treat and praise. Entice him back and forth a few times with more treats.

- Once he learns he can get his feet wet and go through water, start riding him through small puddles and streams.

Get the horse over a phobia about getting his feet wet by leading or riding him around in a field that is being irrigated or is a little flooded after a hard rain. If everywhere he goes is wet, he'll realize it isn't hurting him. After he can handle this, it will be easier to work on water crossings.

 Ride the horse along the edge of a shallow stream, without forcing him right up to it, and patiently wait for him to realize it isn't scary.

PROBLEMS WITH OBSTACLES

- Don't ask him to cross; just keep riding alongside it, or go a little ways away from the water and come back again, until he is relaxed.

- If he acts like he wants to drink from the stream, let him. Work on getting the horse closer and closer to putting his feet in the water, but turn and ride away again before he gets upset and tries to be the one who decides to leave.

- Have him face the stream, and do not put any pressure on him, as long as he's facing it. Use leg and rein cues to turn him back toward the water if he tries to turn away, but leave him alone and let him stand relaxed as long as he's facing it. Eventually most horses facing a stream in this way will step into the water without urging. If he does, let him stand in it or go on across. (If he backs out again, let him, and just bring him right back to facing the stream.)

- After he crosses, let him relax a moment on the other side (or ride a short distance if he's nervous), then come back across it again. Cross back and forth several times, building his confidence. With patience and persistence, the horse will be more willing to try to go across because you are not forcing him.

 If the horse insists on jumping over a narrow stream instead of calmly walking through it, spend some time riding through the widest spots of the stream so he won't be so afraid to put his feet into the water. Choose the spot with the most level and best footing, and approach it at an angle instead of straight on. This makes it more likely you'll be able to get him to walk through it rather than jump over it.

If you feel the horse preparing to jump, turn him away from the stream, ride away, and come back again at an angle, going slowly and calmly. Whenever he does jump, come right back and try to go through the stream again properly, crossing repeatedly in a more controlled fashion.

» **Ride through the widest spot of a stream to encourage the horse to walk through, rather than jump over.**

What If Nothing Works?

When you still have trouble with water crossings, get assistance from a more experienced horse trainer.

REFUSES TO JUMP

Balking at a jump is usually an escape tactic: The horse has been made to think jumping is unpleasant (by a rider who bumped him in the mouth or slammed down hard on his back or caused him pain or discomfort in some other way), or he is insecure about his ability to get over the obstacle. If he gets away with balking, however, his refusals may quickly become habit.

How to Change This Habit

First make sure there isn't a physical reason for his reluctance. If the horse jumped willingly before and suddenly "quits," he may have a subtle injury or source of discomfort or pain. Arthritis, a sore back or feet, or any other ailment are possible causes of a refusal to jump. If he has any physical issues, address those before asking him to jump again.

Consider that the horse may have been made afraid to jump because of sloppy riding, so make sure you are not causing him pain or discomfort when he jumps. Work on your technique, and rebuild his confidence without you on his back. Longe him over low jumps for a while, rather than riding him, if his refusal stems from a riding issue. Once you are more stable in the saddle and he is jumping willingly without you in the saddle, you can try riding over low jumps again.

PROBLEMS WITH OBSTACLES

"Start over" and reintroduce the horse to jumping. Take him over small obstacles that are well within his ability and confidence level. For example, walk, trot, and canter over poles on the ground, and then gradually raise them. The jumps should be very easy for him to hop over even if he is not in perfect position. Encouragement and praise will accomplish more than coercion and punishment. The horse needs time to regain his confidence.

The horse may refuse because he's been burned out by too much drilling over jumps, or he was asked to do more than he was ready for. When you suspect this is the case, give him some time off from jumping. Ride him every day in a nonconfrontational, non-training setting, such as cross-country and on the trail. After a period of relaxing, fun rides, go back to very low jumps (see Solution 3), and only school one or two before stopping and putting the horse away on a good note. Ride him regularly, but do only a few jumps now and then, gradually building up his willingness by doing easy ones until you sense he is ready to start increasing their height again.

It is important that you don't increase the height of the jumps beyond the horse's ability and confidence. Recognize his limitations. Don't push him beyond them or he will refuse again. One way to keep him jumping willingly is to always keep your practice jumps a little lower than what he can handle, working on having him do them correctly. Then on occasion you can ask a little more from him, without stressing and/or burning him out.

» Ride the horse regularly, but do only a few low jumps now and then, gradually building up his willingness.

SOLUTION 5

If the horse has gotten into the habit of trying to avoid a jump by running off to the side ("running out"), go back to lower, easier obstacles (see Solution 3), and just trot him over them slowly, but insisting that he go straight over them. Use your legs and reins to keep him facing the jump. Don't let him run out to one side: If he tries, sidepass back and forth in front of the jump, but keep him facing it. Don't turn him in a circle or let him go off to the side and then make a new approach. He needs to learn that there are no excuses or second tries—he must go over the jump the first time, even if he goes over it from a bad position.

This is why it is important to use very low jumps for the retraining lessons: The horse will eventually "hop" over a very low obstacle from a standstill, once he realizes he can't escape by running off to the side. If you are patient and persistent, he will find that it's actually easier to go over the jump as you approach it from a trot (or canter) than to refuse and have to jump from a standstill.

When the horse jumps properly, praise him and reward him by ending the lesson after one or two successful tries. Keep the jumps very low for a while, and you are well on the way to breaking his avoidance habit.

» The horse will eventually "hop" over a very low obstacle from a standstill, once he realizes he can't escape by running off to the side.

What If Nothing Works?

Assess your horse's jumping ability and attitude. Maybe you are asking something from him that's a little beyond him. If you only jump recreationally or on the trail as needed, choose other activities in the arena and go around natural obstacles when necessary. If you truly think your horse has talent as a jumper, however, and it's just a training problem, get help from a more experienced trainer.

REFUSES TO STEP OVER LOGS/TRAIL OBSTACLES

This habit usually begins because the rider did not take the time to acquaint the horse with different types of terrain before going out on the trail, or the rider did not have the skill or persistence to encourage the horse to go over different kinds of obstacles and the horse learned he could get away with refusal.

> » **Introduce the horse to different kinds of obstacles in an area that is familiar to the horse, such as the barnyard, riding ring, or the horse's own paddock.**

How to Change This Habit

 As is the case with many of the bad habits discussed in this book, you need to go back to basics. Start with an obstacle that is very easy and less confrontational than what you might run into riding across country. Do these lessons in an area that is familiar to the horse, such as the barnyard, riding ring, or the horse's own paddock.

- Start with very inconspicuous small objects, such as a broom handle or a garden hose. Lead the horse around the area in circles, getting progressively closer until you eventually ask him to step over the handle or hose. Many horses won't even think twice about it.

- Move on to something slightly larger, like a single ground pole, and lead him over it both directions.

- Once he handles that, lead him over a pole set up on short blocks (cavalletti) so he has to step higher to get over it.

- Once he leads over these kinds of obstacles, start riding him over them, again using the smallest ones first and gradually working up to the larger ones. If at any time he balks, go back to a previous step that you both know he can handle, and build his confidence again. Before long he will realize he *can* step over a log when asked.

If he is too suspicious of the smallest of obstacles, such as the broom or garden hose (see Solution 1) to step over, give him plenty of time to check it out and smell it before you try to lead him over it. Using advance-and-retreat methods (even allowing him to back up if he wants to, but leading him right back to the obstacle) may satisfy his suspicions, but if he's still leery, try bribery to take his mind off his fears. Bring him up close to the obstacle, but not so close that he "shuts down" his mind and balks. Let him eat a treat while he stands still for a moment, then ask for another step. A series of treats may distract him enough that he stops thinking so much about the scary thing he must step over, or may help him realize that it's not as dangerous as he thought.

A similar way to allay his fears is to lay the hose or broom handle in a grassy area and let him graze up to and around it. Take your time and judge when the timing is right to ask him to step over it, then let him graze again.

» **Treats may distract the horse enough that he stops thinking so much about the scary thing he must step over.**

If the horse is very stubborn and refusing because he's gotten away with it in the past, have a helper walk behind and to one side of him as you lead him up to the obstacle (start with the lowest, least scary one, and make sure it is quite long so the horse can't step around it). As you encourage him to step over it, have your assistant lightly tap his hindquarters with a whip. This usually provides enough encouragement to get him to hop on over the handle or hose. Reward him with a treat.

Once you and your helper have insisted he step over it a few times, and he has been rewarded for doing so, he will realize it's not such a big deal and will step over willingly. From there you can continue to progress with the lessons, using larger and larger obstacles, and eventually riding over them.

When you confront a log on the trail and you can't get the horse to step over it with you on his back, get off and lead him over it. Most horses will lead over an obstacle, even when they won't do it while mounted. Walk beside him over the log, *not* in front of him, or he may jump right into you if he decides to leap over the obstacle instead of step over it. If he still balks, reach back and tap his hindquarters to encourage him to step over it. If necessary, you can improvise and create a "training whip" out on the trail by breaking off a willow switch or dead branch.

When riding with others, have a rider on a calm and willing horse go over the log first. Your horse may then follow because he doesn't want to be left behind. Grab his mane or the horn or bucking strap, as he may decide to jump it, and you don't want to punish him for crossing by knocking him in the mouth or banging the saddle with your seat.

What If Nothing Works?

If even the smallest of obstacles continue to prove unapproachable, have a veterinarian give him a complete physical, checking for soundness issues, as well as his eyesight and/or the possibility of a neurological problem.

Under Saddle Vices

BALKS/SHIES AT LOUD NOISES

Most horses shy or spook at things that startle or alarm them (as an instinctive reaction to something that might threaten their safety), but others take this defensive tactic to the extreme and shy at anything. There are horses that are spooked by loud noises: a car backfiring, a flag snapping in the wind, a paper or plastic bag rustling, the popping and hissing sound of your can of soda as you open it after carrying it in your saddlebag. The horse's instinct is to run first and ask questions later—it isn't really a bad habit so much as it's a survival tactic. But riding these horses can be a challenge!

While many horses shy at something new and different, or at sudden movements or noises, they generally calm down and accept the cause(s) of the "spook" once they find out it's not going to hurt them. Others remain insecure for one reason or another, but often because of lack of trust in their rider or because they sense the rider is tense and nervous. And then there are smart horses that learn that they can avoid having to work by balking or shying, and taking advantage of a timid rider.

How to Change This Habit

Familiarize your horse with loud and strange noises in a noncon-frontational situation. Run a lawn mower, weed eater, or chain saw nearby while he's turned out in his paddock or pen. Start it some distance away and gradually bring it closer. Play loud music in the barn. Make a tape recording of loud noises like dogs barking, sirens wailing, gunfire, noisy trucks, motorcycles gunning their engines, and any other things you can think of that your horse might en-counter. Play the recording by his pen or stall—quietly at first and gradually turn up the volume. Hang a flag by his paddock and let it flap and snap in the wind. When you regularly and gradually desen-sitize your horse to sounds, they won't be alarming out on the trail or at a show.

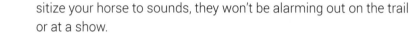

Create some situations in which you can encounter strange sounds while riding in a safe location. Have a friend start up and run the weed eater outside the riding ring while you are mounted. Ride along a pasture fence that borders the road and have a helper drive back and forth.

UNDER SADDLE
VICES

What If Nothing Works?

Lessons to desensitize a horse to loud/strange noises will always help him be a safer riding horse, but some horses always remain a little jumpy. When you are out riding, always be prepared for your horse to react in unexpected ways—and try to keep him calm by staying calm yourself.

BALKS/SHIES AT STRANGE OBJECTS IN PEN/ARENA

You don't have to be out on the trail for things to be "scary" to the horse. Any unusual object or item that appears suddenly, whether it be in his paddock or pen or the riding arena, may spook the horse: a plastic bag blowing and bouncing in the wind; someone's jacket left hanging on the fence; a jump left set up in the arena by previous users; bright light reflecting off a car window—you name it. Whether you ride primarily in the ring or on the trail, you may need to work on some "despooking" lessons if your horse is the nervous type who's suspicious of anything out of the ordinary.

How to Change This Habit

Sensory training is something you can do to help calm the horse and get him over his fear or his spooking habit. You don't need to take him out in the woods or over mountains to start these lessons—you can work on all these things first in his paddock or pen or the arena, and it all starts with groundwork.

"Bombproofing" lessons will help the horse learn to cope with strange or scary situations—whether close to home or out in the big wide world. Spread strange and "scary" objects around the stall, barnyard, paddock, and arena (horse blankets on the fence, flower pots, coiled hoses, garbage cans, stuffed animals—be creative!), and just spend some lesson time leading the horse around them, past them, and eventually up to them. Take whatever time is needed to patiently reassure him and make him feel comfortable touching and smelling the "scary" objects. Approach and stop, approach and retreat—whatever it takes to keep him from feeling pressured.

Start well away from the scary thing and gradually get closer, backing off when the horse gets nervous. Give him a chance to evaluate it from what he considers a "safe" distance.

Once you can lead the horse up to a series of scary objects, progress to mounted lessons: Ride the horse around, past, and up to the items you've spread around, still letting him stop and take a moment to check things out if he needs to. If you've taken the time to do the groundwork, it will be a lot easier to approach the objects when mounted.

» **"Bombproofing" lessons in the barnyard or arena will help the horse learn to cope with strange or scary situations.**

One of the easiest things to use as an aid in getting a horse over spookiness is a flag, small tarp, or a big plastic bag tied to a stick or the end of a dressage-type whip. It should be something that flaps and when it's moved around creates a lot of motion.

- The first step is to get the horse used to having the flag (or tarp or bag) touching and rubbing over his entire body and down his legs. Start out slowly so the flag doesn't flap at first.

- Once the horse realizes the flag is not going to hurt him, move it around him a little more briskly and from all directions. With the flag you can simulate something suddenly coming up behind him or from either side.

- Always do as much sensory conditioning on the right side of the horse as on the left; otherwise, the horse may accept something on one side but still spook at it on the other.

- When the horse is used to having you wave the flag around him in close proximity, have an assistant hold the horse and reassure him while you walk back and forth behind the horse with the flag: Start at least 20 feet behind the horse, and gradually move closer, but stay out of kicking range. Add more movement to the flag as the horse becomes relaxed and accepting, but remain in tune to how your horse is reacting. Don't start waving the flag until he's okay with you holding it still, and don't come closer until he's at ease with some distance away. Scaring him will only defeat your purpose. Spend as many sessions on this as necessary to build his confidence level. Eventually you should be able to wave and snap the flag rapidly while walking in a circle around him.

- Have your helper walk around the horse with the flag while you are mounted.

 Another way to desensitize a spooky horse is to throw a sack, tarp, or some other scary (but harmless) object into his pen or paddock (or a round pen works, as well—see Afraid of Blanket Removal, p. 88). This accomplishes two things: It allows you to gauge the horse's reaction to the sack so you can tell whether he is truly afraid of strange objects and how soon he gets over his fear when left on his own. This method also enables him to deal with the "scary thing" on his own terms, in his own time. Some horses will walk up to the scary object right away to cautiously check it out, while others will keep their distance or circle it a while before gaining confidence and coming close. (Note: Never leave a horse unattended for long periods of time with a sack or tarp loose in his pen, particularly if he is shod as a shoe could catch the material and drag it when the horse moves. He may also start chewing on it.)

» **Turning the horse out in his paddock with a small tarp or sack left on the ground can tell you whether he is truly afraid of strange objects and how soon he gets over his fear when left on his own.**

What If Nothing Works?

If you go about it properly, you can desensitize *most* horses to *most* "scary things." On rare occasion, however, you may encounter a horse that has a serious accident or bad experience in his past that left him with an ingrained phobia related to some particular thing. If that's the case, and he's "mentally scarred," figure out a way to live with it, but only if it's something you can avoid or control. If the horse "loses his mind" over something that you truly can't avoid, and/or he is dangerous, you need help from a professional trainer or a new horse.

BALKS/SHIES AT STRANGE OBJECTS ON TRAIL

We have discussed how many horses spook or balk at strange or startling objects they've never encountered before, but for some, the same "big rock" or "black stump that looks like a bear" that they pass on the trail every day is still cause for a fuss. And there are other horses that shy at anything and everything when heading out on the trail away from home, but then they completely ignore the same kinds of "scary things" when coming back home.

> » **There are horses that shy at anything and everything when heading out on the trail, away from home.**

UNDER SADDLE VICES

How to Change This Habit

First determine whether the horse's fear is "real" or "imagined." Handling a truly frightened horse takes a much different touch than dealing with a "bluffer" that is shying and balking just because he's full of high spirits or wants to see if he can get away with it. A timid horse needs a lot of patient reassurance and encouragement, and he needs to know he can put his trust and faith in *you* and accept *your* guidance and judgment. A bold bluffer, on the other hand, needs a firmer hand and leg to remind him that he needs to pay more attention to business and not use scary objects as an excuse to misbehave.

When encountering something on the trail that might alarm the horse, don't anticipate the worst. If you see something in the distance or ahead along the trail that might scare your horse, don't become tense—this just calls attention to it and also labels it as potentially dangerous. Your horse might not pay any attention to it if you don't. Horses don't think ahead to all the possible bad scenarios like humans do, and in many instances, *a spooky horse is the rider's fault.* Practice relaxing, taking deep breaths, and expelling your breath when dealing with a scary situation while on horseback. Expelled breath—like a big sigh—is a sign of relaxation. Think about it: When a horse relaxes, he sighs, and that's one way you know he's at ease with what's going on around him. And when the horse hears another horse (or you) give a big sigh, he relaxes, too.

» **In many instances, a spooky horse is the rider's fault.**

Prepare your horse ahead of time for some of the things he might see or encounter on the trail. Do groundwork and mounted work at home with a "scary" obstacle course in your barnyard or arena: Get him accustomed to walking over a tarp or a piece of old plywood; walking between sawhorses with rain slickers or tarps draped over them; going by balloons fastened to the fence—use your imagination. Enlist the help of friends to expose your horse to bicyclists, motorcycles, and someone carrying an open umbrella. Have a backpacking friend help you teach your horse about "monsters" he might meet on the trail: The bulky pack can make it hard for a horse to recognize it is just a human, so have your helper talk and sing so the horse can sort it out. (Note: And when you actually do meet backpackers or bicyclists out on the trail, call out to them from a distance and have them talk to your horse as they approach.)

Acquaint the horse with dogs of all kinds, especially barking dogs and those that run up to or behind him. When you encounter a barking, snarling dog along the road or trail, turn the horse around to face it. A horse is usually less afraid of (and less likely to bolt away from) something he can see in front of him. Don't move away from the dog if it is running at you, as the horse might want to run away and the dog could chase you, exacerbating the problem. Face the dog and ride toward it, instead. The dog is more apt to back off if you are coming at him.

If your horse is one of those individuals that is spooky when he leaves the barnyard at the start of a ride and no-nonsense on the way home, it may help to warm him up a little before you head out. Take some of the edge off his exuberance or nervous energy by longeing him or riding him around the arena a few times. After he's settled down a bit, he may not be as silly and jumpy when you leave home. A horse is usually more relaxed and less tense after he's warmed up and his muscles are no longer cold and stiff, and his mind has settled into his work routine.

UNDER SADDLE
VICES

When there's a particular "bugaboo"—something he *always* shies at (a certain rock or stump, for example)—take some time to let the horse check it out. Lead or ride him up to it, then lounge around by it as he has a chance to smell it, lick it, and graze around it. Do this for several days if necessary, until he loses his interest in spooking at it.

One of the most important despooking lessons you can do with your horse is to get him used to having something brushing against and/or "grabbing at" his legs. If you ever find yourself in a snarl of old wire out along the trail or in a pasture, the horse could freak out and panic—injuring himself or you. But, if he's used to having contact around his legs and feet, he will stay calmer in such a situation, which can make it possible for you to get off and extricate him.

Begin with groundwork, using a whip to touch him all over his body and then his legs until he accepts it as harmless. Follow this with a soft rope: Rub the rope all over his legs, then loop it around each one and pull on it. If the horse had a bad experience in wire in his past, this lesson will take longer (and require much patience). Some horses are so "goosey" after getting tangled in wire that they are forever jumpy when riding through low bushes that catch at or tickle their legs. It may take many sessions of patient work to get them over this, and many miles of riding through low brush.

>> **If the horse is used to having things come into contact with his legs and feet, he will stay calmer in potentially dangerous situations on the trail.**

What If Nothing Works?

Patient desensitizing will help, but as mentioned, it may not totally "despook" every horse. If your horse is an extremely sensitive and nervous individual, or if he had a bad experience at some point in his past, you may be able to defuse some of his phobias but not all of them. Know his weak spots, however, so you can work around them and deal with them, planning ahead to either avoid or minimize a serious spooking episode. Plan your rides for still, warm days (especially the first rides in the spring or after a layoff). Spooky, nervous horses will always be more jumpy on a windy, cold day when the air is brisk and everything is in motion around them.

BUCKS IN LEAD CHANGES

Bucking is a dangerous habit that should be halted as quickly as possible. I'll talk about three kinds of bucking on the following pages.

Many horses never try to buck when ridden, and never learn they can. Others are more "ticklish" and may buck once or twice when first saddled and ridden (especially if a trainer skips early groundwork and the horse is not very prepared for transitioning to a rider), but give it up after they find it doesn't gain anything and once they have become accustomed to the saddle. If, however, the green horse ever "dumps" his rider during this early training phase, he may learn that bucking puts *him* in control, and not the rider—and so he continues using it as an evasion tactic.

Some horses buck instantly and without thinking whenever they are startled or annoyed, and this can unseat an unsuspecting rider who is not prepared. Bucking may also be the horse's reaction to pain or irritation from ill-fitting tack. Mixed signals or irritating or confusing cues from the rider can also bring it on. The easiest gait from which a horse can start bucking is the canter/lope. Thus if the horse is not happy with how you ask for a change of lead, he may use it as an opportunity (or excuse) to buck.

>> **Bucking may be the horse's reaction to pain or irritation from ill-fitting tack.**

How to Change This Habit

Make sure there isn't a physical reason the horse might not want to change canter leads. If he is subtly favoring a leg or foot, for instance, he might resist changing to the lead that puts more weight and stress upon the sore one.

Examine your methods and cues for asking for a change of lead. If the horse doesn't understand or finds it difficult to respond properly, he may buck out of frustration. Refine your cues, or try using a slightly different cue that works better for that particular horse (see p. 175 for some ideas).

What If Nothing Works?

Retrain the lead change, going back to asking for a *simple change* of leads from a trot (see p. 181). If the horse still bucks whenever you ask for a *flying change*, get help from a professional trainer who can look at the problem and maybe determine the communication glitch between you and the horse.

BUCKS TO GET RID OF RIDER

Once a horse learns he can buck off a rider, he may try this tactic whenever he doesn't want to do something he's asked. This can quickly become a dangerous habit.

How to Change This Habit

 First make sure there is nothing annoying the horse, such as an ill-fitting saddle, girth, or bridle. Also make sure your riding techniques are not irritating him or causing him discomfort. You want to be sure you are not giving him an excuse to buck so you can work on changing his habit without working against yourself.

 Ride the horse daily and get him into the routine of steady work. Some horses are most prone to buck after they've had time off: They buck due to high spirits or just plain unwillingness to go back to work again. Many of these horses settle down and become more "honest" when working daily.

Avoid situations in which the horse might be likely to buck, especially when first putting him back to work after time off. A horse in high spirits with energy to burn may try to buck when cantering, for instance, so keep your first ride down to a walk or trot. Keep in mind that it's a lot easier for a horse to buck when heading downhill than uphill.

>> **Many horses settle down and become more "honest" when working daily.**

 Improve your riding skills so you are always in control and able to prevent the horse from bucking (or at least from bucking hard enough to throw you off). Constant contact with the horse's mouth, communicating continually with the bit and reins instead of riding on a slack rein, can usually help you thwart a hard buck since you can keep the horse from suddenly putting his head down. The horse has to be able to get his head down at least to the level of his knees in order to buck hard. If his neck is kept at or above the horizontal, he can still leap forward or sideways and kick out with his hind feet, but he can't get enough hump in his back to buck explosively.

SOLUTION 4
If your horse is a strong bucker and you are unsure about your ability to keep his head up in a snaffle bridle, a bit change can give you more control. English riders may find a mild Pelham effective in helping them prevent their horse from dropping his head to buck, and Western riders can transition to a mild curb—both put pressure on the poll and chin as well as the mouth. As mentioned earlier in this book, you must have "light" hands when riding in a Pelham or curb as these kinds of bits are more severe than most snaffles and you want to preserve your horse's sensitivity and responsiveness to the rein aids. Seek advice from a professional instructor or trainer when considering bitting options.

SOLUTION 5
Ride in a Western saddle and put the horse's bridle on over a halter and lead rope. Tie the lead rope to the saddle horn so the horse has only enough slack for normal head and neck movement but not enough slack to put his head down far enough to buck hard. If he can't get his head down to buck, the horse will stop trying.

SOLUTION 6
If the horse tries to buck in spite of good riding and constant contact with his mouth, the best way to halt the bucking action is to quickly pull his head around to the side. He cannot buck while spinning in a circle. If you need a little extra leverage for pulling his head to the side, ride with a halter under the bridle and an extra set of reins snapped to the side rings on the halter, so you can put pressure on his head and nose as well as the bit.

» **The horse cannot buck while he is spinning in a circle.**

UNDER SADDLE VICES

SOLUTION 7

Talk to the horse calmly when he comes to a stop following a buck. If he was bucking because he was startled or frightened, reassure him, and as soon as you get him quiet, praise him for standing still. Never punish him for bucking after he's stopped, regardless of the cause, or he'll think you are punishing him for standing still.

If he's a horse that bucks out of habit to try to get rid of his rider, the time for punishment is when he *starts* the activity, not when he stops. With many horses, a jab with the spur as you pull up their head and spin them around is enough to make them realize bucking is *not* pleasant. After the horse is back under control, go on about your ride and be calm and relaxed; let him know that everything *is* pleasant when he behaves.

> » **When a horse bucks out of habit to try to get rid of his rider, the time for punishment is when he starts the activity, not when he stops.**

What If Nothing Works?

If you continually and consistently head off their attempts to buck, most horses will give up trying. Some, however, are never totally dependable. These individuals must be ridden with constant vigilance and attention so you are never caught off guard. If the horse bucks so explosively you cannot control him, and if he is able to buck you off, he needs to be ridden by a rider who *can* control him; you are better off getting a different horse.

BUCKS WHEN STARTLED/ANNOYED

A green or inexperienced horse may "buck first and ask questions later" when confronted with something that startles him—such as a deer jumping out of the brush, a branch tickling his belly when he goes through a thicket, or a horse fly biting. And as already mentioned, any horse may buck when startled by a rider inadvertently bumping him in the mouth or jabbing a spur in his side (for example) or when annoyed by an ill-fitting saddle or girth that causes him pain.

How to Change This Habit

 If the horse is green, this explosive action may be a defense mechanism he uses when he feels threatened. You must quickly defuse it so it does not continue and become a habit. Try to determine the cause: Check his tack and your technique. If he's ticklish and jumpy when riding through brush or thistles, take time to get him used to things touching his sides or belly. Whatever the cause of his defensive action, address it in a way that either eliminates the cause or gets the horse more accustomed to it.

UNDER SADDLE VICES

 If your horse is "goosey" and prone to buck when startled or annoyed, stay alert. Always ride him with as much conscientious forethought and attentiveness as you would when riding a green horse, so that you are always in control. Don't "go to sleep" on him or sit like a mere passenger. If you are always in control and keeping a constant flow of communication through your reins and bit, you can usually keep the horse from bucking.

>> **If your horse is "goosey" and prone to buck when startled or annoyed, stay alert—don't "go to sleep" in the saddle.**

What If Nothing Works?

If the horse continues to buck at the drop of a hat, and you don't feel capable of getting him over this defensive reaction or you aren't sure of your ability to stay on, get help from an experienced rider or trainer, or get a different horse.

FEARFUL OF NEW SIGHTS/SOUNDS

A young or inexperienced horse is often spooky and nervous when he encounters new things. His shying is normal (and can't be called a "bad habit"...yet). However, *how you handle his shying* can make a great difference in whether or not he continues to be afraid or comes to rely on spooking as an evasion tactic.

How to Change This Habit

The first step in any attempt to teach your horse to be less afraid of things (more willing to trust and obey you) is to have a relaxed and confident attitude yourself so he can follow your cues without fear or resistance. Train yourself to stay calm and in control of your own attitude and actions. If your horse doesn't trust you, he won't look to you for guidance.

Most spooky horses are caused by the rider: The rider anticipates a shy and tenses up, preparing for the horse to jump, and thus transmits anxiety to the horse. Practice taking a deep breath and relaxing your body and your mind. Give the horse a little more slack in the reins whenever you encounter something you think might spook him—instead of tightening them. Your being relaxed helps him realize there's nothing to fear. Controlling your horse is often just a matter of controlling your own emotions and reactions while riding—and doing enough groundwork ahead of time so the horse already has confidence in you as his leader.

When you encounter something that scares your horse and he stops dead in his tracks, *let him stop and stand* a moment—do not force him to go past it just yet.

- Let the horse stand and look at the "scary thing." If he whirls away, turn him back around to face it. Don't let him back up or duck off to the side. Stay calm and relaxed and talk to him reassuringly, patting and rubbing his neck and withers if he's standing still and looking rather than trying to flee.

- Once he relaxes, ask him to go closer to the object in question (or to go on past it) and reward him with praise and a pat if he does— even if it's only a step closer.

- If he absolutely won't go near or past the thing that is frightening him, get off and lead him up to it or past it. Those who consistently do groundwork with their horse will have an advantage: When the horse trusts you when you are leading him, he will probably let you lead him closer to a scary object than you can get while on his back.

- Take as much time as necessary to reassure the horse that "this is nothing to be afraid of." *Do not* punish him for balking or shying, or he will only be *more* convinced that it is a scary, bad thing, and he will be even more afraid the next time he encounters something unusual.

When riding an inexperienced horse in situations where he might be afraid, it helps to go with another person on a calm, willing horse. This gives your timid horse security; he's less apt to "freak out" if the other horse stays calm. The inexperienced horse learns there's nothing to be afraid of and won't be so scared the next time.

As mentioned in regard to other "spooky scenarios," if something scary comes up behind you, like a dog or a plastic bag blowing in the wind, turn your horse to face it. He's less apt to try to bolt if he can see what it is. When something is blowing toward you, keep your horse facing it, even if you have to circle around it. When riding away, try to not have it directly behind you—ride off at an angle or zigzag so you and the horse can both keep the "scary thing" in sight until you are at a safe distance.

What If Nothing Works?

Some horses may always be a little nervous or spooky, either due to poor eyesight (they are unable to figure out what's standing along the trail or to discern what's coming at them) or temperament. But when you make a habit of staying calm and relaxed, you can usually minimize the balk or shy. Always ride in a good, balanced position and be prepared to control the horse if he spooks; however, keep a slightly slack rein, rather than a tight one, so the horse is not under pressure and feels like he *can* relax. In a situation where you think he might shy, hang on to his mane, the saddle horn, or a bucking strap, if you wish, but don't have a "death grip" on the reins that transmits tension to the horse or he *will* do just what you fear.

If the horse does spook and bolt, reach forward, grab one rein, and pull him around in a tight circle (see p. 196).

FEARFUL OF WILDLIFE

Deer bounding out of the brush; jackrabbits zigzagging in front of you down the trail; birds flying up out of tall grass under the horse's feet—any of these may cause your horse to slam on the brakes or spook. Most horses get used to wildlife and the sound and sight of birds after a few encounters, but some horses continue to think they are scary.

How to Change This Habit

Make sure you are not perpetuating your horse's fear or phobia with your own reaction to wildlife encounters. If you are tense because you think he may whirl and dump you, and if you are more intent on keeping him under control than in calming his fears, he may always equate wildlife with something to be afraid of.

» **Make sure you are not perpetuating your horse's fear with your own reaction to wildlife encounters.**

Ride with a friend on a calm horse that's not afraid of wildlife so your horse can take his cues from the other horse. Even if your horse jumps and shies, he won't try to bolt because he won't want to leave his buddy. Have the most experienced horse go first on the trail, especially when riding in a larger group. When the lead horse stays calm, the others are less likely to panic.

Be alert and pay attention. You may spot wildlife along the trail before your horse does. Stop your horse and let him know something is there. If he can see the deer, rabbit, or grouse (for example) *before* it moves, he won't be as startled.

If you encounter a wild animal that doesn't take off but stands its ground (such as a bear, cougar, or bull moose), try to keep your horse still and calm. Face the animal; don't let your horse turn and run, or the animal may chase you. Back away slowly, if you can. Give the animal as much space as possible, while trying to keep your horse under control.

To avoid sudden encounters with wild animals that might be alarming to your horse (or even dangerous), give wildlife advance warning of your presence when riding in the backcountry. Fasten a small tinkle bell to the bottom of your cinch or girth, so that when your horse is moving you are always making some noise.

» **Fasten a small bell to the bottom of your cinch or girth, so that when your horse is moving you are always making some noise.**

UNDER SADDLE
VICES

What If Nothing Works?

Some horses are always jumpy when wildlife startles them. The best way to deal with this type of horse is to reassure him (never punish), and improve your riding skills so you can always stay in balance with your horse and won't be unseated.

If you know the horse is going to shy (if you see an animal or another scary thing before he does), don't "clamp up," or try to hold him steady with the reins, leg pressure, and force. You can't prevent an agile, athletic horse from shying, and using force is counterproductive because he'll panic even more if he feels he can't get away from what he thinks is terrible danger. Just stay in balance as best you can, keeping a light touch on the reins so you won't accidentally jerk his mouth and increase his fear. Keep your attitude under control. Be patient and try to reassure him. Calm, quiet control is the best defense against a shy or spook, and may help keep your horse from falling off the trail (on a steep mountainside) or bashing you into a tree in a panic. When in doubt as to your ability to keep him under control in a bad situation, get off and hold him until the crisis passes.

PANICS IN TRAFFIC/AFRAID OF VEHICLES

Many horses are afraid of traffic and panic when a vehicle comes up behind them or whizzes by. Some get over their fear with practice, but others continue to be afraid (especially if a vehicle is noisy or goes by very fast) and can be dangerous to ride along a road. They may try to whirl or bolt, or may panic when you try to restrain them—rearing or bucking.

> » **Make sure you don't tense up and tighten the reins when you hear a car or truck approaching while riding on the road.**

How to Change This Habit

Make sure you are not the cause of the horse's reaction to traffic. Do you tense up and tighten the reins when you hear a car or truck coming? Do you transmit nervousness to the horse so that he thinks something bad is about to happen? Your horse may be more worried about *your* reactions and *your* fear than he is about the traffic. Try staying completely calm and relaxed. Take a deep breath and keep a little slack in the reins (still maintaining adequate communication and control) while you ask the horse to stand still until the vehicle goes by. Rub his neck and withers and reassure him.

Desensitize the horse to cars and trucks in more familiar surroundings and gradual increments.

- Lead the horse up to parked vehicles along your driveway or in your barnyard. Let him check them out thoroughly in his own time in his home territory.

- When the horse is at ease with automobiles when they are not moving, have a friend drive past you slowly while you are leading the horse. If at any time the horse becomes nervous or afraid, have your friend stop the vehicle so you can lead the horse up to it. Stop and chat with your friend so the horse has a chance to relax and feel at ease.

- Gradually increase the speed at which your friend drives the vehicle past you and the horse. Halt the horse and encourage him to stand calmly as the vehicle passes.

- Repeat the last two steps with you in the saddle.

- Once he can handle vehicles passing at speed in a familiar place, take him out along a road again. Start with a nice, wide road that doesn't have a lot of traffic.

When you have to ride along a road, try to ride with someone on a calm horse. If the other horse is not afraid of traffic, your horse won't panic as violently. When encountering a particularly noisy or fast vehicle, try to get as far off the road as possible and halt both horses, facing the loud or speeding car/truck. Your horse will better handle the situation if he can see what's coming.

What If Nothing Works?

When your horse is extremely afraid of traffic, avoid busy roads if possible. Haul your horse to where you can ride in a safer place. If you must travel along a road for some reason, lead the horse and hold him, facing loud and speeding vehicles until they are past. Be sure you've done enough groundwork with the horse so he trusts you and your leadership so you can keep control of him on the ground. When you know you will be riding along a road, leave his halter on under his bridle and the lead rope looped around his neck so you can lead or hold him using the halter—you will have more control in a panic situation holding him by the halter and lead rope than by the bridle reins.

REARS

Rearing is one of the most dangerous habits a horse can develop. Shying or bucking may result in a rider parting company with the horse and landing on the ground, but a tumble off is not as risky as having the horse go over backward and fall on top of you. The horse that rears is truly dangerous because of the possibility a rider may inadvertently pull him over backward.

>> **Rearing is one of the most dangerous habits a horse can develop.**

How to Change This Habit

First make sure there isn't a physical or equipment problem causing the horse to rear in an attempt to avoid pain. If his mouth hurts when you use the bit (because of an ill-fitting or severe bit, a too-tight curb chain, or a dental problem, for example) he may rear when you pull on the reins. If the saddle pinches him or his back hurts because of stiffness or injury, he may rear when you ask him to move forward. When a horse starts rearing you should try to determine the reason before attempting to deal with the bad behavior.

UNDER SADDLE VICES

If the horse rears because he's afraid—as an avoidance tactic when asked to approach something strange or unfamiliar—he needs patient training to get him over his fear. If he rears when you try to approach a "scary" obstacle, for instance, go back to basics and do groundwork, revisiting cues in hand and then using advance and retreat to eventually get closer to the obstacle without him making a fuss. Once you have worked him through his phobia on the ground, you can again try riding him up to, around, and/or over the obstacle. Have another rider on a calm horse approach the obstacle first to give your horse a feeling of security.

Rearing always begins as a defense against a stressful situation. If you can reduce or remove the stress, you will reduce or eliminate his inclination to rear.

Rearing may be caused by confusion. If you give a horse conflicting aids, such as kicking or squeezing with the legs and at the same time pulling on the reins (perhaps hanging on the reins for balance if your riding skills are poor) the horse may rear. This can be prevented by improving your riding skills through lessons, study, and practice.

Some horses rear to avoid bit control. They often learn this trick because a rider pulls too much (hurting the horse's mouth) or rushes him in training, such as riding a green horse in a curb bit, before he is ready to be transitioned from the snaffle. The action of a curb bit tends to make the horse tuck his chin, and if a rider uses a curb before the horse has learned the basics of reining and control (in a snaffle), and the horse does not know how to respond properly to the action of the curb, he may respond by either tucking his chin too much and going behind the bit (see p. 183) or rearing.

This happens most often when the rider tries to "set" the horse's head ("false collection") by pulling or working at his mouth, rather than pushing the horse forward into the bit. In most cases, a horse that is behind the bit and trying to avoid it has not learned to respond properly to leg and seat cues, and has also been confused by inept attempts by the rider to teach him to respond to the bit. If the horse starts rearing and you've been riding in a curb, examine your riding skills—don't just automatically blame the horse. Take a few steps back, use a milder bit, revisit earlier training, and don't ask him for more advanced work until he is ready and your rein, leg, and seat cues have been improved.

SOLUTION
5

Some horses rear in protest when the rider asks too much of them, pushing them beyond their physical, emotional, or mental abilities. A horse may also rear in an attempt to get his way and run back to the barn or his buddies when the rider tries to make him go somewhere he doesn't want to go or do something he doesn't want to do. If this becomes a habit, the horse may rear whenever he's frustrated or upset.

When rearing is already a habit, work on some specific lessons for keeping control. Remember it's impossible for him to rear unless he's standing still or moving backward (able to plant all his weight on his hind legs). It takes more physical effort to rear (raising his weight and yours) than to move forward. Devising ways of keeping the horse *going forward* keeps you in control. Work on fine-tuning his response to leg, seat, and rein cues so you can always urge him forward when he balks, and you can prevent a rear.

>> **When you sense the horse might rear, redirect his energy into a more acceptable action.**

Teach the horse an alternative movement that you can ask for whenever you think he's about to rear. This does two things: It redirects his energy into a more acceptable action and also puts him into a physical position that makes it impossible for him to rear.

For instance, you can teach him to pivot on his front legs—a *turn on the forehand*—where he swings his hindquarters around while his front feet remain almost in place. This maneuver puts his weight more forward, on his front end, and that helps keep them on the ground. You can teach the horse this maneuver from the ground first:

- Stand at the horse's shoulder and hold his head with a firm but relaxed hand to encourage his front feet to stay in place.

- Ask the horse to move his hind legs away from you by press on his side with your hand, at about the same position your leg would be if you were mounted.

- Pull his head slightly toward you to keep him from moving his front legs as you press on his side. Ask for one step at a time, and release the pressure when he reacts by crossing one hind leg over the other and moving his hindquarters away.

- Repeat until the horse is standing in the same spot (with this front feet), but facing the opposite direction (or you can ask him to complete a full circle so you end in the same position you started).

- Do this from both sides on the ground. Then practice under saddle. When asking him to pivot on his front legs from the saddle, use your reins to cue him lightly with the bit, bending his head and neck slightly away (in the opposite direction) from the direction his hindquarters are moving. Thus your hands are holding his front end relatively still while your leg pushes his hindquarters over—press and release with the leg as you did with the pressure from the ground.

- Ask for one step at a time, coordinating your leg and rein cues so he treads a smooth semicircle (or full circle, if you want to keep him busy for longer) with his hind legs while keeping his front feet in the same spot and maintaining a feeling of forward impulsion. You can ensure he continues to "think forward" by asking him to walk on immediately following completion of the pivot. Once the horse learns to give instant response to your leg cue—swinging his hind end one way or the other upon request—you can ask for a turn on the forehand whenever you think he might be inclined to rear. In this way you keep his trust and cooperation (without fighting him) and substitute an acceptable action for a dangerous one.

>> **It is physically impossible for a horse to rear while moving forward or making a tight circle.**

What If Nothing Works?

If retraining tactics (to defuse the situations in which he would ordinarily rear) don't work, your only option is to learn how to handle his habit so that he won't ever go over backward with you. It is physically impossible for a horse to rear while moving forward or making a tight circle, so if you can sense when he's about to rear, drive him forward sharply with your legs or reach forward on one rein and pull his head to the side and spin him, using leg pressure on the outside of the turn to help force his body around. With some horses it may help if you wear spurs to make your demand for him to go forward forceful enough that he responds instantly.

If the horse does manage to get his front end off the ground before you can drive him forward or into a spin, lean forward toward his neck and loosen the reins to encourage him to get his front end back down on the ground again.

Never lean back as the horse goes up, nor should you pull on his mouth as he rears, as both may upset his balance and pull him right over on top of you. If you don't feel confident in your riding abilities and the horse continues his dangerous habit, get help from an experienced horse trainer or get a different horse.

REFUSES TO BACK UP

UNDER SADDLE
VICES

Most horses that refuse to back up have never been properly taught to do so while being ridden (and some have never learned it during groundwork). Thus they are confused by the cues used to ask them to back up, and they may resist strongly, planting their feet and throwing their heads up in the air, fearful of having their mouths jerked on.

How to Change This Habit

First make sure there isn't a physical problem that makes it difficult or painful for the horse to shift his weight to his front end and back up.

Examine the signals you are giving the horse. In order to back up smoothly, the horse must lower his head and extend his neck, putting more weight on his front end and less on his hind legs. He can't back up properly with his head raised. In a correct backup, the horse moves his legs in diagonal pairs (like a slow trot in reverse). His mouth stays closed. If he opens his mouth or raises his head, you are depending too much on your rein aids. If the horse backs crookedly instead of straight, or if he tucks his chin and rushes backward, you need to work on improving your cues.

> » **If the horse opens his mouth or raises his head when you ask him to back up, you are depending too much on your rein aids.**

Don't use the same cues for backing as you do for stopping (leaning your weight back, pulling on the reins). This is the mistake most riders make; those cues force the horse to raise his head and put more weight on his hind legs, which makes it impossible for him to back up properly.

To cue your horse correctly for the backup:

- Start with the horse standing calmly and squarely. Sit upright and perfectly balanced in the saddle (not leaning back) and get his attention via communication through your reins and bit. His head and neck should be neither too low nor overflexed.

- Use a fixed hand so that you are not actively pulling on the bit but so the horse can gently feel that you are "there."

- Squeeze with your legs to push the horse into the bit. Keep most of your weight in your feet, knees, and thighs, with your back straight and somewhat braced. The horse should be stimulated to move because of your leg pressure, but when he encounters your fixed hand he will realize he can't move forward. So, he will move backward. This is much more effective than pulling on his mouth. Note: Never pull actively on the reins. If the horse doesn't quite "get the picture," give a series of quick give-and-take (vibrating) movements by fingering the reins, to impress upon him that you *don't* want forward movement. He should respond by taking a step backward, and as soon as he starts that step, immediately release the leg and rein pressure so he is rewarded for doing the right thing.

- Ask for one step at a time, and if he gives you two or three backward steps as you request them, ride him forward again and end the lesson.

» **As soon as the horse starts to take a step back, immediately release leg and rein pressure as a reward.**

If the horse had bad experiences that frustrated him with improper backup cues, and he refuses to move, make it easier for him to respond properly.

- Ride up to a wall or fence that can serve as an obstacle to block any forward movement. Halt and stand a moment.

- Once he's standing calmly, take the slack out of the reins (with a rein in each hand) and squeeze your legs as if to push him forward.

UNDER SADDLE VICES

- Since he will see that he can't go forward (into the wall or fence), he might try to go to one side or the other, so use leg and rein pressure to keep him facing straight at the wall/fence as you continue encouraging him "forward" with your legs. He will need to move in response to your leg pressure, and since he can't go forward, he will take a step backward.

- Immediately release your leg and rein pressure as soon as he takes one step back. Praise him.

- Ask for another step—again using leg pressure to drive him into your fixed hand. If necessary, use a give-and-take vibrating action on the bit so he can't brace his jaw against the pressure.

- The instant the horse takes another step backward, release all pressure and end the lesson, praising him. Don't overdo these sessions. One backup lesson each day at some point during your ride is sufficient. He will learn this lesson more quickly if he knows he can get away from pressure by cooperating—and if you don't overdrill him. Eventually you can ask him for more steps backward, but increase the challenge only a little at a time.

- Use the wall or fence for several sessions until you are sure he understands your cues and no longer needs it to remind him he can't go forward when you press with your legs.

» **The horse will learn more quickly if he knows he can get away from pressure by cooperating—and if you don't overdrill him.**

If the horse stubbornly fights your backup cues even when there's a barrier in front of him, go back to groundwork.

- During leading lessons, halt him and stand next to his head facing his tail, giving intermittent short tugs on his halter to encourage him to move away from the pressure by backing up. Don't pull back steadily or he may just brace into the halter—short quick tugs are more effective.

- If he doesn't get the picture, tap on his chest at the same time you apply pressure to the halter, using your free hand or the butt of a crop or whip to give more emphasis to the cue. You can also give the verbal command "back" so he learns to associate it with the halter cues.

- Cease tapping and halter pressure the instant the horse starts to respond by taking a step backward. He needs to be rewarded for doing the right thing by immediate release of pressure. Just ask for one step at a time.

- Once he is backing nicely in hand, try again mounted, and add the verbal command "back" to your leg and rein cues. If he is still confused or resisting, have a helper give him the cues he knows from the ground lessons (intermittent tugs on his halter—worn under the bridle—and taps on his chest with her hand or the butt end of a whip) as you give the leg and rein cues, until he gets the connection.

For a very stubborn horse that refuses to respond to the rider, even with an assistant's help, the assistant can hold a short piece of rope lead (the size and weave of a rope halter) over the horse's nose, and put pressure on the rope in time with the rider's cues to back up. If intermittent pressure on this "nose piece" is not effective, the helper can rub the rope lead against the horse's nose in a sawing motion—the instant the horse begins to respond correctly, all cues and pressures should cease and the horse should be praised.

» **Add the verbal command "back" to your leg and rein cues.**

What If Nothing Works?

If the horse performs well in all other aspects but won't back up (and if you confirmed he doesn't have a physical problem that is causing his reluctance to back), don't use him in competitions that require backing up, and be careful to avoid situations in which he might have to back up on cue. Work on this skill, and other aspects of maneuverability, on the ground so that in an emergency you could get off and back him up in hand, if necessary.

UNDER SADDLE VICES

-4-

Bad Habits
On The Road

Often the problems encountered when hauling horses in a trailer or van are due to past bad experiences. A loading mishap, discomfort related to the size or type of trailer, or a frightening ride due to someone's bad driving can sour a horse on traveling.

Most of the issues encountered with horse transport involve getting the horse into the trailer or van, since the horse's natural instinct is to avoid enclosed areas where he might be trapped.

Without proper training and patient technique, *most horses will not willingly enter a trailer.* If you add to this an unpleasant association (tense or angry humans, being pulled on, pushed, or whipped), the horse may make up his mind *never* to go near that thing again. The trailer becomes something to fear, and he may thereafter fight your efforts to load him. The horse's resistance is merely reinforced if you can't get him into the trailer.

Unloading can also be a problem for inexperienced horses or those that may have scraped or injured a foot or leg as they exited once before. Some horses develop a phobia about stepping back because they can't see where the "floor" ends.

> » **Loading the horse into a trailer is notoriously difficult because his natural instinct is to avoid enclosed areas where he might be trapped.**

And then there are horses that are poor travelers. They may (or may not) load into the trailer willingly, but either way are then nervous or upset during the trip. They may paw, kick, jump around, scramble on corners, or even fall down, and in general make hauling very miserable for themselves and for you. Often "bad travelers" became this way because of frightening or uncomfortable experiences in a trailer—a driver who took corners too fast, slammed on the brakes, accelerated too quickly, drove down bumpy roads without slowing, or in some other way made the horse apprehensive about the experience. There is also the possibility that the horse may have been in a trailer accident.

Problems with Loading

EVADES RAMP/STEPS SIDEWAYS

Some horses find the trailer ramp suspicious and don't want to step on it. They use this as their excuse to not enter the van or trailer.

How to Change This Habit

Groundwork is important before you try to actually load the horse. He should willingly walk forward and halt in hand when asked. If the horse has solid ground skills and his main concern is the trailer itself, it may be that getting him used to the idea of approaching and entering it is all that's needed. This involves patient advance-and-retreat work over many days, perhaps first using a trailer *without* a ramp, and then progressing to one *with* a ramp.

When you have a trailer with a ramp, rather than a step-up, and the horse finds the sound and feel of his feet on the trailer ramp scary, lead him up to the ramp and let him stop. Pick up one of his front feet and place it on the ramp, then the other, and encourage him to just stand there. If he removes a foot, patiently place it back on the ramp again.

Usually after the horse realizes that the ramp is not going to hurt him, he will walk right into the trailer on his own. If he doesn't, continue to place his feet progressively higher on the ramp, encouraging him, one foot at a time, to move his way up it. Always allow the horse to back down again if he wishes—don't force him. Wait until he loses his fear and hesitation and follows you willingly into the trailer.

Another option for working to overcome a phobia related to the ramp itself is to take the ramp off the trailer (if possible—some are detachable) and place it out in the middle of the horse's paddock or in a round pen or arena. (If the actual trailer ramp is not an option, substitute a similar surface that the horse can walk over, such as a piece of sturdy plywood or a solid wooden pallet (without spaces that could potentially catch a hoof). Proceed with lessons to get him over his fear of walking on such a surface or hearing the sound of his feet on it.

- Turn the horse loose in the paddock or round pen with the "ramp" in the center of it, and let him check it out on his own terms.

- When he's at ease with the ramp being in his space, lead him around it at whatever he feels is a safe distance, going both directions.

- Gradually make smaller and smaller circles until you are very close to the ramp. Some horses will eventually walk right next to it and then over it, once they realize it isn't a threat.

- Other horses will still try to avoid stepping on the ramp even when they are no longer afraid of walking right by it. For these individuals, you might try bribery. When the horse will stand quietly next to the ramp, entice him to put a foot on it by having to reach over/across it for a treat or horse cookie. If he does put a foot on the ramp, praise him and give him the treat. Most horses can be persuaded to put both feet on and then walk over to get their reward.

» Use progressive lessons to get the horse used to walking over strange and/or loud surfaces on the ground before asking him to walk up a ramp into a trailer.

What If Nothing Works?

When a horse won't step on a ramp in spite of progressive lessons to get him used to walking on similar surfaces on the ground, use a step-up trailer without a ramp. If you are dealing with a horse that won't enter *any* kind of trailer, there are some other techniques you can try, although usually they can be retrained if you start over and give them lots of time while using nonconfrontational methods (like feeding them in the trailer or more lessons on groundwork and leading). But if you absolutely have to haul a horse that won't load for some reason (to take him to the vet, transport him to a new home, or go on some other trip that cannot be postponed until you can rehabilitate him) there are ways to get him in without a big fight (see Refuses to Enter Trailer/Balks, below).

PROBLEMS
WITH LOADING

REFUSES TO ENTER TRAILER/BALKS

You may have a horse with decent ground manners that isn't actually afraid of getting in the trailer, but while he may not fight your efforts vehemently, he still won't load. He balks when you get him up close to it—he's made up his mind he's *not* going in. And, if you *can't* get him in, his habit of stubborn refusal is reinforced.

How to Change This Habit

Begin by determining whether the horse is balking because he doesn't know anything about trailers (he's inexperienced) or because he has been trailered in the past and didn't like it. If the horse is inexperienced but doesn't seem afraid, a few simple lessons that gradually introduce him to the idea of loading into the trailer will usually work. If he is stubborn because he *has* been trailered before and wants no part of the experience again, it may take longer to overcome his resistance.

The most important thing here is to take some time to work with the horse and work to resolve his resistance habit *before* you are actually in a position where you *have* to load him. This puts less pressure on both you and the horse. When you are much less tense or nervous about the trailer-loading process, the horse will respond positively because he senses that you are relaxed and calm instead of uptight.

» **It takes longer to rehabilitate the horse that had a bad past experience in a trailer than to train the inexperienced horse right from the start.**

Consider the type and size of trailer you use and whether it is appropriate for your horse. If your rig is part of the problem, borrow another setup from an acquaintance to use for retraining purposes. The trailer should be easy for the horse to get in and out of, and tall enough that there isn't any danger of him hitting his head on the ceiling.

It's easier to load a horse into a large, four-horse trailer or a stock trailer than it is to get him into a two-horse trailer with a partition. Note that some of the newer trailers today are designed for easier loading and hauling than their older counterparts. When you are trying to train an inexperienced horse or retrain a spoiled, stubborn one, a spacious trailer without a partition makes it less difficult to convince the horse to enter.

No matter what kind of trailer you use, park it so the sun shines into it during the loading process. (This is so the horse can see where he's going, and it's not so scary.)

SOLUTION 3

Try bribery to overcome the horse's resistance. One of the simplest ways to entice a horse into a trailer is to feed him in it. Depending on the horse's past experience, this may resolve the problem quickly (if he has no reason yet to fear a trailer), or it may take several days or weeks (if he has an ingrained phobia).

- If the horse won't walk clear into the trailer to get at a bucket of feed, start by putting his grain tub on the floor of the trailer near the door, so he merely has to stick his head inside to eat it.

- When he's at ease with that, move the grain back a little away from the entrance so he has to reach for it, then a little further still so he has to put his front feet in the trailer to reach it. Soon he's clear in before he knows it.

- Some people park the trailer in the horse's paddock or pen (be sure to block the trailer tires so they cannot move), so the horse can go in and out of it for food as he wishes—as if it were a small barn. In this situation, the horse "trailer trains" himself.

PROBLEMS WITH LOADING

SOLUTION 4

When trying to lead the horse into the trailer, *don't* pull on his halter; this creates resistance and the horse is more apt to balk or pull backward. If the horse is not afraid of a whip (such as a dressage whip), tap him on his hindquarters as you ask him to step forward so you can keep a little slack in his lead rope. Encouragement to move forward should always come from behind. It helps if you have an assistant to help in this process.

If you must give a tug on the horse's head, don't pull straight forward, or he will pull back. Always tug the halter at an angle (a little to the side to get him to shift his balance and move a front foot), and use tug-and-release. If he is always rewarded by release of pressure on the halter when he moves, he's more apt to take a step.

SOLUTION 5

Use the "buddy system." If the horse has a herdmate or stable pal that loads willingly, load that horse first. When the reluctant loader sees his buddy go right into the trailer (and start eating grain and/or treats inside) he may rethink his reluctance. An insecure horse that wants to be in the company of other horses may load more easily using this method.

When the horse is well-trained on the ground (normally compliant and responsive to leading cues), and if he is not afraid of a long, soft lead rope, he may step right into the trailer with a little urging from a "rump rope" looped around his hindquarters (see p. 63). Some horses bluff and balk if they think they can get away with it, but quickly resign themselves to entering the trailer once they realize you are serious. The rump rope can be particularly useful when loading a very young horse that balks, since you may have recently used it to teach his first leading lessons and he will be likely to remember them and move forward to get away from the rope pressure.

>> **Some horses bluff and balk if they think they can get away with it, but quickly resign themselves to entering the trailer once they realize you are serious.**

When the horse isn't always willing and responsive on the ground, go back a few steps in training and work on his leading lessons so he totally respects your control over his movements. Lead him at the walk and trot, encouraging him to move out freely when he's asked (reaching back with a whip and tapping it on his hindquarters, if needed). Practice stopping and backing up readily on command. This kind of groundwork helps develop trust, respect, and control of the horse's movements, ultimately making it easier to approach and enter a trailer.

Do a lot of groundwork near the back of the trailer with the trailer door closed, so the lesson isn't about "loading." (Note: This solution works best with a step-up, rather than a trailer with a ramp.)

- Lead the horse with an extra-long lead rope to the area well behind the trailer (not so close as to cause the horse anxiety) and direct the horse to walk and/or trot around you in a small circle, as if you are longeing him. Use an appropriate training whip (such as a dressage or longe whip), or swing the free end of the lead rope at his rump as necessary, to make sure he moves briskly.

- When he's calm and attentive, move to stand by the rear left corner of the trailer. Face your horse with your back to the trailer.

- Ask the horse to walk a semicircle in front of you so that he moves to your right and ends up facing the side of the horse trailer.

- Have him stand there briefly, then direct him to turn his nose and come back around you, traveling the other way on the semicircle, until he is on your left side and now facing the (closed) rear trailer door.

PROBLEMS WITH LOADING

- Repeat this pattern, asking the horse to make several part-circles in front of you, back and forth between the side of the trailer and the rear trailer door.

- Change positions so you are now standing at the right-hand, rear corner of the trailer, and repeat the process.

- Once the horse makes these semicircles willingly and is completely at ease (after all, you are *not* trying to make him go into the trailer), return to the area directly behind the trailer, but this time position yourself a bit closer so he is moving between you and the back of the trailer while walking on the mini-longe-circle.

- When he can do this calmly, without rushing or trying to push into you (or hesitating as he approaches the space between you and the trailer), move a little closer so there is just enough room for him to go between you and the trailer.

- Next, open the rear trailer doors and position yourself again at one corner so that when the horse comes around you he faces the open trailer. Let him stop and stand there a few seconds, and invite him to put his head inside and check it out, then quickly direct him away from the trailer and back on the "longe circle" again before he has a chance to think about backing away. Since you're not asking him to enter the trailer, there isn't a "threat," and he's likely to stay calm about it.

- Repeat, bringing him up to the rear of the trailer again and encouraging him to stick his head in. Continue patiently building his acceptance but backing off again so he never becomes alarmed or resistant. As always, these lessons can be spread over several days, if needed, depending on his progress.

- When you feel he is ready, ask the horse to put one foot in the trailer, and praise him if he will. Then ask him to back out again. If you ask him to back out—before he does it himself—you remain in control and he stays more calm and willing.

- Progress to requesting he put both front feet in the trailer. Ask him to step in a little farther or stay in a little longer each time you bring him up to the trailer entrance. If at any point he becomes nervous, alarmed, or uncooperative, let him stand and relax for a moment outside the trailer, or do another longe circle before going back into the trailer.

- At some point, the horse should put one or both hind feet in, but if he doesn't get there on his own, ask him to approach the trailer a little more swiftly and momentum will help take him on in. Use your training whip or the end of the lead rope to gently bump his rump and encourage him forward. *Do not* tap continuously with the whip, or he may feel too pressured. If he balks or backs out, use another brisk trip around you to direct him in again, asking for a little more speed. If he's hurrying, he's more likely to go on into the trailer; if he's walking slowly up to the door he's more likely to stop.

- When the horse does go all the way in, ask him to back right out again before he has a chance to get scared. This takes the pressure off, keeps him willing, and ensures his mind doesn't "lock up" in refusal. Praise him and let him stand outside the trailer and relax (or lead him away for a moment), and then ask him to enter the trailer again. If he stays calm and willing, do it several more times before ending on a good note.

- In follow-up lessons, work on having the horse stay in the trailer longer and longer before asking him to back out, so he learns to wait for you to ask (rather than rushing back out on his own). At this point you can start putting grain or treats inside the trailer so he receives a reward for standing inside. Note: With this solution, feed should be used as a reward only *after* the horse is already in the trailer, rather than as a bribe to entice him into it (see Solution 3).

PROBLEMS WITH LOADING

» **Patiently build the horse's acceptance, backing off as necessary so he never becomes alarmed or resistant.**

What If Nothing Works?

When you absolutely must load the horse before your training or retraining is complete (because of a veterinary emergency, a move, or a sale, for example), you can use this method to get it done without it becoming a fight:

- Back the trailer up so it is close to a barn wall or solid fence on one side, and create another solid "fence" on the other side with a portable panel (like those used in round pens. For safety, drape a rug or tarp over the panel so it presents a solid barrier that the horse is less apt to question. This creates a "loading alley" behind the trailer so the horse can't go anywhere *but* inside it—he can't dodge past it and there isn't a place to escape.

- Lead the horse "down the alley" and toward the trailer while an assistant (or two) encourages him from behind—either with a whip, rump rope, flag (so you can stay out of kicking range), or a bristle broom to poke his buttocks if he balks. If you make it pleasant for the horse to go forward and uncomfortable (or a little scary) for him to back up, most horses will then enter the trailer because they can readily see they can't go any other direction.

RUSHES BACKWARD WHEN APPROACHING TRAILER

Some horses rush backward as soon as you approach the trailer or are unwilling to stand quietly beside it. All they want to do is get away from the trailer, and if you try to lead them closer, they fly backward.

How to Change This Habit

With this bad habit, as with the previous one, one of the best solutions is more groundwork and leading lessons to work on respect, trust, and control. Then work on trailer loading, beginning a little distance away, waiting until the horse is calm and relaxed, then gradually moving closer, using advance-and-retreat methods.

- Reward any forward movement (even just a step or two closer) by letting the horse stop and stand, or even giving him a treat.

- If he backs away a few steps, let him. Just go with him and don't try to pull him forward. Keep his head pointed toward the trailer, and wait until he's relaxed before asking him to go forward again. Judicious use of a whip (merely as an extension of your arm so you can reach back to gently tap his hindquarters and encourage forward movement) rather than putting tension on the halter, is helpful. The tap of the whip provides much better incentive to step forward than pulling on the horse's head because he feels less trapped if he has some freedom of head movement.

- Continue patient work using advance and retreat, getting the horse used to the idea of approaching the trailer calmly (before you try to make him go in it), and he will gradually lose his fear.

» **Keep the horse's head pointed toward the trailer, and wait until he's relaxed before asking him to go forward again.**

Use food as a bribe to take his mind off his fear of approaching the trailer.

PROBLEMS
WITH LOADING

- As you lead the horse closer to the trailer, talk to him encouragingly, and let him stop when he thinks he's reached the end of his comfort zone. Give him a treat or a horse cookie as a reward for standing there quietly and not flying backward in a panic.

- Lead him away and then again come back toward the trailer, giving a treat as he halts and stands quietly. Soon he will start to look forward to the treat rather than thinking about rushing backward, and you can gradually get closer to the trailer before he puts on the brakes.

- Give yourself a lot of time and many days to work on this without *making* the horse go up to the trailer or into it, but allowing him to make the moves forward as he feels comfortable. The horse will soon realize that going to the trailer is not such a bad thing—and he'll willingly walk up to it to get his treat. After that, it's usually just a matter of patience and time to change his mind about loading.

What If Nothing Works?

See my recommendations on p. 275.

STARTS TO ENTER TRAILER THEN BACKS OUT

When first learning about loading, most horses will start in and then back up. They soon get over this, however, once they realize the trailer is nothing to be afraid of—unless they are whipped or forced right back in again. When that's the case they are often convinced that the trailer *is* scary, and they make a habit of rushing back out before they put their hind feet up into the trailer, or backing up again as soon as they enter.

> »   **When first learning about loading, most horses will start into the trailer and then have doubts and back up.**

How to Change This Habit

When working with an inexperienced horse, *do not* try to make him go clear in the first few times he starts to enter the trailer. Let him think that entering it can be his own idea. Allow him to back out again without any reprimand, then ask him to go forward again. Even if it takes several false starts before he goes all the way in, your patience will reassure the horse that nothing hurts him when he goes in and out of the horse trailer. When he knows he is free to back out, he won't feel threatened and is more likely to relax and eventually stay in.

Don't fasten the rump chain or bar (if there is one), nor should you tie his head until he's gone in and out several times and you know he does not feel confined or trapped.

Don't pull on the halter or try to hold the horse in the trailer if he re-ally wants to back out. He will only become more afraid or resistant and fly backward. Make sure there isn't any tension on the lead rope and just move back with him, letting him know there's nothing to be afraid of; as soon as he's calm again, ask him to go right back in.

Take whatever time is needed, and you'll gradually change his mind without having a battle. The loading process should never become a race to see if you can slam the door shut before he tries to back out.

» **Do not try to hold the horse in the trailer if he really wants to back out.**

What If Nothing Works?

See my recommendations on p. 275.

PROBLEMS WITH LOADING

Problems with Hauling

KICKS TRAILER DOORS/WALLS

Some horses resent being confined in a trailer and repeatedly kick while traveling, risking damage to the trailer and/or injury to themselves.

How to Change This Habit

 Consider the style and size of your trailer and whether it is appropriate for your horse. The horse may have started this habit because the trailer was too confining, or he felt irritated by the rump chain/bar (as in a standard two-horse trailer). A larger trailer where he does not feel so cramped may help him travel better. The best solution is a stock trailer or another large trailer where the horse is tied to the wall and has some room behind him.

> » **Consider the style and size of your trailer and whether it is appropriate for your horse.**

 If you have no other choice but to use a standard two-horse trailer with a divider, experiment to see if the horse is less annoyed by changing to a solid rump bar from a rump chain, or vice versa.

The horse may kick if he has balance problems in a tight space, so you can try taking out the trailer divider (if it is solid) or switch to a partial divider that doesn't come clear to the floor so the horse has plenty of foot room.

» **The horse may kick if he has balance problems in a tight space.**

What If Nothing Works?

When you can't change the trailer, always ship this horse in leg wraps and bell boots so he won't injure his hocks or heels or the trailer door when he kicks. You can also pad the trailer door with a rubber mat so he's less apt to damage the door or his legs or feet.

NERVOUS DANCING/NICKERING

Some horses are so ill at ease when a trailer is moving that they stomp around and whinny nervously; tremble or struggle; break into a sweat and have an elevated heart rate. When the trip is a long one, the prolonged stress is detrimental to the horse's health and well-being.

How to Change This Habit

Try to determine the reason the horse is frightened and insecure. Has he had a bad experience in the trailer, such as an accident or jostling from poor driving? Is he in a panic because he feels trapped? Your first goal should be to make sure the trailer is comfortable and non-threatening. A tall or large horse may feel too confined in a small trailer, and some horses that panic in a two-horse trailer with a divider will travel better in an open-style trailer where they have room to move around and can position themselves the way they feel most comfortable and balanced.

Always drive very carefully when hauling a nervous horse. Start very slowly, without jerking, and accelerate gradually. Slow down well ahead of a turn, and don't take a right angle turn any faster than 5 miles per hour.

Plan some short practice trips without having to actually travel somewhere.

- Take as much time as necessary to load the horse in a relaxed, nonconfrontational manner.

- If he becomes nervous in the trailer even before you start the engine, just feed him a treat and talk to him until he settles down again, then unload him, and end the lesson for the day.

- Once he can stand relaxed in the trailer, take him for a very short trip around the block, then come back and unload him again.

- Take a short practice trip every day until the horse is at ease, then start gradually increasing the length of the trip, always returning home and unloading him again before he becomes upset. With time, many insecure horses that have a traveling phobia will learn that there's really nothing to fear.

> » **Haul your horse on short "practice trips" down the road or around the block to build his confidence in the trailer.**

What If Nothing Works?

If a horse absolutely can't handle traveling and freaks out in the trailer, talk to your veterinarian about the possibility of using a tranquilizer when the horse must be hauled.

PAWS

A nervous horse may paw continually while being hauled, damaging the trailer wall or floor, and possibly injuring his feet.

How to Change This Habit

 Most horses paw because they are frustrated about being confined (tied and unable to move around). Anything that helps alleviate the horse's nervous energy and frustration might help, such as giving him a full hay net to work on.

 If the horse continues to nervously paw instead of eating, the best way to resolve the problem is to have him travel without tying him. Let him travel loose in a stock trailer. If he has the space to move around and position himself however he wishes for best balance (such as facing backward), and if he is not worried or frustrated at being tied, he will have less reason to paw. If you are hauling him loose, however, it's safest to do so without a halter on—a halter might catch on something inside the trailer and lead to injury.

>> **You can prevent a horse from pawing during transport by hauling him loose in a stock trailer.**

PROBLEMS WITH HAULING

What If Nothing Works?

If you are unable to haul the horse loose in a large trailer, use bell boots on his front feet during transport, so he is less apt to injure his feet or damage the wall of the trailer when he paws.

SCRAMBLES

One of the most common problems in a two-horse trailer (and even occasionally in a slant-load trailer) is the horse that "scrambles," hitting his feet against the trailer or losing his balance and footing and going down. He may stomp and bang for no apparent reason, or just throw violent fits whenever you go around a corner or come to a stop.

When the horse tries to brace himself for balance and can't spread his legs far enough apart to do so, he leans against the wall or trailer partition and scrambles with his feet on the other side. The scrambling horse is hard on the trailer and hard on himself; he may injure or scrape up his legs when he hits them against the trailer wall, and if he goes down he may be unable to get up again in the confined space.

>> **The horse that "scrambles" may stomp and bang for no apparent reason, or just throw violent fits whenever you go around a corner or come to a stop.**

How to Change This Habit

The easiest solution for a scrambler is to use a trailer without partitions. Most horses that scramble in a two-horse trailer or slant-load don't feel as claustrophobic in a stock trailer or larger trailer with box stalls where they can move around, turn sideways, face backward, and otherwise adjust in order to keep their balance.

Make sure the horse has good footing. Poor traction on a metal floor—or any kind of slippery footing—may cause him to scramble. Use rubber mats on the floor of your trailer, and if that still doesn't provide enough traction, try adding some bedding (straw or shavings) on top of the mats.

Ensure the trailer is level. If your hitch arrangement makes the trailer floor slope up or down, it will be harder for the horse to keep his balance. Take a good look at your tires, axles, and suspension, as well. If your trailer tires (or one or two of them) are over- or underinflated, the trailer might not be level. Broken springs, a bent axle, or other equipment malfunctions can produce an uneven (and bumpy) ride. A thorough inspection of the trailer before hauling horses any distance is always wise.

» **A thorough inspection of the trailer before hauling horses any distance is always wise.**

Evaluate the way you drive when pulling the trailer. Since most scramblers panic and "climb the walls" mainly on turns, always slow way down on curves and don't take sharp corners any faster than 5 miles per hour. Start slowing down well ahead of time, and don't start speeding up again until you are sure the trailer is completely around the corner (and then accelerate *slowly*). Many drivers are careless when hauling horses: They slow down for corners but start speeding up again before the trailer itself is completely around them, throwing the horses off balance with a "crack-the-whip effect."

PROBLEMS WITH HAULING

If the horse doesn't tie well, he may pull back in a straight- or slant-load horse trailer and then feel trapped and start scrambling. Work with the horse on tying in general (see Problems with Tying, p. 75), or haul him in a stock trailer loose (without a halter for safety) to avoid the issue.

» **If the horse doesn't tie well in the trailer, give him some tying lessons around the barn before you try tying him again during transport.**

If the horse scrambles or goes down in a straight- or slant-load trailer and you have removed the partition (see Solution 1) but need to be able to haul another horse with him, do some practice trips with a "buddy horse" without a partition between them. Most horses don't panic when they bump into one another (they are more apt to panic when bumping into the wall or partition). Touching another horse can actually give the anxious horse a sense of security. If you are afraid the horses may step on one another, use shipping boots to protect their feet and legs.

What If Nothing Works?

For the rare few that can't get over their scrambling habit even with trailer and/or partition alterations, you might ask your veterinarian about the possible use of a tranquilizer when travel is absolutely necessary.

TRIES TO LIE DOWN

Occasionally you encounter a horse that wants to lie down during transport. In most instances, this would be cause for concern because it might be an indication of colic or another health problem, but there are a few horses that use lying down as an avoidance technique.

>> **A horse that habitually tries to lie down in the trailer may not do so when hauled in a larger rig or when given more freedom to move during transport.**

How to Change This Habit

Check the horse's health to ensure illness or injury is not what is causing him to want to lie down. Next make sure the horse is comfortable in the trailer: He should not feel claustrophobic and jammed into a stall. A horse that habitually tries to lie down in a two-horse, straight-load trailer, for example, may not feel threatened when hauled loose in a large stock trailer. Having more room will often solve the problem—and if the horse *does* lie down in a stock trailer, he has enough room to get back up again safely (unless there are several other horses traveling with him).

SOLUTION 2 If the horse must be tied, tie him high and short so that he still has some freedom of head and neck, but it is more physically difficult for him to lie down. If you tie to something near the ceiling of the trailer, he can't lower his head enough to lie down.

What If Nothing Works?

When a horse insists on lying down for transport, haul him by himself loose in a large trailer where there's lots of room, and don't worry about it.

TRIES TO TURN AROUND

Some horses are not content to stand in a two-horse trailer facing frontward, and they try to turn around—either because they want to get out of the trailer or because they have trouble keeping their balance while facing forward.

PROBLEMS WITH HAULING

How to Change This Habit

SOLUTION 1 The best solution in this case is to use a style and size of trailer where the horse has more room and can balance himself easily. Horses tend to prefer riding backward or on a slant, rather than facing straight forward. When tied to the wall in a stock trailer, for instance, the horse can position himself at whichever angle he wishes for best balance. If the horse is by himself, or with one other horse he gets along with, he can be loose in a stock trailer, and then ride backward if he wants to.

»   **Horses tend to prefer to travel riding backward or on a slant, rather than facing straight forward.**

If the horse is trying to turn around just because he's ill at ease in a two-horse trailer, have him spend some time hanging around and inside it without being hauled somewhere. Park it in his paddock or the round pen and put his hay and grain inside. Allow him to wander in and out of it as he wishes. If entering the trailer is his own idea, and he can exit at will, he will begin to get over the claustrophobia when you haul him.

Before hauling the horse in a two-horse trailer, make sure he is well halter trained, respects restraint by the halter and lead, and doesn't mind standing tied for long periods when *not* in the trailer. When you do haul him, tie him fairly short (yet with enough length to be comfortable) so he can't bring his head around enough to start turning around.

» **When hauling a horse that likes to turn around in the trailer, tie him short and high.**

What If Nothing Works?

When a horse always tries to turn around in a two-horse trailer, it is best to just haul him in a stock trailer.

Problems with Unloading

RUSHES BACKWARD

Some horses are so nervous about coming out of the trailer that they
rush backward. This can be dangerous for both the horse and the people
handling him.

How to Change This Habit

First make sure you always untie the horse before you undo the
rump chain/bar, open the back door, or lower the ramp so the horse
can't try to rush backward and panic when he discovers he's still tied
in. Untie him and feed him a treat or a horse cookie to get him to
stand for a moment and relax. Don't open the back door or drop the
ramp until the rump chain/bar is unfastened—the horse may try to
come out too soon and put so much pressure on the chain/bar that
you can't unfasten it, and he will get even more nervous and upset.

» **Always untie the horse before you undo the rump chain/
bar or open the trailer door.**

Spend some time just loading and
unloading, halting the horse when
he's only partway into the trailer. Stop
him as soon as he puts his front feet
in, and ask him to back out again
(*you tell him* to back up, rather than
him deciding to rush backward all on

his own). Lead him partway in again, a little farther this time, and back him out again. Repeat the exercise until he realizes he *can* back all the way out of the trailer slowly and safely.

What If Nothing Works?

When a horse continues to panic when it is time to back out of the trailer, use a stock trailer or other large style of trailer that allows you to turn him around first before unloading him.

RUSHES FORWARD

Sometimes you encounter a horse that's so eager to come out of a trailer (particularly a large stock trailer) that he bolts out the door.

How to Change This Habit

 If you are hauling several horses, try unloading the one with the "rushing out habit" first instead of last. He may be so nervous about being left behind that he's rushing out in an effort to follow his buddies. Unloading him first may make him a little more reluctant to career off the trailer because it will mean leaving his buddies.

> » **When hauling several horses together, unload the one that likes to rush out first.**

 Feed the horse a treat in the trailer (something he likes, such as a horse cookie) so he comes to expect it and wants to wait for it before he exits the trailer. Turn him around to face the exit and then give him a treat before he goes out, but be sure to make him stand still for the treat.

Have an assistant hold the trailer door closed while you untie the horse and turn him around, and make him stand patiently facing the closed door for a moment (even if you have to give him a cookie to keep him calm—see Solution 2) before asking the helper to open the door and leading the horse out.

PROBLEMS WITH UNLOADING

More groundwork and leading lessons will help you establish more trust, respect, and control, which will improve the horse in many areas. Specifically work on the horse patiently standing still when asked, wherever you are in the stable, barnyard, paddock, or field. Then when you untie him and point him toward the door inside the trailer, he will be more apt to listen to your "whoa" and walk calmly out—he'll have done it a million times before in all manner of situations.

>> **Revisiting groundwork and "whoa" can help with many trailering issues.**

Practice going in and out of the trailer on days you are not actually hauling him anywhere (see Rushes Backward, p. 295).

What If Nothing Works?

Park the trailer in his paddock or a round pen and feed the horse inside it. Let him wander in and out as he chooses. If he goes in of his own free will to eat, and discovers he can also come out whenever he wants to, he will learn to do so without being afraid or in a hurry.

WON'T BACK UP

Backing out of a two-horse, straight-load trailer can be traumatic for an inexperienced horse if someone hasn't taken the time to load and unload him repeatedly in the course of his training. Backing out can also become a phobia for an experienced horse if he raps or scrapes a hind leg as he exits.

How to Change This Habit

The best way to prevent this problem in an inexperienced horse is to take your time when first teaching him to load and unload. Let him back out several times in his first tentative attempts to enter it. Then he *knows* he can back out and will be less likely to panic or feel trapped because he isn't sure where the trailer floor ends and/ or is afraid of the sound of the ramp (see Evades Ramp, p. 273). By letting him just put his front feet in the trailer the first time and waiting to ask him to step farther in on subsequent tries later in the lesson or over several different sessions, you've allowed him to teach himself how to back out safely.

> » Take your time when first teaching a horse to load and unload from a two-horse, straight-load trailer—the horse needs to learn how to back up and exit correctly and safely.

Groundwork and leading lessons in which you teach the horse to back up on command will help when it comes time to back the horse out of the trailer. You can augment voice cues with a tap on the front of his chest with the butt end of a whip combined with quick tugs backward on his halter (pressure and release, rather than a steady pull) until he very readily backs up on command (see also p. 268). This will make it easier to encourage him to back out of a trailer.

SOLUTION **3**

If the horse is all the way in the trailer and afraid to back up, totally refusing to move, here is one way to get him safely out with the help of an assistant:

- Fasten a long, soft rope to the back end of the trailer at the height of the horse's rump, and pass it forward along the horse's left side (if he is in the left-hand straight stall), across his chest, along his other side, and back out the rear of the trailer. Your assistant should hold the free end of the rope, making sure it never goes so slack as to fall down by the horse's knees or feet.

- Stand near the horse's head, untie him, and reassure him as the assistant unclips the rump chain/bar and opens the trailer door/lowers the ramp.

- Ask the horse to back up as your helper exerts pressure on the rope that goes across his chest. Both of you should go slow and easy, encouraging him to stay calm and think about backing up and where he is putting his feet. The rope is merely used as an additional aid to give him more incentive to back out.

» **When a horse has a true fear of backing out of a horse trailer, the only solution may be to haul him in one where he can always turn around and face forward to exit.**

What If Nothing Works?

When a horse continues to have a phobia about backing out of a trailer, don't use a two-horse trailer with a partition. Take the divider out when you travel so you can carefully turn him around and let him come out facing forward when you unload him. The best solution is to use a large stock trailer or another style trailer with lots of room to turn the horse around.

About the Author

Heather Smith Thomas has raised and trained horses for 55 years, and she has been writing about them nearly that long. She got her first horse at age 9 and began raising horses of her own while in high school, using them in 4-H and to help with cattle work on her parents' ranch.

Heather began writing horse stories for children's magazines and horse care articles for equine publications to help pay her way through college, graduating with a BA in English and history from University of Puget Sound in Tacoma, Washington, in 1966. Her first book, *A Horse in Your Life: A Guide for the New Owner*, was written during the summer between her sophomore and junior year of college and published by A.S. Barnes & Company in 1966.

What began as an expression of interest and love of horses (freelance writing) soon became a career, as a way to help pay the bills on a struggling family ranch—Heather's writing became the equivalent of an "off farm job" that could be done at home at odd hours between riding range to check cattle and delivering calves. Heather rarely leaves the ranch—staying home to take care of "critters" has been a way of life—but she writes regularly for more than 25 farm and livestock magazines and about 30 horse publications. She has sold more than 11,000 stories and articles, and published 20 books. Most of Heather's magazine articles deal with health care, breeding, training, horse behavior/handling, or veterinary topics (horses and cattle). Her goal has been to learn all she can about care and handling of horses and cattle, and to then share this knowledge and experience with her readers.

Heather also currently writes two blogs, sharing her family's ranch experiences with horses and cattle: Notes from Sky Range Ranch appears periodically on the website insidestorey.blogspot.com, and her other blog tells why she wrote the book Beyond the Flames, and keeps readers up to date since that book was published (www.heathersmiththomas.blogspot.com).

Heather and her husband still raise beef cattle and a few horses on a ranch in the mountains of eastern Idaho, where they use their horses for cattle work. These days, she enjoys riding with her youngest grandchildren (age 9 through 16) who live on the ranch. She also appreciates the help of her oldest granddaughter (Heather Carrie Thomas) in training several young horses. Heather Carrie graduated from Carroll College in Helena, Montana, in 2013, and is now training horses professionally. "Grandma Heather" enjoys the special times with her grandchildren who share her love of horses.

Acknowledgments

It would be impossible to try to thank all the people who have influenced my life with horses, but there are several who stand out.

I want to thank my parents who finally gave in to the passionate desire of a small child who wanted a horse—that first very special old gelding started me on a path that has led to a very satisfying life with horses. He changed our lives because one thing led to another, and by the time I was 12 my family had a ranch and cattle, and multiple horses.

Next I must thank Velma and Jerry Ravndal who started the first 4-H horse club in Idaho, dedicating their time and efforts to "their" kids. They had a lasting influence on their first crop of eager riders. Jerry was probably the greatest horseman I was ever privileged to know. His tact, wisdom, and intuitive judgment—and above all his patience—accomplished miracles with horses. He and Velma fostered the ideals of good horsemanship in the budding young horsemen they inspired.

Then I must thank my husband Lynn who has been my teammate in raising horses and cattle—and training horses—for nearly 50 years. Without his help, encouragement, support, and tolerance I would not have been able to devote my life to these animals.

My passion for horses led me on a lifelong quest to learn all I can about them, and then to share what I learn by writing about them. I want to thank the hundreds of people I interviewed over the years in the course of writing articles and books about horses. The knowledge and experiences they shared with me has been a huge part of my ongoing education about horses and horsemanship.

I also thank my daughter Andrea who has been my partner in training our ranch horses, helping me from the time she was old enough to handle a horse. And lastly, I thank my granddaughter Heather Carrie Thomas, who is now a professional horse trainer. She is currently helping me start two young fillies, and I am proud to be learning some new techniques from her!

Index